THE DARKER REACHES OF GOVERNMENT

Perspectives on Southern Africa, 27

THE
DARKER REACHES
OF GOVERNMENT

Access to information
about public administration in the
United States, Britain and South Africa

by

ANTHONY S MATHEWS
BA LLB PhD (Natal)

UNIVERSITY OF CALIFORNIA PRESS

BERKELEY · LOS ANGELES · LONDON

First Printing 1978

University of California Press, Berkeley and Los Angeles
University of California Press Ltd, London

ISBN 0 520 03803 7

LC 78 64475

ⓒ SET, PRINTED AND BOUND IN THE REPUBLIC OF SOUTH AFRICA BY
THE RUSTICA PRESS (PTY) LTD, WYNBERG, CAPE

Preface

My objective in writing this book was to provide the reader with a comprehensive survey, not too encumbered with detail or technical elaboration, of the laws, practices and institutions that either support or diminish secrecy in government administration in America, Britain and South Africa. A major problem at the outset was whether the three societies are not so materially different as to nullify the normal gains of a comparative study. The attempt to portray the living law of each society in a social context has only partially overcome the problem; and my readers may certainly be forgiven if, when all that is written here has been absorbed and evaluated, they conclude that the gulf between South Africa, on the one hand, and Britain and America on the other, is now so great that mutual comprehension and influence is simply not conceivable. Yet the gulf has separated what was formerly, and in part at least, a common intellectual and cultural landscape; and there has been a kind of cultural geologist's fascination in identifying and exposing the forces and stresses that have created the great social divide. The exercise has demonstrated the possibility of a regenerative reform movement in Britain through the influence of American ideas and practices; but South Africa appears to be in a state of unarrestable continental drift from those two Western societies even while it asserts common interests and allegiances with a degree of hysteria proportionate to the distance between it and them.

The subject-matter of this study has proved to be uncomfortably volatile. Some major developments and changes have occurred whilst the book was in the press, and inclusion of all these has not been possible. A postscript on the Department of Information scandal in South Africa has been hastily prepared and this incorporates a brief discussion of legislation authorizing secret funds in any department of government. While in general I have tried to state the law as it was at the end of 1977, a few changes that took place after that date have been incorporated in the text. In the late stages of writing I lacked the use of a good American law library, and this explains the frequent citation of cases from the United States Law Week series.

My indebtedness to others in researching and writing has been great. I received generous grants from the University of Natal, the

v

Human Sciences Research Council, The Attorneys, Notaries and Conveyancers Fidelity Guarantee Fund and the United States Department of State. I wish to record my gratitude to them for making this book possible. A visiting fellowship at Clare Hall, Cambridge, provided me with a congenial and enriching environment for the early stages of the work. During extensive travels in America, individuals and institutions, too numerous to mention here, were extraordinarily helpful and hospitable. Of the colleagues who read parts of the manuscript and offered useful criticism and advice I wish to mention specially Neil Williams, Laurence Boulle, Raphael de Kadt and David Welsh with the usual exoneration of responsibility. Leslie Greenbaum worked with commendable enthusiasm and care to produce the index. Anne Aarsen and Ingrid Lister-James, working from drafts illegible even to the author, were responsible for an impeccable manuscript. Finally, I was much aided by the indulgence of a long-suffering family and understanding colleagues and friends.

A. S. MATHEWS

July, 1978

Table of Contents

PART I

THE PROBLEM

Chapter

PART II

THE LAW

PART III

THE BACKGROUND

PART IV

THE SOLUTION

Bibliography

Aitken, Jonathan	*Officially Secret* (Weidenfeld & Nicholson, London, 1971).
Almond, Gabriel A and Powell, G Bingham Jr	*Comparative Politics: A Developmental Approach* (Little, Brown & Co, Boston, 1966).
Almond, Gabriel A and Verba, Sidney	*The Civic Culture* (Little, Brown & Co, Boston, 1965).
Apter, David	*Political Change* (Cass Paperbacks, 1974).
Atkinson, A B (editor)	*Wealth, Income and Inequality* (Penguin, 1973).
Atkinson, A B	*Unequal Shares: Wealth in Britain* (Penguin, 1974).
Barker, A and Rush M	*The Member of Parliament and His Information* (Allen & Unwin, London, 1970).
Beer, Samuel H	*Modern British Politics* (Faber & Faber, London, 1969).
Bell, Daniel	*The Coming of Post-Industrial Society: A Venture in Social Forecasting* (Heinemann, London, 1974).
Berger, Raoul	*Executive Privilege: A Constitutional Myth* (Harvard Univ Press, 1974).
Bottomore, T B	*Classes in Modern Society* (Allen & Unwin, London, 1970).
Bradshaw, K and Pring, D	*Parliament and Congress* (Constable, London, 1972).
Brzezinski, Zbigniew and Huntingdon, Samuel P	*Political Power: USA/USSR* (Chatto & Windus, London, 1964).
Bunyon, Tony	*The Political Police in Britain* (Julian Freidmann, London, 1976).
Calvin, John	*On God and Political Duty* (Bobbs-Merrill Co Inc, 1956).
Chapman, Richard A and Dunsire, A (editors)	*Style in Administration: Readings in British Public Administration* (Allen & Unwin, London, 1971).
Cloete, J S N	*Inleiding tot die Publieke Administrasie* 3rd ed (Van Schaik Pretoria, 1976).
Cohen, Bernard C	*The Press and Foreign Policy* (Princeton Univ Press, NJ, 1963).
Connerton, Paul (editor)	*Critical Sociology* (Penguin Books, 1976)
Cooper, Kent	*The Right to Know: An Exposition of the Evils of News Suppression and Propaganda* (Farrar, Strauss & Cudany, NY, 1956).
Copeling, A J C	*Copyright Law in South Africa* (Butterworths, Durban, 1969).
Copinger, W A and Skone James, E P	*Copyright*, 11th ed (Sweet & Maxwell, London, 1971).
Coser, Lewis A and Rosenberg, Bernard (editors)	*Sociological Theory: A Book of Readings*, 3rd ed (Macmillan, 1969).
Cowan, Paul Egleson, Nick and Hentoff, Nat	*State Secrets* (Holt, Rinehart and Winston, NY, 1974).
Crick, Bernard (editor)	*Essays on Reform, 1967: A Centenary Tribute* (Oxford, 1967).
Crick, Bernard	*Political Theory and Practice* (Allen Lane, Harmondsworth, 1972).
Crick, Bernard	*The Reform of Parliament* (Weidenfeld & Nicholson, London, 1970).
Cross, Harold L	*The People's Right to Know* (Columbia University Press, NY, 1953).

Crozier, Michael   *The Bureaucratic Phenomenon* (Tavistock Publications, London, 1964).

Dahl, Robert A   *Polyarchy: Participation and Opposition* (Yale Univ Press, New Haven, 1971).

Dahrendorf, Ralf   *Society and Democracy in Germany* (Doubleday & Co Inc, New York, 1965).

Dahrendorf, Ralf   *The New Liberty* (Routledge & Kegan Paul, London, 1975).

De Goede, B and   *Hoe Openbaar Wordt Ons Bestuur* (Vuga Boekerij, The Hague, 1969).
  Van Maarseveen,
  H Th J F

De Klerk, W A   *The Puritans in Africa* (Pelican, 1975).

Dorsen, Norman and   *None of Your Business: Government Secrecy in America* (The Viking Press, NY, 1974).
  Gillers, Stephen (editors)

Drury, Allen   *A Very Strange Society* (Michael Joseph, London, 1967).

Dunsire, Andrew   *Administration: The Word and the Science* (Martin Robertson, London, 1973).

Erskine May   *The Constitutional History of England* (Longman Green & Co, London, 1875).

Erskine May   *The Law, Privileges, Proceedings and Usage of Parliament*, 19th ed (Butterworths, London, 1976).

Fagen, Richard R   *Politics and Communication* (Little, Brown & Co, Boston, 1966).

Franck, Thomas M and   *Secrecy and Foreign Policy* (Oxford Univ Press, 1974).
  Weisband, Edward
  (editors)

Friedrich, Carl J   *Limited Government—A Comparison* (Prentice-Hall Inc, NY, 1974).

Gellhorn, Walter   *Security, Loyalty and Science* (Cornell Univ Press, 1950).

Giddens, Anthony   *The Class Structure of the Advanced Societies* (Hutchinson, London, 1973).

Greenberg, Edward S   *The American Political System: A Radical Approach* (Winthrop Publishers Inc, Cambridge, Mass, 1977).

Griffith, J A G   *The Politics of the Judiciary* (Fontana, 1977).

Griffith, J A G (editor)   *From Policy to Administration: Essays in Honour of William A Robson* (George Allen & Unwin, London, 1976).

Gross, P H   *Legal Aid and Its Management* (Juta, Cape Town, 1976).

Halberstam, David   *The Best and the Brightest* (Barrie & Jenkins, London, 1972).

Halperin, Morton H   *Bureaucratic Politics and Foreign Policy* (The Brookings Institution, Washington DC, 1974).

Halperin, Morton H and   *Top Secret: National Security and the Right to Know* (New Republic Books, Washington DC, 1977).
  Hoffman, Daniel N

Halsbury   *Halsbury's Laws of England*, 3rd ed).

Halsbury   *Halsbury's Laws of England*, 4th ed.

Hartley, T C and   *Government and Law* (Weidenfeld & Nicolson, London, 1975).
  Griffith, J A G

Hartz, Louis   *The Founding of New Societies* (Harcourt, Brace & World Inc, New York, 1964).

Heclo, Hugh and   *The Private Government of Public Money* (Macmillan, London, 1974).
  Wildavsky, Aaron

Herlitz, Nils   *Elements of Nordic Public Law* (P A Norstedt and Soners Forlag, Stockholm, 1969).

Holdsworth, W S   *A History of English Law*, 2nd ed.

Houghton, Bernard   *Bureaucratic Government: A Study in Late Indian Policy* (P S King & Son, London, 1913).

Irish, Marian D and   *The Politics of American Democracy* 4th ed (Prentice-Hall Inc, NJ, 1968).
  Protho, James W

Jewell, Malcolm E and   *The Legislative Process in the United States*, 2nd ed (Random House, New York, 1973).
  Patterson, Samuel C

Johnson, M B   *The Government Secrecy Controversy* (Vantage Press, NY, 1967).

Joubert, W A — *Grondslae van die Persoonlikheidsreg* (A A Balkema, Cape Town, 1953).

Katznelson, I and Kesselman, M — *The Politics of Power* (Harcourt Brace Jovanovich Inc, NY, 1975).

Kilpin, R — *Parliamentary Procedure in South Africa*, 3rd ed (Juta & Co, Cape Town, 1955).

Kinloch, G C — *The Sociological Study of South Africa: An Introduction* (Macmillan, Johannesburg, 1972).

Kolko, Gabriel — *Wealth and Power in America* (Praeger, NY, 1970).

Kornhauser, William — *The Politics of Mass Society* (The Free Press of Glencoe, Illinois, 1959).

Lerner, Max — *America as a Civilization* (Jonathan Cape, London, 1958).

Lippman, Walter — *The Public Philosophy* (Hamish Hamilton, London, 1955).

Lippman, Walter — *Public Opinion* (The Free Press, NY, 1965).

Lucas, J R — *Democracy and Participation* (Penguin, 1976).

Lukes, Stephen — *Power: A Radical View* (Macmillan, 1974).

MacCrone, I D — *Race Attitudes in South Africa* (Oxford, 1937).

Marquard, Leo — *The Peoples and Policies of South Africa* (Oxford Univ Press, 1969).

Mathews, A S — *Law, Order and Liberty in South Africa* (Juta and Co, Cape Town, 1971).

McGrath, M D — *Racial Income Distribution in South Africa* (Dept of Economics, Univ of Natal, Durban, 1977).

Miliband, Ralph — *The State in Capitalist Societies* (Quartet Books, London, 1973).

Millin, Sarah Gertrude (editor) — *White South Africans Are Also People* (Howard Timmins, Cape Town, 1966).

Milton, J R L and Fuller, N M. — *South African Criminal Law and Procedure* (Juta & Co, Cape Town, 1971).

Moodie, T Dunbar — *The Rise of Afrikanerdom* (Univ of California Press, London, 1975).

Morgenthau, Hans J — *Truth and Power* (Pall Mall Press, London, 1970).

Mueller, Claus — *The Politics of Communication* (Oxford Univ Press, NY, 1975).

Nicholson, Max — *The System: The Misgovernment of Modern Britain* (Hodder & Stoughton, London, 1967).

Nordlinger, Eric A — *Conflict Regulation in Divided Societies* (Harvard Univ Centre for Int Affairs, 1972).

O'Higgins, Paul — *Censorship in Britain* (Thomas Nelson & Sons Ltd, London, 1972).

Outer Circle Policy Unit — *An Official Information Act* (London, 1977).

Peters, Charles and Branch, Taylor — *Blowing the Whistle: Dissent in the Public Interest* (Praeger, NY, 1972).

Rose, Richard — *Politics in England Today* (Faber & Faber, London, 1974).

Rosenbaum, Walter A — *Political Culture* (Nelson, London, 1975).

Rourke, Francis E — *Secrecy and Publicity: Dilemmas of Democracy* (The Johns Hopkins Press, Baltimore, 1961).

Rourke, Francis E — *Bureaucracy, Politics and Public Policy* (Little, Brown & Co, Boston, 1969).

Sampson, Anthony — *The New Anatomy of Britain* (Hodder & Stoughton, London, 1971).

Schlesinger, Arthur M Jr — *The Imperial Presidency* (André Deutsch, London, 1974).

Schwartz, Bernard — *Constitutional Law* (Macmillan, New York, 1972).

Shils, Edward A — *The Torment of Secrecy* (William Heinemann Ltd, London, 1956).

Shonfield, Andrew — *Modern Capitalism* (Oxford Univ Press, 1969).

Smith, J C and Hogan, B — *Criminal Law*, 3rd ed (Butterworths, London, 1973).

Snow, C P — *Science and Government* (Mentor Books, 1962).

Sorenson, Theodore C — *Watchmen in the Night: Presidential Accountability After Watergate* (The MIT Press, Cambridge, Mass, 1975).

Strauss, S A, Strydom, M J   *Die Perswese en die Reg* (J L van Schaik, Pretoria, 1964).
  and van der Walt, J C
Strauss, S A Strydom, M J   *Die Suid-Afrikaanse Persreg*, 3rd ed (Van Schaik, Pretoria,
  and van der Walt, J C   1976).
Street, Harry   *Freedom, the Individual and the Law* (Penguin, 1973).
Stuart, K W   *The Newspaperman's Guide to the Law*, 2nd ed, (Butter-
                               worths, Durban, 1977).
Stultz, Newell M   *The Nationalists in Opposition: 1934–1948* (Human &
                               Rousseau, Cape Town, 1974).
Thompson, L and Butler, T   *Change in Contemporary South Africa* (Univ of California
  (editors)   Press, Berkley, 1975).
Ungar, Sanford J   *The Papers and the Papers* (E P Dutton & Co Inc, NY,
                               1972).
Van der Vyver, J D   *Die Beskerming van Menseregte in Suid Afrika* (Juta & Co,
                               Cape Town, 1975).
VerLoren van Themaat, J P   *Staatsreg*, 2nd ed (Butterworths, Durban, 1967).
Vital, David   *The Making of British Foreign Policy* (George Allen &
                               Unwin, London, 1968).
Wade, E C S and   *Constitutional Law*, 8th ed (Longman, London, 1970).
  Philips, G
Welsh, David   *The Roots of Segregation: Native Policy in Colonial Natal
                               1845–1910* (Oxford, 1971).
Westergaard, J and   *Class in a Capitalist Society: A Study of Contemporary
  Resler, H   Britain* (Penguin Books, 1975).
Westin, Alan F (editor)   *Information Technology in a Democracy* (Harv Univ Press,
                               1971).
Wiggins, J R   *Freedom or Secrecy* (Oxford, 1964).
Wigmore   *Evidence*, revised ed. (Little, Brown & Co, Boston, 1961).
Wilcox, Francis O   *Congress, the Executive and Foreign Policy* (Harper & Row,
                               London, 1971).
Wilensky, Harold J   *Organizational Intelligence: Knowledge and Policy in Govern-
                               ment and Industry* (Basic Books Inc, NY, 1967).
Williams, David   *Not in the Public Interest: The Problem of Secrecy in
                               Democracy* (Hutchinson, London, 1965).
Wilson, Woodrow   *The New Freedom* (Chapman & Hall, London, 1913).
Windlesham, Lord   *Communication and Political Power* (Jonathan Cape, London,
                               1966).
Wise, D and Ross, T   *The Espionage Establishment* (Jonathan Cape, London,
                               1968).
Worrall, Denis (editor)   *South Africa: Government and Politics* (J L van Schaik,
                               Pretoria, 1975).
Wraith, Ronald   *Open Government: The British Interpretation* (Royal Inst
                               of Public Administration, London, 1977).
Young, Hugo   *The Crossman Affair* (Hamish Hamilton, London, 1976).

Table of Statutes

UNITED STATES OF AMERICA

FEDERAL

STATE

UNITED KINGDOM

Table of Cases

Introduction

One of the surprising features of twentieth-century politics is the apparent compatibility of democracy with secrecy in public administration. The 'open' society can coexist with a passion for, and the application of, secret policies and procedures. The authority for practices of secrecy in government, and sometimes their justification as well, are generally found in legal rules of a statutory origin. Societies which do not hesitate to style themselves democratic frequently maintain broad and vague laws which authorize or require the secret administration of public affairs.

This book describes and analyses such laws in three countries—the United States of America, Great Britain and South Africa. The focus is upon laws which either support or proscribe the secret conduct of executive government. The management of public affairs in the legislative and judicial branches of government is in general public and open; but even here there are dark areas. The problems, legal and political, involved in bringing more light into such areas will be discussed supplementally to the central task of this work—an examination of secrecy and publicity in the administration of public business at all levels of the executive branch. The extension of democracy in the last decades of the twentieth century is heavily dependent upon letting the sunlight into that sphere of government.

Contextual treatment of the laws under analysis is obviously essential where their subject-matter is related to crucial, social and political issues of the day. The exposition of the governing legal rules will therefore be preceded by a discussion of the relevance of an effective right to information about public affairs to democratic government and a broad survey of contemporary social forces that have raised the problem of secrecy in government to a crisis point; and followed by an attempt to integrate those rules into a broadly sketched socio-political context. An integration of that kind seems essential not just for an appreciation of the origin and functions of the operative rules but more importantly for a realistic assessment of the chances of, and strategies for, legal reform.

A word of warning to the reader on the philosophical and political starting-points of the ensuing study seems desirable. The entire work rests upon the belief that the liberal-democratic system of government (perhaps better described as 'libertarian democracy' to avoid out-moded nineteenth-century connotations) is capable by reformation of meeting and successfully accommodating the many legitimate demands for change that are being voiced in Western capitalist societies. These demands have been articulated more insistently in contemporary Marxist critiques of the Western democracies which have in common a belief in radical 'restructuring' of such societies involving at the very least a 'full-scale public appropriation of the bulk of the private economy'.[1] In contrast, the reasoned assumption that liberal democracies are better capable of coping with social man's need for material welfare, political participation and personal liberty, underlies this work. It may be true that a 'tension between promise and its practical denial runs deep in all capitalist societies';[2] but it runs far deeper in contemporary Marxist societies, though for different reasons. Until Marxist societies demonstrate a convincing capacity for accommodating substantially the full *complex* of human needs as opposed to inflated aspects of them, reform of the much abused democracy with a mixed economy promises the most hopeful prospect. Before then it would be foolish to replace liberal democracies with more failed Marxist systems, the creation and maintenance of which have exacted greater human costs than can be laid at the door of Western societies.

NOTES

[1] J Westergaard & H Resler *Class in a Capitalist Society: A Study of Contemporary Britain* (Penguin Books, 1975) 216.

[2] Ibid 7.

PART ONE

The Problem

Democracy and the Citizen's Access to Information

Of the three countries whose laws feature in this book, two are self-evidently democracies.[1] The political systems of the United States of America and Britain are of the liberal-democratic type, though neither conforms to all the prescriptions implied by the model. The third, South Africa, has a political system in which the democratic elements are severely limited by White hegemonic rule and the liberal elements barely exist at all. Yet the political rulers in South Africa, if not the less fortunate of their subjects, insist that their governmental system is in the Western democratic tradition. While an objective criterion test may make this insistence appear either grotesque or comical according to the observer's temperament, the subjective orientation of South Africa's political rulers towards Western democracy does not make it unsensible to ask, in a work devoted to all three societies, whether democracy implies the right of the citizen to be informed about public affairs. Being 'informed', in this context, does not mean that the citizen is provided by his governors with information about their administration. It means rather the right to self-information: the right to acquire by access to documents or deliberations, exercised either personally or through agencies independent of the government (such as the press), an accurate knowledge of administration and its background. Does democracy incorporate the right to be self-informed in this sense?

The adjective 'democratic' could scarcely be applied to a country whose parliamentary proceedings were secret or whose administration of justice took place behind closed doors. As a matter of history, the public (or 'strangers' as they were known in parliamentary terminology) were freely admitted to the English Parliament in the late eighteenth century but their presence in the House of Commons was recognized by official orders of the House only in 1845.[2] The right to publish debates was finally won, after a protracted struggle, at the end of the eighteenth century.[3] The courts of law have always been open, with minor exceptions, throughout the course of English legal history.[4] The early British rule of legislative secrecy was extended to the

1

American colonies,[5] but legislative assemblies in the United States have
been open to the public from the earliest times, though the committees
of the legislature (of Congress, for example) frequently meet behind
closed doors.[6] Secrecy in congressional committees has been strongly
defended on the ground that it promotes sincerity, frankness and
compromise,[7] but there are nevertheless proponents of legislation
designed to require the committees to admit members of the public.[8]
The committee system characteristic of legislative activity in the United
States does not detract from the general rule that legislative assemblies
and courts in that country operate under the full glare of publicity.
The question that is central to this study is whether democracy demands
that the business of the executive arm should likewise be subject to the
scrutiny of the general public.[9]

The question just posed has become a serious issue in Western
political and legal writing only in the past two or three decades. In
the United States, for example, the first legislative 'charter' conferring
upon subjects a right of access to government papers and documents
at the federal level was enacted in 1966.[10] The congressional investigation that preceded the Act originated about a decade earlier; and the
first major studies of the problem in America were products of the
fifties.[11] Concern over the problem of secrecy and information in
government is a much more recent phenomenon in the United Kingdom. There is no British legislation comparable to the Freedom of
Information Act and the first major writings emerged in the sixties.[12]
In South Africa there has barely been a ripple of interest.   Prior to
modern times the only exception in the Western democracies to the
lack of association between open government and access to executive
records is Sweden where such a right was constitutionally established
in 1776.[13] Since that time the right has existed almost unbroken to the
present and has been developed into a cornerstone of Swedish
democracy.

If access to government files and deliberations is an essential aspect
of democracy, the realization of its importance has dawned very late
in the history of political theory or practice. On reflection this tardiness
is not at all surprising. The domination of parliaments by the executive
and the gargantuan growth of administration are both comparatively
modern phenomena. Before the executive established its ascendancy
it was more effectively subject to control by representatives of the
people and to the legislature's power of enquiry. After an extensive
review of the power of enquiry of the British Parliament, Professor
Raoul Berger expresses the conclusion that there were no 'executive
limits on that power in English history . . .'.[14] Congressional power to
enquire as an aid to the legislative function and a means of supervising
the executive branch has long been exercised and judicially recognized
in the United States.[15] While separation of powers in America has
prevented the executive branch from grasping the reins of power to

the extent that is characteristic of parliamentary democracies, that country has experienced equally with the others the growth of public administration to the point where it is for the average citizen the most important activity of government: 'American bureaucracy takes its place as an equal partner with the President, Congress and the Judiciary.' A contemporary challenge to democracy of crucial significance to its survival is that of extending responsiveness to the new partner in government.

Does theoretical writing on the liberal-democratic model support the contention that a right to know about the actions and decisions of the executive and its administration (and indeed about those of the other branches of government) is an essential attribute? No doubt a measure of secrecy is a necessity to any government however defined or constituted; but few contemporary exponents of democratic theory would support Bagehot's view that democracy can be made to work only 'if its real rulers are protected from vulgar enquiries'.[16] The writings of Walter Lippmann, who was an ardent champion of liberal-democracy, may appear to stand as an exception to this last statement. Declaring that an elected executive official's main duty is to his office and not to the people who elected him, Lippmann denounced popular control of government in memorable words: 'Where mass opinion dominates government, there is a morbid derangement of the functions of power. This derangement brings about the enfeeblement, verging on paralysis, of the capacity to govern.'[17] In a later work Lippmann's approach to democracy precludes the recognition of a general right to know. Proceeding from the argument that public interests can be managed only by a specialized class, he adds: 'This class is irresponsible for it acts upon information that is not common property, in situations that the public at large does not conceive, and it can be held to account only on the accomplished fact.'[18] These quotations, without any doubt, express some of the central tenets of what has been styled 'Tory democracy'. Its basic features are the belief in hierarchy as a condition for order, the acceptance of authoritative leadership and the duty of the masses to obey their elected leaders.[19] Of special concern to the citizen's right to information is the belief that democracy is essentially the right to select parliamentary representatives: 'Continuous direction of policy is not within the Tory concept.'[20]

Clearly the Tory view of democracy is a limited and ageing notion. Modern democratic government is more of a two-way process and should preclude 'a deliberate attempt to operate the system behind the scenes as an essentially hierarchical, one-way mechanism'.[21] The Tory or élitist concept is seriously flawed in a number of ways. It contemplates an inert electorate except at election times when the citizenry fleetingly emerge from a condition of somnambulance to confirm their representatives in office or to replace them with others deemed more suitable. But even this anaemic form of democracy implies the right to, or at least the importance of, knowledge about the actions and decisions of the officers of government. Prior to the Watergate disclosures President Nixon was returned to office in 1972 by the largest majority in the history of American presidential elections. The information which Watergate brought to light destroyed the credibility of the President and his administration and demonstrated to the nation their unworthiness for office. Arthur M Schlesinger has said that 'by the 1960's and 1970's the religion of secrecy had become an all-purpose means by which the American Presidency sought to dissemble its purposes, bury its mistakes, *manipulate its citizens* and maximize its power'.[22] The preceding facts demonstrate graphically the great importance of access to detailed information about public administration even for the limited purpose of exercising a choice of representatives in government. As Andrew Dunsire[23] has observed, though the theory of responsible government 'can accommodate a high degree of secrecy, or lack of publicity, without logical self-contradiction', it does imply a duty of *ex post facto* accountability. Accountability, as he says, 'presupposes a measure of openness' and the extent of that openness in a system that is genuinely responsible will be determined by the sovereign. In a responsible democracy the sovereign body is the people and it is to them that the governors are accountable. Without an adequate flow of information even *ex post facto* accountability is meaningless. The élitist concept is also flawed by reason of its inability to provide an answer to perhaps the most pervasive problem of the democratic government of mass societies—the problem of alienation and anomie. (Alienation in this context refers to the feeling of citizens that they are impotent, that 'the powers that be are unreachably remote'.[24] The sense in which anomie is used has been well described by Claus Mueller as 'the breakdown of loyalties tying [citizens] to established institutions and the values of society at large'.)[25] The Tory notion may indeed be seen as a partial cause of contemporary citizen alienation so that its stubborn survival in many Western societies stands as a major obstacle to democratic reform.

If élitist democracy rests on the assumption that the information upon which the governing class acts cannot and should not be shared with the citizenry because the capacity to govern will thereby become debilitated, it is vulnerable to yet a further serious criticism. Exponents of the Tory notion such as Walter Lippmann write as though citizen participation and the sharing of information presupposes a transfer of the decision-making power from the government to the masses. This is a confusion, since what is claimed is a right to know and to influence— not a right to know and to decide. The government must still govern; but it must do so to the greatest degree possible in the open and with the advantage of the public canvassing of the issues to which policy and administration give rise. Modern democracy, except perhaps in more extreme variants,[26] does not seek to neutralize the exercise of power but rather to balance the need to govern by the need for a responsiveness to citizens.[27] The élitists have frequently bolstered their cause by unjustifiably denigrating responsiveness as an abdication of authority when it might reasonably have been seen as a means of legitimizing and stabilizing power.

The logic of the development of the argument thus far is that the right to know is entitled to a place in 'the catalogue of democratic rights'.[28] Recent analyses of democratic theory and practice tend to vindicate this view. Almond and Verba have said that the common thread in all definitions of democracy is that 'ordinary citizens exert a relatively high degree of control over their leaders'.[29] This view, it must be emphasized, goes beyond an emphasis on citizen participation which would be characteristic also of totalitarian democracies, and stresses in addition the right to oppose and, to some degree, to control. Robert A Dahl takes as the key constituents of polyarchies—societies marked by governmental responsiveness to the needs of the citizens— the right of participation and the right to engage in the public contestation of issues and policies.[30] The same idea is expressed by writers who insist that democracy is a system which allows alternative answers to be given to social questions: 'But the principle remains the institutional safeguarding of liberty by effective protection from the dogmatic establishment of one-sided positions.'[31] While it may be true that the Western democracies have limited the choices available to citizens by keeping certain issues off the agenda,[32] this is an argument for broadening the agenda;[33] it is not an argument which seeks to deny that democratic society should be characterized by the reality of alternative choices.

Whether democracy is expressed in the form of the right to engage in public contestation or to offer policy alternatives, certain ancillary rights are logically implied. Dahl speaks of these as the ability of the citizen to formulate preferences, to express them (individually and collectively) and to have them weighed without discrimination.[34] This ability clearly depends on the existence of certain formal rights such as organizational freedom, freedom of expression and the freedom to have 'alternative sources of information'. Almond and Verba, in similar vein, testify to democracy's historic connection with 'a high level of information about public affairs'.[35] Once it is conceded that a vital aspect of democracy is the right of active participation by citizens both at and between elections—whether on the ground that such participation is necessary for the protection of interests[36] or that participation elevates those who undertake it[37]—it follows as a logical necessity that the participants require access to information to make their involvement effective and rational. In a debate in the House of Lords in 1916, Lord Parmoor declared that there could be no popular government in a true sense unless 'you allow the people of a country to have sufficient and adequate knowledge on which to act rightly and think justly'.[38]

A 'democracy' in which the citizens act on false, distorted or incomplete facts will be a perversion of the principle of open government and will deprive the system of democracy's claim that it facilitates rational resolution of disputes. There is clearly much substance in Harold L Cross's dramatic pronouncement that without freedom of information 'the citizens of a democracy have but changed their kings'.[39]

The liberal-democratic model also incorporates the principle of constitutionalism by which we mean the existence of legal limitations on the exercise of public power. 'Information power', for reasons that will be discussed later, is threatening to become an uncontrollable and uncontrolled force in modern society. Constitutionalism cannot afford to limit itself to traditional forms of power if it is to remain an institution in the service of democracy. 'In a democracy, the public is the ultimate source of social power, and information power, accordingly, is ultimately a public trust.'[40] Therefore, if we approach the problem from the angle of democratic constitutionalism, we get the same answer; the citizen's democratic rights incorporate access to official sources of information.

An imaginative grasp of the spirit of modern democracy also yields the same answer. Professor Bernard Crick has said that the making of government decisions known in the form of law was historically the first victory of democracy and that the task for contemporary times is to ensure that 'the reasons for . . . decisions will be made known and even, more and more, the consequences of decisions evaluated critically and publicized and popularized intelligently'.[41] To refuse to accept this is to restate (unconsciously perhaps) the Tory view of democracy. 'What is rarely noted is that government in essence has switched from being something imposed on people from above to something demanded by people below.'[42] Denial of an information right seems to spring from inadvertence to the transformation of democracy in our times.

THE SPECIAL POSITION OF CONSOCIATIONAL DEMOCRACIES

Up to this point democratic systems have been discussed as if they constituted a single type sharing the same features. Arend Lijphart has suggested that stable Western democracies fall into two categories, namely, the Anglo-American, old Commonwealth and Scandinavian type, and consociational democracies exemplified particularly by Switzerland, Holland and Belgium.[43] In consociational democracies, unlike those of the first category, the political culture is deeply fragmented and the phenomenon of cross-cutting memberships and allegiances which is supposed to account for stability in the Anglo-American model is usually absent. Where consociational democracies are stable,[44] this is attributable to the co-operative efforts of political élites. This élite collaboration which overcomes the mutual tensions and differences inherent in the fragmented political cultures is the essence of the consociational model of democracy.

The question that arises is whether a citizen's right to information about public affairs is equally a vital aspect of consociational democracy. The relevance of the question in a study devoted to Britain, America and South Africa is seriously in doubt. Britain and America are examples of the non-consociational model; and South Africa hardly belongs in any democratic camp except perhaps in the aspirational sense. Yet it has been suggested that the model for political accommodation in South Africa is the consociational one on account of the society's deep subcultural cleavages. Two factors which favour the successful application of consociational democracy—a multiple balance of power as opposed to a dual balance or clear hegemony by one subculture and a relatively low social load on the decision-making apparatus[45]—are noticeable more by their absence from the South African context. Yet the consociational model, or an adaptation of it, offers more promise in this setting than the other democratic form. As it probably has more to offer to the solution of the political problems of culturally plural societies, it is worth examining whether and to what extent a citizen's right to information is implied.

The problem with this question is that the consociational model is not normally associated with any specific institutional variations. Lijphart has in fact declared that '[t]he essential characteristic of consociational democracy is not so much any particular institutional arrangement as the deliberate joint effort by the élites to stabilize the system'.[46] The institutional variations that are present in the consociational system such as coalition cabinets, alternating presidencies and the sharing of lower offices have no direct bearing upon a right to information which they appear neither to favour nor to disfavour. Nevertheless, the idea of the consociational democracy—the accommodation of political differences at the élite level—appears to be hostile to an active citizen participation or to any notion of citizen self-government. Eric A Nordlinger has accentuated the necessity for leaders to predominate over their subjects in consociational systems and has said that political acquiescence and deferential attitudes on the part of the subjects are often the basis of domination.[47] This appears to imply that participation and access to information will take place at the élite level only and that in practice no right of access to information will be conferred upon individual citizens or groups of citizens.

The last proposition should perhaps be expressed more positively in the form that consociational democracy does require that all subcultures *through their chosen leaders* shall have access to official information.[48] This is to some extent implicit in the sharing of offices, but it also seems essential to the attitude of mutual trust and co-operation on which the system depends. In the non-consociational model in which government and opposition are aligned against each other in an almost perpetual state of conflict, secrecy is used by the party in power as a means of disadvantaging the opposition. While this may not be a logical implication of the two-party style of politics, such a system does appear to differ from consociational democracy in that a sharing of power, including information, between the political leaders is *positively* implied in the latter system. This means that in South Africa the extent of the government's commitment to consociational politics might be tested *inter alia* by the extent to which a real sharing of information is taking place with recognized black leaders.[49] Citizen access to information, as opposed to élite access, is consistent with consociational democracy only to the extent that the élite management of government will not be disturbed thereby.

AUTOCRATIC, AUTHORITARIAN AND TOTALITARIAN SYSTEMS AND THE RIGHT TO INFORMATION

The purpose of this first chapter has been to demonstrate that it no longer makes sense, if it ever did, to speak of democracy without at least implying a popular right to information or, in the case of consociational democracies, at least a shared access to information. It will be helpful now to look briefly at the political models with which democracy is normally contrasted—models which stand as a negation of the idea of democracy—in order to see how they approach the information right. As might be anticipated, the denial of a popular right to information is a feature of all systems that are autocratic, authoritarian or totalitarian. This statement is not as tautologous as it might at first sound, except perhaps in the case of an autocratic political system which is characterized by the absence of institutions of participation and in which the citizens are regarded as needing to know only that which is necessary to secure compliance with decisions.[50] Where the political structure is authoritarian, both institutions of participation and some measure of sub-national institutional autonomy may exist, the 'leading stratum' claiming merely the ultimate right to decide.[51] Nevertheless, because of the control exercised by the rulers over ultimate decisions and because of belief of authoritarian élites that they know better than the citizens what is good for society, information flow both up and down the communication lines may be substantially curtailed or distorted.[52] In totalitarian systems, the content of communications, like everything else, is subject to pervasive control and 'all channels of communication are at the service of the élite for the conveyance of approved information'.[53] This affects primarily the downward flow of information, from state to citizens; but there is evidence that communication up the line in totalitarian governments is frequently distorted as a by-product of centralization and terror, frequently leaving both citizens and rulers in possession of distorted or false information.[54] If the three types of system are compared with respect to the downward flow of information—the subject of this study—then it appears that the differences are as follows: Autocracies permit no participation, including the sharing of information; authoritarian rulers control information as a means of retaining power over matters that are 'ultimate'; totalitarian governments assume absolute control over the downward flow of information, thereby making the state its only 'authentic' source.

The purpose of contrasting such societies with democracies is not to induce a sense of complacency among supporters of the latter. Information distortion is known to take place in democratically styled systems in which, it has been suggested, the manipulation is less visible and more subtle: '. . . is it not the supreme exercise of power to get another or others to have the desires you want them to have?'[55] The great virtue of democracies is that institutional means exist for the correction of information distortion and other power imbalances; but unless they are used the subjects of democratic states can become the victims of far-reaching manipulation by reason of the government's control of modern communications systems. Francis E. Rourke has spoken of the danger that democratic leaders will 'acquire the ability to manufacture the consent upon which their authority is supposed to rest'.[56] An important counter to this tendency is a meaningful right of access to information about public administration. Without it the democracies will move uncomfortably close to those systems with which they like to contrast themselves.

NOTES

[1] Bernard Crick has wisely said that 'democracy is only—but no less than—a necessary element in good government which is always, in turn, mixed': see Bernard Crick *Political Theory and Practice* (Allen Lane, Harmondsworth, 1972) 138. Following him, Britain and America should perhaps be described as being sufficiently democratic to merit the title.

[2] Erskine May *The Constitutional History of England*, (Longman Green & Co, London, 1875) vol 2, 27 et seq. See also Erskine May's *The Law, Privileges, Proceedings and Usage of Parliament*, 19th ed (Butterworths, London, 1976) 221–3.

[3] Erskine May *The Constitutional History of England* 34–53.

[4] Holdsworth *A History of English Law* vol 14, 181–2. The question whether the public ought to have more information about the workings of the courts than is presently available is not within the scope of this work. Justice William H Rehnquist in an article entitled 'Sunshine in the Third Branch' published in (1977) 16 *Washburn LJ* 559 has said that the courts are sufficiently open—'all of the business of the Supreme Court of the United States comes in at the front door and leaves by the same door'. He argues cogently against publicity for judicial conferences prior to judgment on the ground that this would be injurious to candour and harmony between the judges and would subject them and their judgments to undesirable outside pressures. On the other hand, it is known that judges sometimes make representations to the other organs of government, usually on the subject of legislation. The need for secrecy in respect of these representations is not so persuasive. Such secrecy appears to facilitate an undesirable breach in the separation of powers between the judicial and other branches of government. When judges become a pressure group on matters of broad public policy, their insistence on the desirability for secrecy begins to ring a little hollow.

[5] William R. Wright, 'Open Meeting Laws: An Analysis and Proposal' (1974) 45 *Miss LJ* 1151 at 1155.

[6] J R Wiggins, *Freedom or Secrecy* (Oxford, 1964) 13–14. In recent times Congress has conducted a greater percentage of committee meetings in the open.

[7] Francis E Rourke *Secrecy and Publicity: Dilemmas of Democracy* (The Johns Hopkins Press, Baltimore, 1961) 105.

[8] See 'Project: Government Information and the Rights of Citizens', (1975) 73 *Mich L Rev* 971 at 1214. Many states in America have adopted legislation requiring committee sessions (with exceptions) to operate in the open.

[9] This study does not incorporate an examination of the right to attend meetings of the numerous and varied tribunals, boards and advisory committees set up under legislation. However, to the extent that the records of such bodies are part of the executive arm of government, the citizen's right (or the lack of it) to learn about their proceedings from papers and documents is dealt with in the ensuing analysis of both law and practice.

[10] The Freedom of Information Act 5 USC 552. The Administrative Procedure Act (60 Stat 238) had previously (in 1946) conferred a limited and ineffectual right of access to federal papers and documents.

[11] For example, Harold L Cross's *The People's Right to Know* (Columbia Univ Press, NY, 1953) and Kent Cooper's *The Right to Know: An Exposition of the Evils of News Suppression and Propaganda* (Farrar, Strauss and Cudany, NY, 1956).

[12] For example, David Williams's *Not in the Public Interest: The Problem of Secrecy in Democracy* (Hutchinson, London, 1965).

[13] Stanley V Anderson 'Public Access to Government Files in Sweden' (1973) 21 *Am J Comp Law* 419.

[14] Raoul Berger, *Executive Privilege: A constitutional Myth* (Harvard Univ Press, 1974).

[15] *McGrain v Dougherty* 273 US 135 (1927). See also Bernard Schwartz *Constitutional Law* (Macmillan, New York, 1972) 67–73.

[16] Quoted by Anthony Sampson in 'Secrecy News Management and the British Press' in *Secrecy and Foreign Policy*, eds Thomas M Franck and Edward Weisband (Oxford Univ Press, 1974).

[17] Walter Lippmann *The Public Philosophy* (Hamish Hamilton, London, 1955) 21 and 52.

[18] Walter Lippmann *Public Opinion* (The Free Press, NY, 1965) 195.

[19] Samuel H Beer, *Modern British Politics* (Faber & Faber, London, 1969) 91–101.

[20] Loc cit 101.

[21] Max Nicholson *The System: The Misgovernment of Modern Britain* (Hodder & Stoughton, London, 1967) 340.

[22] Arthur M Schlesinger Jr *The Imperial Presidency* (André Deutsch, London, 1974) 345 (emphasis supplied).

[23] Andrew Dunsire *Administration: The Word and the Science* (Martin Robertson, London, 1973) 167–9.

[24] Bernard Crick *Political Theory and Practice* 135.

[25] Claus Mueller *The Politics of Communication* (Oxford Univ Press, NY, 1975) 10.

[26] Radical democrats, for example, believe that voters should 'originate policies as well as decide between them': See Samuel H Beer op cit 96. This view is not acceptable if it means that executive power cannot be exercised without citizen *concurrence*.

[27] Almond & Verba *Civic Culture* (Little, Brown & Co, Boston, 1965) 340–1.

[28] Lord Windlesham *Communication and Political Power* (Jonathan Cape, London, 1966) 185.

[29] Op cit 118–19.

[30] Robert A Dahl *Polyarchy: Participation and Opposition* (Yale Univ Press, New Haven, 1971) 4–7.

[31] Ralf Dahrendorf *Society and Democracy in Germany* (Doubleday & Co Inc, NY, 1965) 12, 14 and 147.

[32] Stephen Lukes *Power: A Radical View* (Macmillan, 1974).

[33] While one may accept the proposition that there is a 'mobilization of bias' in all organizations which precludes the consideration of certain issues, it is unreasonable to expect liberal-democracies to accept as an issue on their agenda policies which involve their own destruction.

[34] Op cit 2–3.

[35] Op cit 9.

[36] On the basis that interests not defended will be overlooked.

[37] L J Sharpe 'Instrumental Participation and Urban Government' in *From Policy to Administration: Essays in Honour of William A Robson*, ed J A G Griffith (George Allen & Unwin Ltd, London, 1976) 115–17.

[38] Quoted by David Williams *Not in the Public Interest* 207.

[39] Harold L Cross *The People's Right to Know* XIII.

[40] Harold Sackman 'A Public Philosophy for Real Time Information Systems' in *Information Technology in a Democracy*, ed Alan F Westin (Harv Univ Press, 1971) 223.

[41] Bernard Crick *The Reform of Parliament* (Weidenfeld & Nicholson, London, 1970) 253.

[42] Max Nicholson op cit 418.

[43] Arend Lijphart, 'Consociational Democracy' (1968–9) 21 *World Politics* 207 at 211.

[44] They were not stable in societies like Weimar Germany or France.

[45] Arend Lijphart loc cit 216–19.

[46] Ibid 213.

[47] Eric A Nordlinger *Conflict Regulation in Divided Societies* (Harvard Univ Centre for Int Affairs, 1972) 79–80.

[48] Access to information through leaders creates the danger that they will use this privilege to manipulate their position within the community supporting them and thereby dilute democratic control.

[49] Those that I have spoken to are emphatic that no such development is taking place.

[50] Richard R Fagen *Politics and Communication* (Little, Brown & Co, Boston, 1966) 30.

[51] Ralf Dahrendorf op cit 407.

[52] Richard R Fagen op cit 115 and 141.

[53] Ibid 32.

[54] Almond & Powell *Comparative Politics: A Developmental Approach* (Little, Brown & Co, Boston, 1966) 164, 171 and 184; Harold L Wilensky *Organizational Intelligence: Knowledge and Policy in Government and Industry* (Basic Books Inc, NY, 1967) 112.

[55] Stephen Lukes op cit 23. See also J Westergaard and H Resler, *Class in a Capitalist Society: A Study of Contemporary Britain* (Penguin Books, 1975) 145: 'In fact no control could be firmer and more extensive than one which embraced the minds and wills of its subjects so successfully that opposition never even reared its head.'

[56] Op cit vii.

CHAPTER II

Contemporary Social Realities and Access to Information

The arguments of the first chapter suggest that extensive secrecy in the executive branch and its departments is incompatible with democracy.[1] Ironically the recognition of the relationship between access to executive information and democratic government has come at a time when certain social and political developments have strengthened the foundations of secrecy almost to the point where reform seems totally precluded. A clear understanding of the forces that have conspired to produce this situation is needed to avoid a surrender to pessimism and to create the conditions for a broader and more effective citizen right of access to executive branch information. The developments particularly hostile to a citizen information right are the growth of executive power, of official bureaucracy and the practice of news management; secrecy policies flowing from intelligence, defence and internal security programmes; the maintenance and even expansion of secrecy in foreign policy and, finally, the impact of science on the flow of information.

THE GROWTH OF EXECUTIVE POWER

The accretion of power to the executive branch of government is a commonplace of politics and constitutional law in this century. While secrecy may not be an unavoidable concomitant of enhanced power, it is an unfortunate fact that power and secrecy have developed together.[2] This is partly because executives have themselves tended to interpret public interest in terms of efficiency rather than responsiveness to the electorate.[3] Though it is disputable that secrecy necessarily means better executive government—'[t]he law of ascending secrecy in administrative behaviour assures abuses that more than cancel the gains'[4]—there is no denying the prevalence of the belief that more secrecy promotes improved administration. What subscribers to this belief really intend to express, or perhaps ought to express, is the proposition that greater secrecy leads to *stronger* executive government. The less accountable a public body is the greater its freedom to act as it pleases: 'The exeeutive branch thrives on secrecy because secrecy frees it from congressional, judicial and public oversight.'[5] Secrecy, it has

12

been said, may alter the whole power balance between the different branches of government in favour of the executive.[6]

Even without excessive secrecy practices, the exigencies of modern government have necessitated a transfer of considerable power to the executive from other branches, notably the legislature. Among the many causes of this transfer there are three which are especially prominent, namely, the increasing role of technical decision-making in modern societies;[7] the extensive welfare and management operations assumed by governments which because of their complexity and detail are practically beyond legislative control or even supervision; and the tendency of foreign policy—the oldest and most traditional area of government secrecy—to impinge heavily on contemporary domestic policy-making. These factors alone have disturbed power relations and threatened the position of the legislature and judiciary vis-à-vis the executive. If in addition the new powers of the executive are exercised behind a veil of secrecy, the conditions of executive dominance, if not tyranny, have been finally created. The claim that this stage has been reached in some of the Western democracies can no longer be dismissed as one-sided and alarmist.

Cabinet government has aggravated the position for those democracies that practise it as opposed to the presidential executive. Walter Bagehot once referred to the cabinet as 'the efficient secret of the English Constitution'. For reasons that are partly historical and partly constitutional 'there is no secret like a cabinet secret'.[8] So much has secrecy become part of the essential style of the cabinet that it operates even within the cabinet where, for example, only the Prime Minister, the Home Secretary and the Foreign Secretary in Britain are fully in the know in respect of security matters.[9] Cabinet secrecy has an exceptionally tenacious hold in Westminster-style democracies because its justification goes beyond arguments based on the sensitivity of the information which is suppressed. It is said to be necessary to maintain the solidarity of the cabinet and is related to the convention of collective responsibility in whose name volumes of innocuous information have been suppressed. The emphasis on solidarity in cabinet government has been wittily expressed by Max Nicholson in his statement that '[i]t is of the essence of the cabinet's power, and one of the main reasons for its successful take-over of this from the Commons, that it needs, and passionately desires, to hang together rather than to risk hanging separately'.[10] Without a rule of secrecy to cover up the divisions within the cabinet, they will not be seen to 'hang together' with the result that secrecy is maintained as a principle of internal management without reference to its objective justification based on requirements such as national security. It follows that the secrecy of cabinet-style government is more deeply entrenched and more pervasive in scope than that practised by presidential executives. The situation is aggravated further in Westminster democracies by the weakness of parliamentary committee systems which appear to lack effective power to obtain information and generally to supervise the executive. In this area of government the facts cry out for a reform designed to achieve a more open and adversary discussion of issues in executive government.

THE GROWTH OF BUREAUCRACY

Modern governments invariably operate a large and involved bureaucratic machinery. In theory this machinery is at the service of the executive to carry out its policies. The truth is that a large measure of the power which the executive branch has inherited has passed to the bureaucracy itself. Max Weber's references to bureaucracies as institutions characterized by virtues of precision, reliability and efficiency have been criticized as attributing to them a falsely neutral role. Philip Selznick, for exmaple, has said:

> 'But what Weber seems to have only partly understood is that the dynamics of the administrative apparatus itself created new personal influences—those of the administrators themselves seeking their own ends and engaging, as newly powerful participants, in power relationships.'[11]

The notion of bureaucratic neutrality has been vigorously attacked by Ralph Miliband, who argues that the upper layers of the administration are inevitably involved in policy-making from which it follows that they act as 'politically' as the executive. He adds that the higher civil servants 'constitute a considerable force in the configuration of political power in their societies'.[12] There is today a wealth of authoritative political writing to support the proposition that bureaucracies in parliamentary democracies have secured substantial power over law-making,[13] over the Ministers that are nominally in control over them[14] and over parliament itself.[15] On parliament's power, Anthony Sampson observes that 'in practice the sovereignty of parliament gets lost in the intricate labyrinths of power that surround it . . .'.[16]

The bureaucracies, it is now clear, have become centres of power in all Western democracies, including those that have presidential-type executives. Viewed from the perspective of access to information this is an alarming development since official secrets were the invention of the bureaucracy. Secrecy has been, and remains, one of the most effective techniques which officials have employed to enhance their power.[17] The key to the taming of bureaucratic power and to the introduction of bureaucratic accountability is an effective right of access to official information available both to legislatures and individual citizens.

There is an inherent tendency towards secrecy and secretiveness in all bureaucratic institutions. The tendency has structural roots in the organization of bureaucracies. Institutions of this kind are always hierarchical, to a greater or lesser degree. Hierarchical structures undoubtedly facilitate the distortion and suppression of information. David Apter has said that where accountability is low and access to sources of information limited, the political system will show a high degree of hierarchy and reliance on coercion.[18] Centralization within bureaucracies also produces information pathologies by distorting the flow of accurate information both up and down the line.[19] Information becomes harder to get because centralization reduces open conflict between rival departments.[20] There is also a direct correlation between specialization within bureaucracies and secrecy policies. Secrecy is frequently a by-product of expertise and is resorted to by specialized departments to secure an advantage over rival departments.[21]

The extensive secrecy practices of bureaucracies are attributable also to various factors of a non-structural kind. Most of these can be grouped together under the label 'bureaucratic mentality'. The cautiousness of bureaucrats is a fact that has frequently been commented upon. The traditional attitude of caution usually results in a decision not to disclose information even where the official has a discretion.[22] Caution is probably attributable largely to the official's dependence on the state and fear of harming the interests of the benefactor from whom his security is derived.[23] Officials also exhibit a tendency that is probably natural everywhere—that of covering up mistakes by practices of secrecy; but in the case of public bureaucracies the tendency is endemic.[24] The desire for promotion and influence may explain the practice of covering up mistakes and withholding unpleasant information from superiors.[25] Another attitude of great significance is reflected in the widespread belief of officials that secrecy promotes efficiency.[26] Most bureaucrats would probably not accept Francis E Rourke's dictum that 'Responsiveness no less than competence is the hallmark of a successfully functioning democratic bureaucracy'[27] even though, as he persuasively argues, the gains of secrecy are frequently illusory. The extent to which a belief in the virtue of secrecy is embedded in the official mind is starkly revealed by instances of bureaucratic vindictiveness towards colleagues who have made embarrassing disclosures. A vicious campaign was launched against a Pentagon official who revealed practices of gross inefficiency to a Congressional Committee even though the wastage of millions of dollars of the nation's money was at issue. As the victim ruefully observed after the loss of his position and failure to regain employment: 'If you must sin, sin against God, not against the bureaucracy. God may forgive you but the bureaucracy never will.'[28]

In a revealing study Morton Halperin has demonstrated how information is frequently 'doctored' to make it conform to established bureaucratic positions or to shared images within the bureaucracy. The techniques of doctoring which he documents include the selection of favourable facts, the solicitation of reports from those known to favour a proposed plan, the exclusion as participants of persons who might disagree and the use of coercion to obtain back-up opinions.[29] While Halperin's particular concern is the distortion of information which flows up the bureaucratic line to the highest executive officers,

the practices he describes may also result in the suppression of information given to or sought by outsiders. His finding that shared interests
and beliefs within bureaucracies lead to information suppression
(frequently of an unintentional kind) reveals a significant cause of
information pathologies in democratic societies. Bureaucracies confront believers in liberty in general, and the right to know in particular,
with a task of great magnitude. In his Reith lectures Ralf Dahrendorf
summed up the task in the following way:

> 'An agenda for recovering public control and individual rights from bureau-
> cracies, while preserving their service for solutions of problems of scale and citizen-
> ship is one of the primary tasks in the search for a new liberty.'[30]

Reflecting on his experience of bureaucracy in India a British writer
has declared pessimistically that bureaucracies from their nature are
hostile to popular movements and incapable of self-reform.[31] Creating
an effective right to information therefore incorporates the enforced
reformation of the most recalcitrant of institutions—the public
bureaucracy.

NEWS MANAGEMENT

One of the historic functions of the press is to provide the public
with authentic and accurate information about the management of
public affairs. At first blush the phenomenal development of the
communications media—especially the press and television—in this
century is a sign that this function is being adequately fulfilled, at least
in democracies where control of news is not officially claimed or
acknowledged by governments. It seems paradoxical then that in the
development of modern communications media a serious threat to the
general public's right to know about government affairs has grown up
and attained alarming dimensions. The reason for this threat is that
the newly powerful executives and bureaucracies described in the
preceding sections have developed the art of news management to a fine
degree. The situation to which this has brought us is described in the
following words by a commentator:

> 'The state, in other words, now goes in more and more for "news management",
> particularly in times of stress and crisis, which means for most leading capitalist
> countries, almost permanently; and the greater the crisis, the more purposeful
> the management, the evasions, the half-truths and the plain lies.'[32]

News management appears to have originated in 'off the record'
briefings that were started after the First World War and increased
during and after the Second.[33] These led to the custom of providing
news on 'a not for attribution' basis[34] and eventually to the phenomenon
of the press lobby which today provides the source of most press and
television information about government affairs.

The distinguishing feature of all 'managed' news, whether in the
form of briefings, lobby discussions or leaks, is that it is news provided
by officials about the activities of their government. The purpose of

providing news through lobbies, leaks or briefings is often the laudable desire to temper secrecy in the interests of democracy;[35] and there is no doubt that much information that would not otherwise get out reaches the public in this way. But it is vital to remember that for news that gets abroad by this process 'the public must rely on sources that have some vested interest in the information that is given out'.[36] Unless lobbies, briefings and leaks coexist with an independent right of information they could become one of the chief techniques by which governments in democracies produce a contrived or manufactured consensus. The Westminster press lobby, in which the leading British newspapers participate, has in fact been described even in non-radical literature as a new and insidious form of secrecy.[37]

There is little doubt that the right to authentic and accurate information is seriously jeopardized when the communications media are forced to rely exclusively or largely on official handouts or upon 'unofficial' briefings and leaks by officers of government. As the controller of information, the government is in the prime position to promote a certain point of view by releasing some secrets and not others.[38] It has been shown that news released in the United States during the Cuban missile crisis was expressly aimed at producing a newspaper response that the administration desired.[39] While this may be excusable in a crisis of that magnitude, its dangers as a regular practice of government are obvious. During the American involvement in Vietnam news management was continuously and extensively practised by the government so that 'the facts would be fitted to Washington's hopes'.[40] The programme included suppression or distortion of reports relevant to the weakness of the Saigon government, the effect of the bombing, the effect of committing more troops and even the *fact* of further troop commitments.[41] Of the many *ex post facto* revelations on the war, one of the most interesting is the fact the CIA policy advice rejected the domino theory on which commitment to the war was publicly based and was pessimistic about the success of the war strategy.[42] This has led a writer to remark that 'if the Senate Foreign Relations Committee, the press and the public had known of the extent of the intelligence community's doubts, there would have been a genuine uproar about going to war'.[43] Public support for the war was for long sustained by a policy of secrecy combined with news management; but, as Theodore Sorensen has said, that policy in the end produced a great backlash of political anger and bitterness.[44]

If it is true that 'a posture of guerilla warfare . . . should characterize relations between the press and government'[45] in order that the press should be able to fulfil its function of informing the public, it is clear that that lobby system undermines that state of relations by making reporters the willing captives of officialdom. An observable consequence of journalists getting on to a basis of confidentiality with Ministers and officials in exchange for 'off the record news' is a system of self-censorship, all the more dangerous because it carries none of the marks of a system of news control. A co-opted press eventually acts as an unwitting public relations branch of government;[46] and it creates a public that is 'spoonfed with government pap'.[47] Managed news is provided on the assumption that only a limited and privileged class is entitled to know[48] and is usually accepted on the tacit understanding that it will not be used in a way which embarrasses the government. This makes it hostile to, and subversive of, a general right of information.

INTELLIGENCE, INTERNAL SECURITY, NATIONAL DEFENCE AND THE RIGHT TO INFORMATION

Government intelligence, internal security and defence operations are traditional areas of secrecy and therefore pose hard problems for a democratic society:

'A democratic society is confronted with the problem that some intelligence activities require maximum secrecy and that its missions may be spoilt by publicity, whereas democratic government requires publicity.'[49]

A society that demonstrates no concern for this problem has ceased, or is ceasing, to be democratic. The conflict between the requirements of democracy and of a society's intelligence and internal security programmes was not so critical before such programmes became a regular, co-ordinated, efficient and massively financed feature of government. An organized intelligence service was introduced in Britain in 1573 by Sir Francis Walsingham on behalf of Queen Elizabeth I and reputedly consisted of fifty-three agents placed in the courts of foreign monarchs.[50] Modern intelligence services in the United Kingdom appear to go back to a few years before the First World War when MI 5 and MI 6 were set up.[51] Officially and even legally (there is no express common law or statutory creation) these services do not exist. The creation of a modern-type, systematically organized intelligence service is officially credited to Frederick the Great.[52] Later Bismarck developed intelligence as a military staff function.[53] During, between and after the world wars intelligence activities made great strides and began to assume something of the massiveness and efficiency of contemporary programmes. One of the most significant causes of their post-war growth was the 'cold war' of the fifties. The dimensions of present-day intelligence and security operations constitute a grave threat to the right of access to information and more generally to democratic institutions and practices.[54]

The special danger of intelligence and security programmes lies in their inherent tendency towards expansion beyond the original or prescribed goals. A major Congressional investigation into the American intelligence community reached the following conclusion:

'The tendency of intelligence activities to expand beyond their original scope is a theme which runs through every aspect of our investigative findings. Intelligence collection programmes naturally generate ever-increasing demands for new data.'[55]

The Committee made a similar finding on the expansiveness of internal security programmes and secret police activities and cited with approval the testimony of a witness who spoke of the tendency 'to move from the kid with a bomb to the kid with a picket sign to the kid with the bumper sticker of the opposing candidate'.[56] The Congressional Committee made eight major findings on abuses in the administration of American intelligence and security operations and these included one of special relevance to this study: the failure to account to appropriate authorities adequately for their activities.[57] This took place, the Committee said, because of the excessive secrecy practised by the agencies, thus depriving the Congress, the executive and the public of knowledge of abuses and illegal practices.[58] A circumscribed and legitimate secrecy is very readily expanded into broader secrecy practices under the cover of which new and authorized functions are assumed by intelligence communities. Worthy of special note is the fact that the dangers just alluded to were found to be a serious problem in a society in which the constitution and the law impose many limitations on the powers of the intelligence community. Where intelligence and security officials are subject to no or few legal restraints, they very easily constitute themselves into new and unaccountable centres of power in the state.

Certain specific dangers have been found to flow from lack of accountability and of parliamentary and public knowledge of intelligence operations. The essential functions of these agencies is the collection of intelligence material and its evaluation. The tendency of the agencies, both those concerned with external and internal intelligence, to extend their functions under the shield of secrecy to covert *operations* has almost everywhere proved irresistible. These operations have been found to include financial assistance to foreign governments or opposition groups for military or non-military purposes, direct intervention in local or foreign politics to produce changes in power positions, and even assassinations.[59] Apart from the obvious danger to foreign relations and even international peace in such unsanctioned activities, they constitute, in the words of President Truman, a threat to the maintenance of a free and open society. Another major danger is that the super-secrecy which intelligence agencies like to practise, and are frequently allowed to practise, generally impairs rather than enhances the critical judgement of those who evaluate intelligence and of those who act on the evaluations. This is so for various reasons which include the fact that secrecy encourages the worst kind of agents for objective reporting and discourages the consideration of alternative sources of information and views. Discounting the claims made for the superiority of special knowledge derived from secret reports, Carl J Friedrich has said that 'the knowledge of the insiders, of the investigators, administrators and policy makers is woefully inadequate, and certainly does not justify any confidence in their judgment about what constituted the right kind of action, that is to say the rational road to security and survival'.[60]

Just as uncontrolled intelligence activities threaten access to information and democratic rule, so expansive internal security programmes produce similar evils. This because, as a writer has remarked, '[o]nce the government controls the definition of national security, there is no limit to what information it may decide falls within this category'.[61] Controlling the definition of security also enables the authorities to manipulate information to enhance their power or weaken that of their opponents, a problem to which the limitation of secrecy is the only effective answer. Broad security laws and the creation of an extensive security apparatus—another feature of contemporary government in many societies—gravely injures the citizen's right to know.

War, defence and military matters in general have no doubt always contained elements of secrecy and concealment. The increase in the destructive capacity of weapons and the contemporary involvement of science and the military have aggravated an ancient problem to a critical level. In pre-democratic societies it was taken for granted that subjects sent into battle need not know about or participate in political decisions that led to war. If democracy means anything at all it must imply a substantial measure of involvement of citizens called upon to pay the ultimate price in decisions concerning war and peace—'those who are to bleed and die have a right to be consulted'.[62] Consultation is meaningful only if it takes place on the basis of real information; but there is the cruel dilemma that real information designed to increase citizen participation may advantage an enemy or potential enemy. While the public clearly do not need to have the design specifications of actual weapons or the precise location of missile sites to exercise an effective influence on defence and war policy, there is little doubt that the scientific nature of modern warfare has cast defence policy deeply into the shadows. The policy of 'no incineration without representation' is today more difficult to attain than ever.

The needs of defence have a tendency to shroud more than military matters in secrecy. The modern phenomena of the undeclared war and the so-called 'low intensity' war have led to the imposition of drastic curbs on the citizen's general liberty, including his right to know about or participate in matters only indirectly connected with defence. Madison expressed this with great force and clarity when he said: 'Perhaps it is a universal truth that the loss of liberty at home is to be charged to provisions against danger, real or pretended, from abroad.'[63] One only has to be a South African to discover how dangers 'real or pretended' have diminished citizen knowledge of and participation in the whole spectrum of political affairs. The consequential secrecy extends even to facts that are known to the enemy with the result that the government tends to dupe its own people rather than outsiders.

American experience in the war in Vietnam and the Cuban affair demonstrate that even bodies with constitutional authority over questions of war and peace can become the victims of defence secrecy. In the Bay of Pigs episode, the CIA concealed vital information from President Kennedy; and in the Vietnam War Congress was consistently kept in the dark. All wars necessitate some measure of secrecy but surely not to the degree that will impair the judgement of the executive and the legislature in the determination of defence policy. In an authoritative study Francis E Rourke concludes that secrecy practices have the effect of precluding scrutiny of such vital matters as the adequacy of national defence, the possibility of disarmament and the effectiveness of American foreign policy.[64] Concealment has these and other dangers which could easily make it injurious to the very interests it seeks to protect.

Élitist attitudes of the irrelevance of mass opinion in military and defence matters are not lacking, even in societies that confidently claim to be democratic. Walter Lippmann is representative of such attitudes in his expressed belief that popular opinion cannot be right on the large questions of war and peace since these matters require a knowledge and experience which ordinary people lack.[65] His view is fallacious for several reasons. It ignores the moral right of the citizens in a democracy to have relevant knowledge of and influence upon the terrible decisions of war—a right which no one has expressed more cogently than Jefferson:

> 'It is their sweat which is to earn all the expenses of war, and their blood which is to flow in expiation of the causes of it.'[66]

But apart from the moral question, Lippmann fortifies his case by a concealed assumption that the citizen's right to information is virtually the right to take the final decision. The final decision will inevitably be taken by the constituted authorities of the general public. What is demanded is not that these authorities be deprived of their constitutional authority to act but that their judgement on behalf of the people be conditioned by as full an adversary discussion of the issue as the philosophy of the open society implies. The question of exactly how much and what kind of information can safely be provided to government bodies and the general public is without doubt a difficult and complex one. The *New York Times* in a memorable leader declared, 'this is a problem that no society but our kind of open democracy faces; and it is because the maintenance of our kind of open society is so precious, that the dilemma is so terrible'.[67] Therefore, while the problem may be difficult and complex, no society committed to freedom can afford to shirk it.

MODERN SCIENCE AND ACCESS TO INFORMATION

As we have seen, the dependence of military superiority upon science has broadened the range of secrecy in public administration.

But the impact of science on secrecy practices extends far beyond military questions and is evident in the whole range of modern governmental activities. Science in this context includes technology and refers to all the major elements of what Daniel Bell has characterized the 'knowledge society'. These include the development and uses of computers in planning and computer systems of information storage, retrieval and communication; and cybernetics—elaborate control systems based on mathematical foundations and involving the use of electronic technology.[68] Daniel Bell's own words point up sharply the main features of all these developments:

> 'What has now become decisive for society is the new centrality of *theoretical* knowledge, the primacy of theory over empiricism, and the codification of knowledge into abstract systems of symbols that can be translated into many different and varied circumstances.'[69]

The phenomenon that the author here describes is not just a by-product of modern science and technology as it affects government; it involves the conscious utilization by government of the theories and techniques of science and technology in social planning. The result is the increasingly technical and complex nature of government decision-making. This new style of government has the danger, alluded to by Habermas, of concealing latent ideological functions which are 'imbedded in the functions of a presumed system of purposive rational action'.[70]

The negative impact of the knowledge society on general access to information is one of its most depressing features. A society of that kind requires a new class of specialists ('knowledge workers') and they are coming to constitute an influential élite within government. This raises the danger that power will gravitate into the control of a 'new élite of information keepers'[71] whose specialized skills decrease the possibility of accountability and, following Habermas, of the determination of the interests they actually serve. A consequence that has already occurred, it has been said, is the passing of power from legislative bodies to the executive,[72] thereby strengthening the aggrandisement of such power described earlier in this chapter. At the same time the esoteric nature of the knowledge of this class raises the spectre of a permanently uninformed public. Another observable consequence of the new kind of bureaucratic specialization implicit in sophisticated governmental planning is that it introduces new tendencies towards hierarchical structures within government branches; and hierarchy and low levels of information tend to run together, as we have seen. The combination of a specialist élite and a new esoteric language of planning and decision-making could have a devastating impact on informed citizen participation in the most important activities of government.

A consequence of the developments just outlined is that the 'relationship of technical and political decisions' becomes a crucial problem of public policy calling for both theoretical and institutional responses.[73] The nature of possible solutions is best postponed for later discussion;

but it is worth observing at this stage that the new forces threatening both the balance of power within government and the right of the citizen to be informed are to be seen, like computer technology, not as an enemy, but as creating a power to be harnessed for the right purposes.[74]

FOREIGN POLICY AND THE AVAILABILITY OF INFORMATION

The discussion of war and defence policy has demonstrated that the managers of foreign policy, of which the former is an aspect, submit to a reduced level of public scrutiny.   From the earliest times external relations have been conducted in an atmosphere of mystery and secrecy on the explicit or implicit assumption that 'foreign policies bloom better in quiet conference rooms'.[75] The grip of secrecy in foreign affairs is so tenacious that the law and the courts have usually come down squarely on its side. In the American decision of *United States* v *Curtiss-Wright Export Corporation*[76] the court expressed the position in terms that although subsequently criticized as too simplistic and uncompromising, still substantially accord with judicial attitudes:

> 'In this vast external realm, with its important, complicated, delicate and manifold problems, the President alone has the power to speak or listen as a representative of the nation.'[77]

The court partly rested its finding on the secrecy required in foreign negotiations. The common law, under the doctrine of state privilege, exempts from disclosure in courts of law a category of information known as 'state secrets', and this category includes matters relating to international relations.[78] Where statutes have specifically required public disclosure of official information, an exemption in favour of matters concerning foreign relations is usually made. The Freedom of Information Act in America, which compels the disclosure of a broad range of government information, specifically exempts material required to be kept secret in the interest of foreign policy.[79] Secrecy, it seems, has always been, and will continue to remain, a powerful element in the conduct of foreign relations.

While the lack of information about foreign policy and relations is not new, recent developments have heightened the significance of such secrecy for democratic government. In earlier times the distinction between foreign policies and domestic issues was (or at least, seemed) clear-cut; but today that distinction has broken down and there are few foreign policy decisions that do not have an impact on national politics. This is so whether the decision is in the realm of economic foreign policy (the imposition of import quotas or to join the EEC, for example) or one that will inevitably lead to war; in either event, there will obviously be a repercussion on internal affairs. An inevitable result is a broadened range of secrecy for domestic issues and, more than that, the possibility of deliberately extended secrecy policies. This is due to the ease with which any issue 'can somehow be clothed in a foreign affairs cloak', so as to permit the exercise of executive authority' with unrestrained secrecy'.[80] The pervasive nature of foreign policy affairs in the modern state has produced a major new dilemma for those who seek more extensive information about internal politics.

The tendency of foreign policy to move to the centre of the stage of national politics, and to occupy so large a part of it, has baneful consequences similar to those produced by the other modern developments adumbrated in this chapter. Power gravitates naturally to the executive in these circumstances and into the hands of the officials who act as guardians of the information.[81] External relations are generally handled by specialists who can cope with the speed of events and the complexity of issues—a factor that increases both secrecy and the concentration of power.[82] In turn, these make possible covert operations by the intelligence agencies which can have an influence on the shaping of foreign relations which is quite unknown to the public or even the legislature; and the general deception of the citizens as to the causes of, and reasons for, decisions in foreign affairs.[83] Healthy opposition in foreign policy-making is generally absent because dissent is more easily labelled 'treason' and there are no foreign policy interest groups corresponding to domestic interest groups that give internal politics its competitive nature.[84] 'Subtle and powerful pressures' are frequently put on journalists who 'cause embarrassment' in foreign relations.[85]

It is no exaggeration to say that foreign policy has produced a crisis for democracies; and that this problem is particularly intractable because, although democracy demands exposure, effective foreign policy frequently requires secrecy. Bernard C Cohen has said that the two demands in their purest form are incompatible.[86] Nevertheless, the secrecy that surrounds decision-making in the foreign policy area is often unnecessary or too extensive, and more democratic procedures can certainly be devised. In the light of the attitude of the law and courts already referred to, the solution is essentially a political one for citizens, interest groups and legislatures.

NOTES

[1] This is not to suggest that secrecy is never justified and that all executive business must be conducted in the open. The issue is discussed below.

[2] See *None of Your Business: Government Secrecy in America* eds Norman Dorsen and Stephen Gillers (The Viking Press, NY, 1974) 13–14.

[3] David Williams op cit 9.

[4] Harold L Wilensky op cit 137.

[5] Morton H Halperin & Jeremy J Stone 'Security and Covert Intelligence Collection and Operations' in *None of Your Business: Government Secrecy in America* 117.

[6] Thomas M Franck and Edward Weisband, 'Executive Secrecy in Three Democracies: The Parameters of Reform' in *Secrecy and Foreign Policy* 8.

[7] Daniel Bell *The Coming of Post-Industrial Society: A Venture in Social Forecasting* (Heinemann, London, 1974) 311–12.

[8] Anthony Sampson *The New Anatomy of Britain* (Hodder and Stoughton, London, 1971) 67.

[9] Patrick Gordon-Walker, 'Secrecy and Openness in Foreign Policy Decision-making: A British Cabinet Perspective' in *Secrecy and Foreign Policy* 44.

[10] Max Nicholson op cit 178.

[11] See Lewis A Coser and Bernard Rosenberg's *Sociological Theory: A Book of Readings* 3 ed (Macmillan, 1969) 464.

[12] Ralph Miliband *The State in Capitalist Societies* (Quartet Books, London, 1973) 107. See also 47, 53 and 59.

[13] Richard Rose *Politics in England Today* (Faber & Faber, London, 1974) 104. The author says at this place: 'The result is that the Whitehall machine, rather than parliament, is the prime law-making body.'

[14] Max Nicholson op cit 407. See also Jonathan Aitken, *Officially Secret* (Weidenfeld & Nicholson, London, 1971) 36 and 211.

[15] Anthony Sampson op cit 7–8.

[16] Ibid.

[17] *International Encyclopaedia of the Social Sciences* vol 2, 214.

[18] David Apter, *Political Change* (Cass Paperbacks, 1974) 109. See also *International Encyclopaedia of the Social Sciences* vol 11, 323–4.

[19] *International Encyclopaedia of the Social Sciences* vol 11, 325–6.

[20] Anthony Sampson 'Secrecy News Management and the British Press' in *Secrecy and Foreign Policy* 221.

[21] *International Encyclopaedia of the Social Sciences* vol 11, 315.

[22] Richard Rose op cit 233.

[23] Lewis A. Coser and Bernard Rosenberg *op cit* 456.

[24] Max Nicholson op cit 476.

[25] Morton H Halperin *Bureaucratic Politics and Foreign Policy* (The Brookings Institution, Washington DC, 1974) 92.

[26] See, for example, David Williams op cit 55.

[27] Op cit 40.

[28] Ernest Fitzgerald 'Blowing the whistle on the Pentagon' in *None of Your Business: Government Secrecy in America* 254.

[29] Morton H Halperin op cit 150–67.

[30] Ralf Dahrendorf *The New Liberty* (Routledge and Kegan Paul, London, 1975) 41.

[31] Bernard Houghton *Bureaucratic Government: A Study in Late Indian Policy* (P S King & Son, London, 1913) 177–8.

[32] Ralph Miliband op cit 208.

[33] Kent Cooper op cit 277.

[34] M B Johnson *The Government Secrecy Controversy* (Vantage Press, NY, 1967) 24 and 51.

[35] Patrick Gordon-Walker loc cit 47.

[36] William S Moorhead 'Operation and Reform of the Classification System in the United States' in *Secrecy and Foreign Policy* 107.

[37] See, for example, Stanley de Smith 'Official Secrecy and External Relations in Great Britain: The Law and its Context' in *Secrecy and Foreign Policy* 321.

[38] Haynes Johnson 'The Irreconcilable Conflict Between Press and Government: "Whose Side are You On"' in *Secrecy and Foreign Policy* 175.

[39] M B Johnson *The Government Secrecy Controversy* 72.

[40] Raoul Berger op cit 275.

[41] Ibid 265 et seq.

[42] Sanford J Ungar *The Papers and the Papers* (E P Dutton & Co Inc, NY, 1972) 34–5.

[43] David Halberstam *The Best and the Brightest* (Barrie & Jenkins, London, 1972) 668.

[44] Theodore C Sorensen *Watchmen in the Night: Presidential Accountability After Watergate* (The MIT Press, Cambridge, Mass, 1975) 20.

[45] Quoted by M B Johnson op cit 119.

[46] J R Wiggins op cit 238.

[47] M B Johnson op cit 95.

[48] In an interview with a prominent Fleet Street foreign editor, I was informed that lobby news was so written up in the newspapers that those who were 'entitled to know' could discover the truth by reading between the lines.

[49] *International Encyclopaedia of the Social Sciences* vol 7, 42.

[50] David Wise and Thomas Ross *The Espionage Establishment* (Jonathan Cape, London, 1968) 94.

[51] Ibid 97. MI 6 is basically responsible for espionage overseas. MI 5 handles internal security and counter-espionage at home.

[52] *International Encyclopaedia of the Social Sciences* vol 7, 416.

[53] Ibid.

[54] 'The more secrecy, the smaller the intelligent audience, the less systematic the distribution and indexing of research, the greater the anonymity of authorship, and the more intolerance for deviant views and styles of life.' See *International Encyclopaedia of the Social Sciences* vol 11, 327.

[55] 'Final Report of the Select Committee to Study Governmental Operations with Respect to Intelligence Activities' US Senate 94th Congress 2nd session (Report no 94–755) Book II 4.

[56] Ibid 4. See also 23.

[57] Ibid 265. 'On numerous occasions, intelligence agencies have, by concealment, misrepresentation, or partial disclosure, hidden improper activities from those to whom they had a duty of disclosure.'

[58] Ibid 292.

[59] See, for example, Morton H Halperin and Jeremy J Stone 'Secrecy and Covert Intelligence Collection and Operations' in *None of Your Business: Government Secrecy in America* 109 et seq; David Wise and Thomas Ross op cit 167.

[60] Carl J Friedrich, *Limited Government—A Comparison* (Prentice-Hall Inc, NY, 1974) 90.

[61] David Wise 'Pressures on the Press' in *None of Your Business: Government Secrecy in America* 234.

[62] Raoul Berger op cit 345.

[63] Quoted in *None of Your Business: Government Secrecy in America* 23.

[64] Francis E Rourke op cit 16.

[65] Walter Lippmann *The Public Philosophy* 29.

[66] Quoted by J R Wiggins op cit 92.

[67] *New York Times* 28 April 1961.

[68] Zbigniew Brzezinski and Samuel P Huntingdon *Political Power: USA/USSR* (Chatto and Windus, London, 1964) 123.

[69] Daniel Bell op cit 343–4. I am aware that Daniel Bell's general thesis has been criticized as, for example, by Anthony Giddens in *The Class Structure of the Advanced Societies* (Hutchinson, London, 1973) 254 et seq. However, the criticism does not focus on the assertion that theoretical knowledge is of central importance but rather on Bell's argument that the technocrats constitute a newly emergent dominant class.

[70] See Claus Mueller's discussion of Habermas's essay 'Technology and Science as "Ideology" ' in *The Politics of Communication* 109 and Jurgen Habermas 'Theory and Practice in Scientific Civilization' in *Critical Sociology*, ed Paul Connerton (Penguin Books, 1976) 330.

[71] Emmanuel G Mesthene 'How Technology will shape the Future' in *Information Technology in a Democracy* 157.

[72] Daniel Bell op cit 311–12.

[73] Ibid 364–5.

[74] Alan Westin 'The Technology of Secrecy' in *None of Your Busines: Government Secrecy in America* 322.

[75] Bernard C Cohen *The Press and Foreign Policy* (Princeton Univ Press, NJ, 1963) 78.

[76] 299 US 304 (1936) 81 L ed 255 (see also *Chicago and S Airlines v Waterman SS Corp* 333 US 103 (1948), 92 L ed 568 at 576).

[77] Ibid 262.

[78] *Wigmore on Evidence* revised ed (Little, Brown & Co, Boston, 1961) § 2378.

[79] 5 USC 552(b)(1)(A) (April 1976 suppl).

[80] Richard A Frank 'Enforcing the Public's Right to Openness in the Foreign Affairs Decision-Making Process' in *Secrecy and Foreign Policy* 281.

[81] David Vital *The Making of British Foreign Policy* (George Allen & Unwin Ltd, London, 1968) 92.

[82] Ibid 73.

[83] It has been shown, for example, that the Nixon administration was intensely pro-Pakistan in private while claiming to be neutral in public.

[84] Francis E Rourke op cit 204–5.

[85] David Vital op cit 80.

[86] Bernard C Cohen op cit 264.

CHAPTER III

Politics, Power and Secrecy

Extensive secrecy practices are objectionable chiefly because they are harmful to democratic government which, as Woodrow Wilson said with permissible exaggeration, 'ought to be all outside and no inside'.[1] Modern democracy emphasizes the actively participating citizen,[2] while secrecy is a factor strongly responsible for what Eric Fromm has called a 'pathogenic feature' of modern society—the alienated passive man.[3] The other side of reduced public participation and apathy caused by excessive secrecy is the diminished accountability of men in public office. 'Secret power', it has been said, 'is not easily controlled—the levers of such power too often become hidden with the rest of the machinery.'[4] The democratic process is clearly undermined when government is so much on the inside that its officers cease to be accountable for their actions.

The baneful effects of secrecy are not limited, however, to its tendency to weaken democratic government. Too much secrecy has dangerous consequences for all societies, not just those that adhere to democratic values and procedures either fully or in a qualified sense. It is important that these consequences be fully understood.

THE GENERAL DANGERS OF GOVERNMENTAL SECRECY

Although the justifications for governing 'by cloud and by night' are often plausible and even laudable, it is a fact that secrecy and misgovernment tend to be associated. A quotation from President Wilson constitutes the best text for a discussion of this proposition:

'Everyone knows that corruption thrives in secret places, and avoids public places, and we believe it a fair presumption that secrecy means impropriety.'[5]

A public that acquiesces in broad secrecy practices on the part of its government is in effect signing a warrant that will authorize corruption, graft, nepotism and like evils. Other evils, falling short of corruption, are common by-products of secrecy. These may be subsumed under the label 'official lawlessness' and include such practices as illegal wiretapping, bugging and break-ins of the kind revealed by Watergate.

Such lawlessness, it has been observed, becomes routine when governments are permitted to conceal their activities as official secrets.[6] The
misgovernment encouraged by secrecy includes also the more venial
practice of concealing or minimizing the errors of men exercising
power.[7] Secrecy, it is abundantly clear, constitutes a licence to forms of
mismanagement ranging from the false appropriation of public
property to concealment of official lawlessness or bungling. The cure
is not to suppress information about maladministration because it
destroys confidence in government, as a South African politician has
suggested,[8] but rather the rigorous limitation of official secrecy
practices.

Secrecy and the deceptions that go with it harm the relations between
government and citizen and ultimately create a general corrosion of
trust in the authorities. The abuse of secrecy laws frequently produces
the unintended result that the people cease to attach credibility to
government information and statements by officials.[9] The atmosphere
so created is one in which the public is willing to believe anything and
disbelieve everything. Though this situation, on the surface, will
concern only democratic rulers, it does contribute to what Arthur M
Schlesinger has called 'the draining away of truth' to the extent that
nobody, not even those at the top, can distinguish truth from falsity.[10]
In any event, the society that distorts the downward flow of information creates information pathologies which result in cognitive failures
among the leaders as well as in the subjects. This explains in part why
rulers in totalitarian and authoritarian societies lack information about
failures and problems and cannot therefore improve the programmes of
reform inaugurated and controlled by them. 'A dictatorship', it has
been said, 'seems efficient only because it shoves its inconsistencies and
errors beneath the surface.'[11] An atmosphere of misinformation or
limited information also tends to produce opposition motivated by
misunderstanding[12] and simplistic and extreme responses from the
general public. Such responses or opposition may constitute obstacles
to reform desired by leaders even in non-democratic and quasi-
democratic societies.

Yet another danger inherent in expansive secrecy laws or practices
is that progress in science and technology may be jeopardized. Governments became anxious about the open tradition of science as soon as it
seemed clear that military strength was directly dependent upon
scientific progress.[13] An immediate consequence of that anxiety was
the introduction of secrecy programmes designed to protect scientific
secrets from enemies or potential enemies. Inevitably those programmes affected the circulation of information within the scientific community itself and even within the scientific community internal to the
nation applying the curbs. Science has maintained a tradition of internal
publicity and free admission to the profession based on qualifications
only.[14] Security policies designed for preserving scientific secrets have

qualified both aspects of that tradition by curtailing publicity and
limiting access to the scientific profession on grounds that are primarily
ideological. While the consequences of such policies are hard to
measure, it seems reasonably clear that excessive secrecy practices
hamper the discovery of new ideas or the application of existing ones.
This is so because the free flow of data encourages speculation and
experimentation and the possibility of the 'chance discovery' which is
widely recognized as the essential process of scientific innovation.[15]
This process is characterized by 'dramatic leaps from one body of
discovery to another'[16] and is less likely to occur where there is an
impeded access to relevant bodies of data. Secrecy also hampers
scientific and technical achievement by fragmenting knowledge and
narrowing the range of expertness with the consequence of needless
repetition of work and the pursuit of 'blind alley' research results.[17]
The scientific workers who is limited to his own speciality and to what
the authorities decree he 'needs to know' will inevitably be deprived of
sources of inspiration (and these are frequently cross-disciplinary) that
facilitate new discoveries or developments. It has been suggested that
if the security provisions that were introduced in the United States
during and after the Second World War had been applied in pre-war
Germany, the work leading to the discovery of nuclear energy might
not have been possible.[18]

Some governmental controls on the publication of research and on
the access of scientists to classified material is probably inevitable; but
stringent controls may be counter-productive as Walter Gelhorn has
concluded in his authoritative study of the problem:

> 'Secrecy is antithetical to the spirit of science . . . only for brief periods can it be
> practiced without destroying the scientific superiority it is intended to preserve.'[19]

No government, whether democratic or otherwise, can afford to
disturb the conditions necessary for successful research or to discourage
its best scientific minds by irrational restraints on the exchange of
information within the community of science.

Some of the dangers of secrecy are based on (possibly questionable)
psychological assumptions, for example, C P Snow's argument that the
keepers of secrets are likely to become arrogant and dangerous: 'It takes
a very strong head to keep secrets for years, and not go slightly mad.
It isn't wise to be advised by anyone slightly mad.'[20] At the other
end of the scale, the public, from which the secrets are kept, is likely
to suffer a lowered morale in times of crisis if it suspects that information is being suppressed. The suggestion has been made, for example,
that the only thing that seriously upset the British people during the
Second World War was to be denied the true facts even when they
were disconcerting.[21] Moreover, when suppressed news does leak out
it tends to cause more panic than if it were not withheld in the first
instance.[22]

If secrecy policies do carry the burden of the disadvantages just outlined, why are they so appealing to governments and leaders, including those in the so-called open societies? The answer to that question is essentially a twofold one. First, the exercise of power and the use of secrecy have been immemorially linked; and, second, secrecy is sometimes necessary for effective government in the sense that legitimate and laudable goals could be frustrated by the open conduct of governmental business.

SECRECY AND POWER

Secrecy, it has been said, is the 'natural ally and stuff of authority'.[23] When political leaders wish to extend their power they almost inevitably extend the scope of official secrecy. Knowledge is a form of power and a secret knowledge is conducive to absolute power.[24] The association between power and secrecy is frequently overlooked by critics who simple-mindedly condemn governmental secrecy as an evil in politics. Rather than simply condemn, it seems more realistic to recognize, as Hans Morgenthau has said, that '[p]ower in order to be effective, must appear as something other than what it actually is. Deception—deception of others and of self—is inseparable from the exercise of power.'[25] Once the association is understood, the futility of merely wishing secrecy practices away can be replaced by the construction of programmes and practices designed to ensure that power is 'informed and restrained by truth'.[26]

Perhaps the most important way in which secrecy serves power is to conceal the interests which political rulers seek to advance by their decisions. If political leaders can invest their actions and decisions with the quality of neutrality and detachment they increase their legitimacy and enhance the chances of the general acceptance and painless implementation of policies and programmes. Some political decisions may be genuinely neutral in that they represent an overt compromise or accommodation between competing interests; but frequently the quality of neutrality with which politicians manage to invest their programmes is due specifically to the concealment of sectional interests advanced by such programmes. The concealment may be conscious or unconscious, and is perhaps most frequently a mixture of both. But whether intentional or not, there is no denying that secrecy is regularly employed to frustrate or inhibit recognition of the interests which particular policies actually advance or prejudice. The recognition that secrecy strengthens power in this way is a first step towards meeting the criticism that Western democracies are irremediably biased in favour of the interests of capital and against 'working-class' demands.[27] Full appreciation of the way in which power tends to conceal the interests which it serves is a necessary preliminary to the task of providing what Andrew Shonfield has called 'a visible forum for the work of the specialized bodies of senior bureaucrats'.[28] Where the forum of decision-making is more open, power will be less able to masquerade in a false apparel of neutrality and the goal of informing and restraining it by truth will become realizable.

A factor which has strengthened the link between power and secrecy is the difficulty of governing in a modern system of competitive politics with opposition parties being ever ready to frustrate the ruling party by capitalizing on official information. In such a situation it is perhaps inevitable that the government in power will attempt to deny its opponents information which can be forged into political weapons to bring it down. Even where democratic theory unequivocally compels disclosure political leaders tend to conceal what they believe would be politically damaging and thereby bring the practical necessities of power into conflict with the values of the open society. Realism dictates recognition of the fact that every party in power consciously or unconsciously strives to maintain itself in office and that concealment, although contrary to the requirements of good government, may assist it in that task. Confidentiality, as J R Lucas has said, as often as not reflects the concern of decision-makers 'that the government should be, and should be thought to be, doing a good job'.[29] Staying in office depends in part on the ability to cultivate what he describes as '[a] general sense of euphoria and satisfaction with the government', and there must be few political rulers who do not actively seek to achieve a contented public. Their use of secrecy for this purpose demonstrates that at certain points the needs of power inevitably conflict with the ethical requirements of government.

Untimely disclosure by a government may hamper its task of carrying through policies that have had the broad approval of the electorate and which implementation may prove to be generally beneficial. Opponents will often seek to stifle in the cradle newly formulated plans of the governing party and concealment in the early stages may be crucial if these plans are to have a chance of implementation.[30] Information is sometimes leaked from a department of government in order to 'increase the domestic cost' of taking a particular decision and thereby frustrate its execution.[31] Here again the requirements of power, in the form of the ability to formulate and put through new government plans, drive men in office towards a policy of secrecy rather than of disclosure.

EFFECTIVE GOVERNMENT AND THE NEED FOR SECRECY

Secrecy is often resorted to by governments not as an outgrowth of power but on account of functional necessity. In such cases secrecy does not conflict with the requirements of good government—it becomes rather a means of furthering it. A balanced analysis of secrecy and openness in government requires positive support for secrecy where it is functionally necessary rather than the grudging respect that is sometimes conceded. It should be readily conceded, for example,

that the maintenance of a country's defensive capacity and the effective
pursuit of wars into which it may be drawn require secrecy concerning
such matters as tactical plans, weapon design and troop movements.
Excessive demands for publicity have sometimes overlooked such
needs as Arthur M Schlesinger has shown in relation to the American
civil war. 'The confederates', he says, 'got more information from
Northern reporters than they did from Southern spies';[32] and he adds
that this included information about the location of Grant's guns in
the siege of Vicksburg.

Diplomatic negotiation is another area of governmental activity
where concealment is frequently a functional necessity. Without
secrecy diplomatic bargaining will either end in failure or yield less
satisfactory results. This is because publicity forces the bargainers to
'increase their opening demands' and to 'stick to their guns when the
going gets rough'.[33] Where negotiation takes place in secrecy, on the
other hand, 'the participants can bargain more easily and more quickly
come to agreement without loss of face'.[34] Similar considerations apply
to the formation of policy within governments. Publicity in the
embryonic stages of policy-making discourages free and candid
advice and is not conducive to the exploration of all policy alternatives.
If advisers were to be made publicly accountable for the airing of
possible policy positions, advice could be chilled and better alternatives
left out of the reckoning.

These examples of the benefits of secrecy are not intended to exhaust
the instances of its functional necessity. Others such as budgetary
decisions until official release and anti-crime measures might easily be
added. At this stage it is necessary only to underline the point that
certain government operations depend for their effective realization
on a measure of official secrecy.

THE ADVANTAGES OF OPEN GOVERNMENT

A rehearsal of the arguments for secrecy may appear unnecessary in
view of the enthusiasm with which governing parties accept and apply
them in their administration. Despite the popularity of secrecy practices
in government, a restatement of justifications for it is desirable for two
main reasons. The first is that only by examining such justifications can
we appreciate that the need for secrecy, though undoubtedly real, is a
necessity that is strictly limited and circumscribed. The second reason
for taking arguments in favour of secrecy seriously is that only by so
doing can a supporter of open government convert critics and sceptics
to a belief in the principle of citizen access to official information. A
blind and unquestioning faith in open government is likely to produce
a reaction towards the other extreme.

It is in this spirit that we may now proceed to examine the advantages
of open government with, however, a few words of caution. J R
Wiggins has perceptively remarked that the harmful consequences of

concealment are *deferred* and *cumulative* and therefore less easily recognized.[35] Conversely, the advantages of secrecy have a quality of concreteness and immediacy which may make them fatally attractive to politicians whose inclination towards the short-term and the expedient are almost a defining characteristic. The gains of secrecy seem fated to a better understanding than the losses.[36] The ensuing account of the benefits of open government will accordingly be more attractive to the reader, and especially the leader, who possesses in some measure the far-seeing quality of the statesman as opposed to the politico whose horizons lie not far beyond his feet.

Some of the benefits of openness in government will have more relevance for societies that are actually or aspirationally democratic. This is especially true of the argument that informing the citizen strengthens the legitimacy of particular policies or even of entire governmental programmes. Bernard Crick has remarked that states 'who can carry the voluntary enthusiasm of their populations with them' are much stronger than autocracies;[37] and this strength may be built up through greater knowledge of and participation in government. Particular policies will be correspondingly stronger as citizens are informed about them and give them voluntary support. Wise leaders will reject the maxim that it is legitimate to deceive the public into doing the 'right' thing, and will seek to build a broader base of legitimacy for their policies by seeking informed support. The United States' experience in Vietnam supports the statement that 'no foreign policy that does not have its roots in public opinion, that cannot be endorsed and sustained by the elected representatives in parliament, can long endure'.[38] The same appears to be true of the initially secret South African invasion of Angola over which voters were clearly deeply divided. Maintaining policies through misinformation of the public may be successful for a while, especially before the policy starts to go wrong; but when the misguided nature of ill-chosen and non-legitimized programmes becomes generally obvious, the reaction of disillusionment and wrath is likely to harm the political leadership and to poison relations between government and citizen in a variety of perceptible or imperceptible ways. This frequently causes suspicion about and rejection of future policies even when they are beneficial to society. However, it has to be conceded that legitimacy for parties or programmes is something which has little appeal to leadership groups that are autocratic or totalitarian.

The same is not true of the second and central benefit of the open conduct of government business. Any government whether democratic, authoritarian or totalitarian must wish its formulation of law and policy to be effective and efficient in the sense that they correctly express the desired goals and achieve them in the process of administration. Programmes of energy conservation and agricultural development, for example, may be advanced by certain policy decisions and hampered by others. The methods employed in the administration of such programmes may be of a kind that either limit or increase their effectiveness. Even though ideological considerations may impinge on such questions there is an irreducible element of instrumental rationality in governing that will be sought by all governments, whatever their ideological colouring. The ascertainment of the rationally correct solution to problems of government (energy and agriculture, for example) tends to be frustrated by secrecy and facilitated by an open style of governing. This constitutes one of the most significant reasons for keeping secrecy practices down to an essential minimum.

Excessive secrecy in government confines planning to a small coterie of 'reliable' experts. Because 'no government of the day has a monopoly on what little wisdom is going on the subject',[39] the deleterious effects of so limiting the formulation and application of policy may be serious. Opening up the processes of government will contribute to increased rationality and effectiveness in several ways. When outsiders, and particularly outside experts, gain access to relevant official information, the inadequacy of advice to government frequently becomes manifest and much-needed supplemental advice can then be made available to those in office. Openness also tends to create 'centres of outside analysis'[40] which frequently enrich planning by enlarging the known policy options, proving accepted theories wrong and facilitating adjustments to plans from time to time. When too much secrecy surrounds government institutions, the implementation of its policies discourages a feedback of relevant information and increases the tendency of 'pushing through its programmes come hell or high water'.[41] A more open style of planning has the additional advantage of reconciling governments to the inevitability of initial failures and errors in social administration and helps them to avoid the pretence that plans were bound to succeed from the start and the danger of adherence to them purely to save face.[42] Access to information may also enhance rationality and effectiveness by 'narrowing the gap between intent and performance'.[43] The goals of laws are frequently distorted or nullified by their administration; and it is here that the constitutional right of Congressional enquiry into the actual operation of laws has proved valuable in adjusting the practice to the legislative intent. No such enquiries are feasible without a right of access to official information. Finally, the right to scrutinize the actions of government improves administration by keeping officials to a 'pitch of duty'[44] whereas secrecy provides a convenient screen behind which slackness and incompetence may flourish undetected.

The foregoing arguments for open government may be supplemented by still others; for example, the dangers of secrecy outlined earlier in this chapter are advantages from the perspective of the right of citizen access to official information. The jeopardy in which excessive secrecy may place the development of science may be contrasted with

the incentives to scientific progress which the free exchange of information tends to provide. However, sufficient has been said to validate the
argument that for societies that have reached, or seek to attain, a
democratic destination, open procedures of government confer
extensive benefits and advantages that far outweigh the gains of
governing 'by cloud and by night'.

CONCLUSIONS

Openness in the process of governing is a prime value for democratic societies. The application in practice of that value, in addition to
its broadening effect on democracy, produces other benefits unrelated
to the realization of democratic goals. The additional advantages are
of a kind that are sought even by non-democratic societies since they
are conducive to greater rationality and effectiveness in government.
On account of the restrictive political framework of non-democratic
societies the benefits of rationality and effectiveness tend to be elusive
whereas democratic societies are in a position to capitalize on them
and thereby give themselves a strong edge of superiority over other
societies. The advantages of open government, however, depend on
due recognition being given to the legitimate claims of secrecy, and
excessive publicity may be as harmful to good and efficient government
as obsessive secrecy. Moreover, extravagant demands for publicity set
in motion counter-pressures for secrecy and a situation of extremes is
the usual result.[45] The words of Edward Shils on this danger are particularly relevant:

> 'The tradition of liberal, individualistic democracy maintained an equilibrium of
> publicity, privacy and secrecy. The equilibrium was enabled to exist as long as the
> beneficiaries and protagonists of each sector respected the legitimacy of the other
> two. . . .'[46]

Those who wish to maintain open government as a leading virtue of
democracy injure its claims by unrealistically deprecating secrecy which
has a place, though a qualified one, in the governance of all societies.

NOTES

[1] Woodrow Wilson *The New Freedom* (Chapman & Hall Ltd, London, 1913) 111.

[2] Carl J Friedrich 'Reflections on Democracy and Bureaucracy' in *From Policy to
Administration: Essays in Honour of William A Robson* 40.

[3] Erich Fromm 'Humanizing a Technological Society' in *Information Technology in a
Democracy* 202.

[4] David Wise and Thomas Ross op cit 290.

[5] Woodrow Wilson op cit 112.

[6] M L Stein 'The Secrets of Local Government' in *None of Your Business: Government
Secrecy in America* 178–9.

[7] Lord Windlesham op cit 184.

[8] Mr Volker, National Party MP for Klip River, is reported to have said '[I see]
little merit . . . in newspaper exposés of government malpractice. . . . Too much knowledge might shatter public confidence in institutions of this nature.' See W B H Dean
'Whither the Constitution', inaugural lecture delivered at the University of Cape Town
on 2 October 1975, 9.

[9] William S Moorhead, 'Operation and Reform of the Classification System in the United States' in *Secrecy and Foreign Policy* 112.

[10] Arthur M Schlesinger Jr op cit 358.

[11] Marian D Irish & James W Protho, *The Politics of American Democracy* 4 ed (Prentice-Hall Inc, NJ, 1968) 88.

[12] M L Stein 'The Secrets of Local Government', in *None of Your Business: Government Secrecy in America* 164.

[13] Edward A Shils *The Torment of Secrecy*, (William Heinemann Ltd, London, 1956) 182.

[14] Ibid 176.

[15] Walter Gellhorn *Security, Loyalty and Science* (Cornell Univ Press, 1950) 36.

[16] Ibid.

[17] Ibid 40–1.

[18] Edward Shils op cit 189.

[19] Walter Gellhorn op cit 75.

[20] C P Snow *Science and Government* (Mentor Books, 1962) 65.

[21] Kent Cooper op cit 199.

[22] Ibid 194–7.

[23] *Secrecy and Foreign Policy* XV.

[24] *None of Your Business: Government Secrecy in America* 5.

[25] Hans J Morgenthau *Truth and Power* (Pall Mall Press, London, 1970) 14.

[26] Ibid 28.

[27] See, particularly, J Westergaard and H Resler op cit *passim*. Reducing secrecy will also help to mitigate what these authors describe as the 'unspoken assumptions' and the 'anonymous, institutional and routine' exercise of power in Western democracies (pp 246–7). However, their apparent belief that all bias can be eliminated from a political system—and this by the simple expedient of the public appropriation of private property —is here rejected as unrealistically utopian.

[28] Andrew Shonfield, *Modern Capitalism* (Oxford Univ Press, 1969) 391.

[29] J R Lucas *Democracy and Participation* (Penguin, 1976) 104–5

[30] J A G Griffith 'On Telling People' in *Essays on Reform, 1967: A Centenary Tribute* ed Bernard Crick (Oxford, 1967) 17. In his book *Democracy and Participation* 156, J R Lucas has said: 'If the public does not get to hear about what is being done, it cannot protest until the decision has been both taken and carried out, by which time protest is futile and will therefore be only half-hearted.'

[31] Morton H Halperin op cit 183.

[32] Arthur M Schlesinger op cit 335.

[33] Zbigniew Brzezinski and Samuel P Huntington op cit 200.

[34] Ibid.

[35] J R Wiggins op cit 74.

[36] Walter Gellhorn op cit 34.

[37] Bernard Crick 'Participation and the Future of Government' in *From Policy to Administration: Essays in Honour of William A Robson* 65.

[38] George Ignatieff 'Secrecy and Democratic Participation in the Formulation and Conduct of Canadian Foreign Policy' in *Secrecy and Foreign Policy* 58.

[39] Hugh Heclo and Aaron Wildavsky op cit 380. Cf Kent Cooper op cit 281: 'All genius is not confined to those in charge of government.'

[40] Ibid.

[41] J R Lucas op cit 155. As the author points out many government enterprises go wrong because unpalatable facts are screened out and mistaken decisions consequently go unreviewed.

[42] Donald N Michael 'Democratic Participation and Technological Planning' in *Information Technology in a Democracy* 298.

[43] J R Wiggins op cit 72–3.

[44] Ibid.

[45] Edward A Shils op cit 147.

[46] Ibid 26–7.

PART TWO

The Law

CHAPTER IV

The United States—
Laws Restricting Access to Information

The law relating to the control of information about public affairs may have either a negative impact by seeking to restrict the flow of information to persons or groups other than those who control it; or its effect may be positive by affording to such persons or groups a right of access to the information. While this criterion does not neatly divide the relevant law into two clear parts, it should make the ensuing description of American law more comprehensible. The law which restricts or curtails the flow of information falls in this analysis under three main heads: (*a*) Statutory enactments; (*b*) Executive privilege; and (*c*) The classification system. Taken together, the three areas are a compound of common and statutory law, of legislation and administrative regulation, and of constitutional and regular (or non-fundamental) law. We proceed to examine each of these areas before turning to the positive right to information.

STATUTORY ENACTMENTS

United States federal legislation limiting the use of or access to official information is dominated by the so-called Espionage Statutes.[1] Together with the Espionage Statutes we may bracket one or two related provisions of the United States code.[2] Apart from the measures so bracketed, there is a host of specific provisions incorporated into diverse statutes which either restrict information or authorize or prohibit non-disclosure. Since these specific prohibitions run into the hundreds, only a sample analysis and exposition will be attempted.

THE ESPIONAGE STATUTES AND RELATED LAWS

INTRODUCTION

A vital feature of the American law, as distinguished from comparable legislation in the other societies considered in this book, is its limited range and effectiveness. In general, the Espionage Statutes touch only upon defence and related information and avoid the danger of cosmic coverage to which legislatures in these other societies have so

39

readily succumbed. Considered together, and given their broadest interpretation, the Espionage Statutes are in no sense Official Secrets Acts of British and Commonwealth style. Though such wide-ranging laws are probably not conceivable in the American constitutional context, it is noteworthy that they were never intended to have a universal sweep.

THE SCOPE AND EFFECT OF THE ESPIONAGE STATUTES

The Espionage Statutes were first enacted in 1917[3] and, with minor changes, have remained in force every since. There are provisions which, on their face, deal only with classic espionage—the transmission of defence information to a foreign power.[4] There are others which taken at face value penalize acts that are intended to or might conceivably be preliminaries to classic espionage.[5] The ensuing discussion will focus first on the provisions which deal with true spying and will then turn to preliminary or related offences. The publication elsewhere of detailed and authoritative accounts of the American law[6] makes it unnecessary to present more than a broad, impressionistic account of the relevant enactments and interpretative decisions.

CLASSIC ESPIONAGE

The essence of the crime created by the most important and frequently used provision of the Espionage Statutes[7] is the communication to a foreign nation (or agent thereof) of documentary or other information 'relating to the national defense' with intent or reason to believe that it is to be used to the injury of the United States or to the advantage of a foreign nation. The provision is clearly directed at traditional spying whether committed in times of peace or war. This being so it is not surprising that the law easily passed the test of constitutional challenge in *Gorin* v *United States*;[8] and that it has been successfully employed against a number of spies.

Guilt depends upon proof of intent or *'scienter'* which consists of an intention to injure the United States or bring advantage to a foreign nation, or of reason to believe that this will be the result of the communication.[9] The 'or' separating the two parts of the statutory phrase prescribing *'scienter'* has to be read disjunctively with the result that it will be sufficient for the prosecution to prove that the accused intended or contemplated either injury to the United States or advantage to a foreign power. It follows, as the court indicated in *United States* v *Heine*,[10] that the scope of the prohibition is greatly broadened by the words 'to the advantage of a foreign nation' since many acts can be imagined which benefit a foreign nation without injuring the United States. The prohibition has a broad application in two other respects. The advantage intended or within the accused's contemplation refers not just to a hostile nation but to any foreign nation. In *Gorin's* case the Supreme Court declared: 'No distinction is made between friend or enemy. Unhappily the status of a foreign government may change.'[11] Furthermore, it was held in the same case that the expression 'national defense' is a 'generic concept of broad connotations, referring to the military and naval establishments and the related activities of national preparedness.'[12] Though this finding indicates that all kinds of information are covered, not just defence information in the technical and narrow sense, there is an important limitation imposed by the court in *United States* v *Heine* in which Justice Hand said that 'whatever it was lawful to broadcast throughout the country it was lawful to send abroad'.[13] Heine's conviction was therefore quashed by the court because he had collected and sent abroad to agents of an enemy nation information which could be published lawfully in the United States. It appears to follow that the range of material covered will depend partly on the extent to which the government has classified information and withheld authority for its release. On this precise ground the Court of Appeals in *United States* v *Soblen*[14] confirmed the conviction, saying that 'the fact that the source of the information was classified as secret distinguishes this case from *United States* v *Heine* . . . upon which appellant places reliance'.[15] However, classification does not conclusively determine the question of the accused's guilt as the jury will have to decide whether the information is defence related in the broad sense adopted by the courts.[16] But defence-related information not classified or otherwise protected from disclosure is outside the prohibition.

There is nothing unreasonable in interpreting 'national defense' broadly where guilt is conditional upon proof of a guilty mind in the sense already described. As Professors Schmidt and Edgar have said, 'purposeful assistance of the agents of foreign governments may properly be regulated broadly, even though the assistance pertains to matters at the periphery of military affairs'.[17] Excessive overbreadth has been avoided partly by excluding information lawfully in the public domain. Furthermore, it seems that publication in the media of information relating to defence does not constitute criminal espionage even if the information thereby reaches a foreign power, either by reason of Congressional intent[18] or possibly on account of First Amendment requirements. This limitation on liability demonstrates the high value placed in the United States on the right to canvass publicly the great issues of politics even if they are highly sensitive. At the same time, understandably enough, true spying is not left unpunished as in *United States* v *Rosenberg*[19] where the accused were convicted of communicating to the Soviet Union information about an atomic experimental station. In this area of law the balancing of conflicting interests represents at the lowest a defensible compromise.

Still under the heading of classic espionage may be grouped a second provision of the Espionage Statutes which, on account of infrequent use (and, perhaps, even uselessness) deserves only brief treatment. This provision[20] makes it criminal in times of war to collect, record, publish or communicate certain specifically described information relating to the public defence (such as the description or disposition of armed forces, the plans or conduct of military operations or measures taken for the defence or fortification of any place) which might be useful to the enemy and with the intent that it shall be communicated to the enemy. In so far as this crime deals with the communication of defence information to a foreign power, it appears to punish nothing that is not already covered under the first provision criminalizing classic espionage. Indeed, the first provision is more effective for this purpose as the intent requirement is less strict (it does not require an intent to communicate to the *enemy*) and the information covered is broader (that is, not limited to specific categories of information or by the *eiusdem generis* rule of interpretation in its reference to 'other information'). The first provision is not limited to times of war and is also wider in this additional respect.[21] But the crime now under discussion reaches beyond the act of communicating information to a foreign power and also covers the acts of collecting, recording or attempting to elicit the specified information with intent to communicate it to the enemy. The broader reach is of doubtful advantage since proof of intent to communicate to the enemy may be very difficult where no communication has been attempted or taken place; and the intent does not appear to be present where publication in the media takes place with a view to furthering public knowledge or debate, even if the information is certain thereby to reach the enemy. With respect to the prohibition on publication, as opposed to communication, Professor Schmidt has described the provision as being 'so limited as to be, in actual practice, insignificant'.[22] The conclusion that the legislature was unwise to incorporate in the provision, and thereby confuse, both classic espionage and activities that might be preliminary or related to it, seems inescapable.

ACTS PRELIMINARY TO ESPIONAGE

The provisions discussed in the section are collected under a statutory heading which refers to gathering, transmitting or losing defence information.[23] Because diverse and notionally complex crimes are involved, explanation will be clarified by rearranging them under the following rubrics: (1) Gathering with intent; (2) Gathering without intent; (3) Wilful communication or retention; and (4) Negligent loss. In each of these categories, the information protected is defence information.

(1) *Gathering with intent*[24]

There are two crimes which punish the gathering of defence information with intent. The first declares guilty of criminal conduct any person who with intent or reason to believe that the information is to be used to the injury of the United States or the advantage of a foreign nation 'goes upon, enters, flies over or otherwise obtains information' concerning certain specifically described defence places and installations for the purpose of obtaining information respecting the national defence. The second makes it a crime to copy, take or make plans, blueprints, photographs, models et cetera of anything connected with the national defence with like purpose and intent. It is immediately observable that whereas the information covered (defence information) and the intent requirements are materially similar, if not identical, to their counterparts in classic espionage, the activity proscribed here is different. In classic espionage communication to a foreign nation was the act made criminal; here it is 'gathering' that is proscribed.

Because the nature of the information protected and the intent are similar, the decisions reviewed when dealing with classic espionage are relevant. Indeed, in many of these judgments, for example the leading case of *Gorin* v *United States*,[25] the indictment covered both the offences now under consideration and classic espionage. It follows that 'information respecting the national defense' is broadly interpreted on account of the requirement of guilty intent.[26] The disjunctive reading of the intent requirement—either injury to the United States or advantage to a foreign nation may be proved—also governs the gathering offences. In these respects the legal problems that arise are essentially similar. The most significant difference is that the activity of 'gathering' is broader than that of communication to a foreign nation and may more readily encompass actions that have little connection with espionage. This fact might well justify a narrower reading of the expression 'respecting the national defense', but the courts have not so far adopted one.

By far the most critical problem that the gathering offences give rise to is their application to gathering for purposes other than communication to a foreign nation; for example, gathering for publication in newspapers or books in order to focus attention on national defence policy. According to the plain meaning of the provisions in question, a gatherer who realizes that publication will injure the United States or benefit a foreign nation is guilty even if his real purpose is the more laudable one of drawing attention to and correcting the defence policy decisions of the government. It is here that the allowable weight which may be given in the American legal system to legislative history and constitutional prescriptions becomes crucial and helpful. Authoritative analyses of the legislative history demonstrate with fair clarity that while the enactments in question authorize the punishment of the gatherer who intends or contemplates evil use of the material (that is, for transmission to a foreign power) the innocent gatherer is free from legal guilt.[27] A less generous reading is bound to raise serious constitutional difficulties.

(2) *Gathering without intent*

A single provision[28] makes it criminal to receive (or to agree or attempt to receive) documents, notes, plans, sketches et cetera which relate to the national defence and which the recipient knows, or has reason to believe, have been (or will be) received contrary to any provision of the Espionage Statutes.[29] Guilt is therefore conditioned on knowledge that the documents have been received or will be disposed of contrary to the other provisions of the Statutes. Unlike the second espionage section analysed above which commences with the words 'Whoever, for the purpose aforesaid, and with like intent or reason to believe . . .,' the provision now under discussion begins with 'Whoever, for the purpose aforesaid . . .'. The purpose of collecting information respecting the national defence remains a requirement, but the requirement of an intent to injure the United States or advantage a foreign nation has been dropped.

Notwithstanding the clear import of the introductory words to the section now under discussion, an authoritative commentary on the Espionage Statutes argues that the intent requirement should be read into the law.[30] The authority given for this reading is legislative history but it seems doubtful that a conscious and deliberate omission of the words used in earlier provisions to prescribe an intent requirement can be so nullified. It is therefore safer to assume that the only culpability requirement of the crime punishing receipt of defence information is knowledge that the information has been received (or will be received) contrary to other sections of the Espionage Statutes. Even so, the scope of the prohibition is limited by its reference to information of a documentary type only and possibly also by the narrow construction of the other sections to which it refers.[31]

(3) *Wilful communication or retention*

Two provisions[32] of the Espionage Statutes make it a crime to communicate defence information to *any person* not entitled to receive it. In the circumstances prescribed, retention of such information is also an offence. Since what is punished here is wilful communication or retention without any evil intent, these two provisions approach most closely the British-type official secrets laws. Nevertheless, there are important differences. The British laws protect all official information whereas the provisions under discussion refer only to defence information—a limiting factor however broadly the expression is interpreted. Secondly, whereas the British laws can and will be applied by the courts free from constitutional restraints, these particular provisions of the Espionage Statutes are fraught with constitutional difficulties, to speak only mildly.

What precisely is declared illegal by the prohibitions now under discussion? The first prohibits the wilful communication, delivery or transmission, by a person in lawful possession or control thereof, of documentary or other tangible information relating to national defence, or of non-tangible information relating to the national defence which the possessor has reason to believe could be used to the injury of the United States or the advantage of a foreign nation, to any person who is not entitled to receive it. Furthermore, if such a lawful possessor wilfully retains and fails to deliver such information on demand to an officer or employee of the United States entitled to receive it, he is guilty of an offence. The second prohibition is similar but deals with unauthorized possessors rather than lawful possessors. The offence of wilful communication is defined in precisely the same way for the unauthorized possessor but the offence of retention is not conditioned upon prior demand; simple retention constitutes a crime if the possessor is not authorized to have the documents.

On the face of the statutory language the culpability requirement is clearly different from the intent to injure the United States or advantage a foreign nation that is specified in other sections. While some writers have boldly declared that a similar intent governs these provisions by implication,[33] others have laboured manfully to justify a reading of wilful communication that falls somewhere between simple consciousness of the act committed and an intention to cause injury or advantage.[34] The only court decisions on the question regard the intent requirement as being satisfied by proof of a knowingly unauthorized transfer of defence information,[35] though it ought to be noted that the question arose almost tangentially in these cases. Without doing violence to sound principles of statutory interpretation it is hard to conclude that the intent required is any more than a knowingly unauthorized transfer or retention. This must necessarily result in a different reading of the words 'information relating to the national defense' because, as we have seen, a broad construction of these words was regarded as permissible only when linked with an evil intent. But it is extraordinarily difficult to settle upon a narrower reading, and the existence of other provisions protecting more narrowly defined categories of defence information compounds the difficulty. The conclusion seems almost inevitable that the wilful communication and retention provisions are void on their face.

The conclusion was not deemed inevitable by Justice White in some surprisingly incautious *obiter dicta* in *New York Times* v *United States*.[36] The government, in this case, sought an injunction against the *New York Times* to restrain further publication of the Pentagon Papers and based its arguments on the inherent powers of the Executive to prevent publication of material gravely injurious to the United States. Though the government had not relied on the power to restrain breaches of the Espionage Statutes, Justice White went out of his way to declare that newspapers would be subject to punishment under the communication and retention provisions. While he was willing to join the majority in refusing the injunction, he was also at pains to assert the relevance of the Espionage Statutes and, without the advantage of full argument concerning their import and scope, assumed their constitutional validity. In the circumstances this judgment is hardly dispositive of the question. The prosecution of Dr Daniel Ellsberg under the Espionage Statutes might have produced an authoritative pronouncement from the Supreme Court on all these issues, but the government's case came to a premature conclusion for procedural irregularity and resolution of the complex problems of interpretation and constitutionality must await another day.

The broad prohibitions on wilful communication and retention are pregnant with other difficulties of interpretation. The sections in question proscribe communication of defence information to persons not entitled to receive it but offer no statutory guidelines for determining when a person has authority to receive. A problem of equal difficulty has arisen in relation to the British Official Secrets Acts which *inter alia* prohibit the unauthorized communication of official documents and information. The Franks Committee, which was appointed to investigate the provision in question, was unsure whether information is 'unauthorized' only when communication has been specifically forbidden or whether 'unauthorized' meant that everything was unauthorized except communications specifically sanctioned.[37] The Committee decided that the latter was probably the intended result. In the United States there is a temptation to make the question turn on the presidentially authorized classification system but this solution is less simple than it superficially appears.[38] Another difficult question that arises is whether publication in the press of defence information is a prohibited communication. In general the position of the press in relation to these offences is a difficult one and will have to be decided in the light of the uncertain scope of First Amendment requirements.[39] The retention offence has its own special problems since it is not restricted to documentary-type information and appears therefore to penalize even the retention of recollections! The law is clearly ripe for repeal or amendment if not for a declaration of constitutional invalidity.

(4) Negligent loss

It is a criminal offence for anyone in lawful possession of documentary or other tangible information relating to national defence by gross negligence to permit the loss, theft or removal thereof or to fail to report such loss, theft or removal to a superior officer.[40] The provision refers primarily to government officials (and, perhaps, government contractors to whom defence information has been entrusted) and despite the use of the word 'information' appears to be limited to loss of tangible kinds of defence data by reason of the *eiusdem generis* rule and the inapplicability of the acts punished (theft, loss, removal, etc) to non-tangible information.

RELATED OFFENCES

The United States Congress has also enacted a number of more specific offences which criminalize the transmission of information without evil intent. In general these provisions have a restricted scope and should accordingly be immune to constitutional attack. The first makes it an offence for any person to knowingly or wilfully communicate to an unauthorized person, to publish or to use prejudicially to the United States any classified information concerning codes, cryptographic systems or apparatus, communications intelligence activities or material obtained from foreign governments by the processes of communications intelligence.[41] The information protected is narrowly defined and all key expressions are elaborated by specific definition. The information must have been classified, but provided that it relates to the specific categories enumerated by the section the courts are unlikely to allow the propriety of classification to be challenged since this might involve the government in revealing what the provision was designed to conceal.[42] Though drawn in commendably tight language, the prohibition could have been used to limit public discussion about the propriety of U2 spying over the USSR and the Pueblo incident off North Korea until the government had made the information public. These events clearly constituted 'communications intelligence activities' and the simple act of unauthorized publication (as in fact occurred) is within the reach of the law. Thus even narrowly drawn statutes may impede public discussion of important policy issues and decisions. However, express provision is made for the participation in such decisions by committees of Congress since the prohibition does not extend to the disclosure of information to such committees upon lawful demand.[43] No other provision of the Espionage Statutes is characterized by such precision in drafting or by so thoughtful a balancing of competing interests.

A provision applying mainly to officers or employees of the United States makes it a criminal offence for such persons to knowingly communicate to an agent of a foreign government or to an officer or member of a communist organization any information that is classified as affecting the security of the United States unless such disclosure has been authorized by proper authority.[44] Two features of the crime indicate that it is of narrow application: its reference to government employees and its concern with classified information. In *Scarbeck* v *United States*[45] the government proved that the accused, whilst on the staff of the United States Embassy in Warsaw, had communicated classified documents to a representative of the Polish government. The accused argued in his defence that guilt depended upon a showing by the government that the documents had been properly classified as affecting national security. In confirming the conviction of Scarbeck, the court rejected the proposition that the propriety of the classification had to be established by the prosecution. It said that 'neither the employee nor the jury is permitted to ignore the classification given under Presidential authority'.[46] *Gorin's* case was distinguished as applying to 'the entire population' whereas the section at issue in *Scarbeck* was aimed at a small group.[47] The judgment demonstrates the sensible partiality of American courts for precisely drawn criminal statutes.

Wilful and unauthorized communication or publication of diplomatic codes or matters prepared therein, or of material obtained while in the process of transmission between a foreign government and its diplomatic mission in the United States, by a person who obtained such material by virtue of federal employment, is also a criminal offence.[48] The limited application of this section is again indicated by its reference to a narrow class of person (present and past federal employees) and a restricted class of subject-matter (codes and diplomatic transmissions).

The Espionage Statutes authorize the President to define 'vital military and naval installations and equipment' as requiring protection in the form of a prohibition on the communication of information concerning such installations or equipment.[49] It then becomes an offence to make photographs, pictures, drawings et cetera of the designated installations or equipment without authority[50] or to reproduce, publish, sell or give away the photographs, pictures or drawings without authority or an indication thereon that it has been censored by proper authority.[51] The President has designated installations and equipment as requiring protection but has included not just 'secret places and hardware' but also all classified documents.[52] Because the prohibitions apply to all persons, require no evil intent and include publication as an offence, it seems doubtful that this broad definition of installations and equipment will be proof against legal challenge.[53] However, the prohibition on the dissemination of information about 'secret places and hardware' is of undoubted validity.

EVALUATION OF THE ESPIONAGE STATUTE AND RELATED LAWS

The preceding exposition of United States statutory laws falling under the above heading has revealed that this branch of the law consists of an unfortunate compound of provisions directed at classic espionage and those directed at more innocent forms of revelation; and also of broadly ranging sections and more tightly drawn provisions. Judicial construction has validated the broad provisions where espionage is involved, and the law is clearly effective against classic spies. Court interpretation is likely to be less generous where no evil intent is required by the law (as in the case of the offences prohibiting wilful communication or retention) unless the prohibitions are narrowed by reference to the class of person or material involved. The present uncertainties affecting several provisions of the espionage statutes are due in part to the confused compounding of notionally distinct offences.

The principles of desirable legal reform appear to be the following: (1) The separation of spying offences from other forms of revelation; (2) the retention of a broad definition of protected material for true espionage offences on the assumption that a person who intends to benefit a foreign power may properly be punished for transmitting even slightly sensitive information; (3) the restriction of the gathering, retention or communication offences to narrowly defined categories of highly sensitive information such as codes, communications intelligence and military weapons and plans. Detailed suggestions are best reserved for later elaboration.

SPECIFIC PROVISIONS PROHIBITING DISCLOSURE OR AUTHORIZING NON-DISCLOSURE

Over the years Congress has enacted many statutes which incorporate provisions that prohibit disclosure of specified information, exempt material from disclosure or authorize some person or body to withhold information. When the Freedom of Information Act was passed by Congress in 1967 it was estimated that there were nearly a hundred statutes of this kind in existence.[54] The Freedom of Information Act sought to preserve the non-disclosure which these other statutes directed or authorized in an exemption which has proved to be both cloudy and controversial. The exemption declared that the provision of the Act requiring mandatory disclosure should not apply to matters that are 'specifically exempted from disclosure by statute'.[55] Though the intention of this exemption was to preserve the restrictions on access to information enacted in diverse statutes, many courts felt themselves obliged to qualify the exemption in order to give some meaning to the words 'specifically exempted' and to further the legislative policy behind the Freedom of Information Act. In general these courts concluded that to fall within the exemption the statute must have identified some class or category of information that is protected from disclosure.[56] The result in many cases was that the non-disclosure provisions of existing statutes were nullified by court rulings. The ruling of the Supreme Court in FAA Administration v Robertson[57] overturned all such rulings[58] and held that the effect of the exemption under the Freedom of Information Act was to preserve unqualified the non-disclosure provisions of other statutes. The Federal Aviation Administration (FAA) had declined to make available to a suitor under the Act reports on the maintenance performance of certain commercial airlines and cited as authority a section of the Federal Aviation Act which authorized the Administrator to withhold any information which in his judgement would adversely affect the interests of an objecting party. Though this section referred to no specific class or category of protected material and prescribed no guidelines for the exercise of the Administrator's judgement, the court held that it fell within the exemption and was effective to prevent disclosure. In the words of Justice Stewart, 'it seems . . . clear that Congress intended to leave largely undisturbed existing statutes dealing with the disclosure of information by specific agencies'.[59] The word 'specifically' in the exemption to the Freedom of Information Act was therefore held to mean no more 'than that the exemption be found in the words of the statute rather than the implication of it'.[60] However, the effect of this Supreme Court ruling was modified by an amendment to the exemption protecting statutory exclusions passed in 1976 as part of the government in the Sunshine Act. As modified by Congress the exemption now protects material specifically exempted from disclosure by statute 'provided that such statute (A) requires that matters be withheld from the public in such a manner as to leave no discretion on the issue or (B) establishes particular criteria for withholding or refers to particular types of matter to be withheld'.[61] Thus a mandatory prohibition on disclosure in another statute continues to be effective, but where non-disclosure is discretionary the statute is effective only if criteria for the exercise of discretion are provided or particular types of matter are identified as protectable by the statute.

The statutory restrictions on the provision of information that were in force when the Freedom of Information Act was enacted are too numerous and varied to be surveyed here. They range from income tax returns through social security materials to data about atomic energy. Two of these restrictions merit brief examination either because of their inherent significance or for their value in illustrating the effect of the amended exemption governing statutory restrictions on disclosure. The first applies to all employees of the United States (including any department or agency thereof) and prohibits them under criminal penalty from divulging or publishing information received in the course of employment relating to trade secrets or commercial or financial matters.[62] Though early court decisions uniformly declared that the third exemption of the FOIA was not broad enough to validate the prohibition on disclosure in this section,[63] the Supreme Court ruling in *FAA Administrator* v *Robertson*[64] by implication affirmed its legal effectiveness.[65] The amended third exemption has no effect on this ruling since the prohibition of disclosure in the section is mandatory; and in any event the types of information which may not be released seem to be adequately described in the statute.

The second statutory restriction meriting special discussion is one of great inherent significance—the protection of information relating to atomic energy. The technical expression for the material protected is 'restricted data', which is defined to include all data relating to the design, manufacture or utilization of atomic weapons, the production of special nuclear material or the use of special nuclear material in the production of energy.[66] The Atomic Energy Commission is vested with power to protect restricted data *inter alia* by regulation;[67] and also with power to declassify material so that it falls outside the protected category of restricted data.[68] The Commission's power to protect information is discretionary but the power appears to be valid because the 'particular types of matter to be withheld' are described as required by the amended Freedom of Information Act. The Act furthermore declares that consistently with the requirements of common defence and security, the dissemination of scientific and technical information on atomic energy should be encouraged to advance scientific and industrial progress. The criminalization of the transmission or misuse of restricted data is reasonably restrained considering the sensitivity of the topic. The two main offences punish the disclosure of restricted data to any person 'with intent to injure the United States or . . . to secure an advantage to any foreign nation' and the disclosure to any person of such data with reason to believe that it will be utilized to bring about such injury or advantage.[69] Other provisions penalize the receipt of restricted data (or tampering with it) with similar intent.[70] Mere unauthorized disclosure of restricted data is also made an offence but only in respect of employees, ex-employees, contractors, ex-contractors and the like.[71] An injunction may be brought to restrain violations of these provisions or regulations made under the Act.[72]

Despite the limited nature of the criminal sanctions, the statutory regulation of information relating to atomic energy has been criticized for the blanket definition of all atomic data as restricted. The result, it has been said, is that all atomic energy information is 'born secret' and a heavy burden is put on the Commission of justifying disclosure rather than concealment.[73] This has kept top officials of government and allies in ignorance, the latter even in respect of 'the capability upon which, soundly or unsoundly, they are greatly relying'.[74] Another consequence of major importance is the distortion of the democratic process consequent upon the 'superabundance' of secrecy.[75] The recognition of these dangers to democratic processes was probably responsible for amendments in 1974 providing more extensively for full reports to Congress by the Committee and for the presentation of such reports to be 'to the maximum possible extent in open sessions and by means of unclassified written materials.'[76] But the differentiated treatment of atomic data for the purpose of providing a criterion for disclosure[77] has not yet become a reality.

The nearly one hundred statutes at the federal level of government which criminalize the disclosure of information, restrict access to it or authorize in broad terms the power to withhold, stood until 1976 in sharp contrast to the judicially controlled standards for the concealment of information under the Freedom of Information Act. The 1976 amendment will now force a review of these laws to determine how far they are consistent with the FOIA. It seems, for example, that the unlimited disclosure provision, with criminal penalties attached, protecting returns and reports obtained by the Department of Health, Education and Welfare unless the secretary of the Department decided otherwise,[78] is in a format now nullified by the FOIA. In *Stretch* v *Weinberger*[79] the court ruled that the provision was in effect nullified by the Act; but that judgment was itself nullified by the Supreme Court.[80] The amended Freedom of Information Act appears to restore the finding in *Stretch* since prohibition of disclosure is not mandatory and the prohibition neither provides criteria for withholding nor determines the types of matter that are to be protected.[81] A general review of specific concealment statutes seems essential in the light of the amendment, which appears to relegate to history the sweeping controls over disclosure that many laws permitted.

EXECUTIVE PRIVILEGE

The rule or doctrine of law known as executive privilege is an instrument for withholding or restricting access to information in the control of the executive branch of government. The doctrine has also been invoked to justify the alleged immunity of the President from legal process;[82] but this aspect of it is only indirectly relevant to this discussion. Executive privilege in the informational sense has been asserted to deny information to litigants in court proceedings—the rule of evidentiary privilege—and to prevent Congressional access to material controlled by the executive. The ensuing discussion will focus on denials of information which the Congress has sought for the performance of its functions. The narrower right to material required for litigation will be referred to incidentally and analogically since it is concerned more with the protection of litigants than with the right to know in the political sense.

Relying on the doctrine of executive privilege, the executive branch in America has with increasing frequency claimed a right to withhold information in its control from Congress or its committees. The information alleged to be protected from disclosure by this privilege has usually fallen into identifiable categories such as military and foreign affairs, investigative files and reports, information made confidential by statute and internal opinions and advice.[83] In early times assertions of the privilege were infrequent, but in the past two or three decades denials have swelled to a veritable flood. A report of the Library of Congress discloses 49 assertions since 1952 (double the number of *all* prior instances) and at least 20 denials in four years under the Nixon administration.[84] The frequency of executive denials runs parallel with, and is probably largely attributable to, the growth in power of the executive arm of government and the proliferation of its records. This fact underlines the relation between power and knowledge and the importance of access to information as a means of limiting power. The tendency to convert denial into a rule, with disclosure as the exception, is perhaps a less dramatic and disturbing development than the broadening of the privilege 'to everybody in the executive branch' in contrast to the historical doctrine that the President alone had authority to invoke it.[85] Regular use of the expanded doctrine has brought into being a dangerous engine of executive usurpation and lawlessness.

Behind the statistics of demands for information and their refusal there lay brewing a conflict of major dimensions between the legislature and the executive. Though these two branches of government were the nominal parties to the dispute, it affected no less the right of the people at large to learn fully about major decisions of government. While not all material confided to Congress is thereby made available to the public, and while Congress is empowered to protect information coming to it,[86] the people's right to know was as much at stake in this conflict as that of the legislature. Certainly in the Watergate tapes case, in which the Supreme Court brought to a resolution some of the major legal issues in the dispute over executive privilege, the resultant gain was as much the public's increased knowledge of those murky events as that of the special prosecutor who brought the suit.

The major issue of absolutely fundamental importance was the claim made by the executive that it had sole power to decide what information it was entitled to withhold as executively privileged. Expressed in this extreme form, the doctrine warrants the stricture of Professor Berger that it needs to be lifted from the field of legal esoterica and viewed in terms of underlying reality: as a shield for executive unaccountability.[87] Early denials were not expressed in absolutist language,[88] but as the conflict sharpened the privilege of the executive was couched in increasingly unqualified terms. Attorney-General Rogers, in a memorandum to the Senate Sub-committee on Constitutional Rights, spoke of 'an uncontrolled discretion to withhold information and papers in the public interest';[89] and similar assertions of an unreviewable discretion were put to the courts in the Watergate tapes cases.

Though the interest of a private litigant to information that will assist his suit appears to be of less weight than the right of Congress to material necessary for the performance of its vital functions, evidentiary privilege has not been cast in absolute terms by judicial precedents. Even in *United States* v *Reynolds*,[90] where military secrets were involved, the court reserved to itself the final decision as to the validity of an assertion of executive privilege, though it has to be admitted that the language of the judgment is at times ambivalent and contradictory. The plaintiff was the widow of a civilian killed in the crash of an airforce plane carrying highly secret electronic equipment and sought the production of investigative reports into the accident by Air Force experts. The court denied production but reserved the power to determine how far it should 'probe in satisfying itself that the occasion for invoking the privilege is appropriate'.[91] In criminal cases, where the interest in ensuring a full and fair trial is involved—an interest more momentous than that of the civil litigant but arguably of lesser significance than the broad oversight and investigative powers of Congress[92]—

the courts have displayed an equal or greater reluctance to defer to executive judgment. In *United States* v *Burr*[93] the production of papers in the hands of President Jefferson was sought by the accused in a treason trial. Chief Justice Marshall expressed both his discomfort and his awesome duty in these words: 'It cannot be denied that to issue a subpoena to a person filling an exalted position of the Chief Magistrate is a duty which would be dispensed with more cheerfully than it would be performed; but, if it be a duty, the court can have no choice in the case.'[94] Later in his judgment he envisaged protecting only matter 'not essential to the defence';[95] and in due course Jefferson left it to the court to determine what parts of the papers should be protected as not relevant. Professor Freund has said that this and the other Burr judgments establish the principle that there is no absolute privilege in a criminal case and that the court will weigh the competing interests involved in the assertion of the right to withhold.[96]

The culminating judgment in the judicial history of the problem is that of the Supreme Court in *United States* v *Nixon*[97] in which the special prosecutor appointed to investigate violations of the law in the Watergate affair sought production of taped conservations between the President and his advisers. The district court overruled the President's motion to quash the subpoena on the basis of executive privilege in confidential discussions and advice and ordered production of the tapes for *in camera* inspection. The Supreme Court affirmed the district court ruling and held that the interest in the confidentiality of the decision-making process, even if backed by the doctrine of the separation of power, could not 'sustain an absolute and unqualified Presidential privilege of immunity from judicial process under all circumstances'.[98] The court, it is true, put outside the reach of its decision cases in which the need arose to protect 'military, diplomatic, or sensitive national security interests';[99] but even in those cases the logic of judicial evaluation holds and is vital though it might not extend beyond the determination of whether the assertion of the privilege is in fact based on the protection of military, diplomatic or security interests. Significantly, the Court of Appeals for the District of Columbia has recently said that none of the authorities referred to it establishes that courts are foreclosed from acting with respect to disputes involving national security.[100] The extreme caution of courts where such sensitive interests lie behind executive privilege hardly weakens the recognition in *United States* v *Nixon* that the doctrine raises a dispute about 'the scope of intersecting powers' and that the judiciary has power to make a binding determination.[101] The court has since reaffirmed this approach in *Nixon* v *Administrator of General Services*[102] in which a Congressional statute providing for the seizure, classification and ultimate disposition in accordance with law of the papers of ex-President Nixon by an official of the executive branch was declared valid. The court balanced the intrusion into the confidentiality of the papers that was implicit in the process of control and classification authorized by Congress against the interests that Congress sought to achieve by the legislation and concluded that the intrusion was too limited to override these interests.[103]

The conclusion that disputes raised by a claim of executive privilege are ultimately subject to judicial resolution does not validate Professor Berger's view that the doctrine is a myth. In *Senate Select Committee on Presidential Campaign Activities* v *Nixon*[104] the court held that conversations that take place in the performance of presidential duties are presumptively privileged even from *in camera* inspection. The court declared that the President and his direct advisers should continue 'to work under a general assurance that their deliberations would remain confidential'.[105] The presumption should hold unless countered by a strong showing of contrary need. Asking whether the taped conversations which had been subpoenaed were 'demonstrably critical to the responsible fulfillment of the Committee's functioning',[106] the court found that the need demonstrated was too attenuated and tangential to the Committee's functions and it confirmed the judgment of the district court in which an order for production was refused. Congressional resort to the court carries no certainty of success, least of all where the disclosure sought is contested on the basis of executively privileged military, diplomatic or national security information. What has been shown to be mythical is the executive assertion that it has an unfettered and unreviewable power to determine what information may be withheld from Congress or the courts. In the words of a recent commentary on the history of executive privilege, '[t]he claim that the President has unlimited power to withhold material sought by Congress or the courts is as untenable as the assertion that he has no power to do so'.[107]

The protection of advice within the executive branch will clearly continue to receive court approval despite the stricture that candid exchange is 'merely another testimonial to the greedy expansiveness of power, the costs of which patently outweigh the benefits'.[108] But because candid exchange may be abused to conceal corruption, inefficiency or crime, the privilege needs to be qualified by certain limitations. Among the limitations proposed by commentators on the privilege are the restriction of the privilege to advice as distinct from actual decisions or factual material, and the exclusion of criminal or corrupt advice from the protected area. The procedural limitation that the privilege may be asserted only at the personal direction of the President has also been suggested by the same commentators.[109]

Where the conflict over information is between the executive and legislative branches rather than a problem of evidentiary privilege, communication and co-operation between the branches offers a more sanguine prospect of reasonable accommodation than too ready an appeal to the judges.[110] Courts are more comfortable in cases of evidentiary privilege 'where relevance and materiality are more focused in the search for defined facts than in a wide-ranging enquiry either to furnish a basis for legislation or to probe into mal-administration'.[111] The sanction most likely to guard against misuse of executive privilege is knowledge that the courts are prepared to assume the role of the ultimate arbiters of such a boundary-of-powers dispute. Indiscriminate resort to litigation to compel disclosure could weaken that sanction.

While evidentiary privilege is a doctrine of the common law, executive privilege appears to be an attribute of the principle of separation of powers and therefore constitutionally based.[112] In *Nixon v Administrator of General Services*[113] the Supreme Court referred to the privilege as one which 'derives from the supremacy of the Executive Branch within its assigned area of constitutional responsibilities'. The distinction is significant in at least one setting—the interrelation between executive privilege and the Freedom of Information Act. That Act provides for mandatory disclosure of information subject to nine exemptions of which some protect against disclosure the same categories of information that fall under executive privilege. However, the range of protection may not be identical and the question could arise whether executive privilege may be used to withhold information that is not exempt from disclosure under the Act. Despite the suggestion that the 'constitutional underpinnings' of executive privilege have not been fully articulated,[114] the court judgments recognizing it appear to be premised on the implications of the constitutional allocation of power to the executive. If that be so, Congress may not by statute withdraw the implied power and executive privilege will prevail in a conflict with the Act.

In the broad sense, executive privilege can be (and has been) invoked to deny information to the courts, Congress and the public. The courts, it has been suggested, have asserted the right to weigh the need for the asserted privilege 'across the entire spectrum of evidentiary privilege'.[115] The invocation of the broader doctrine, covering the rights of Congress and people to information about executive decisions, is now in principle subject to the same independent weighing by the judiciary. This advance in the application of the rule of law to executive as well as to evidentiary privilege is of momentous significance.

CLASSIFICATION

Classification is essentially an internal instrument of administration designed to limit and control access to government material thought to be so sensitive as to require special protection. Systems of classification invariably establish categories (top secret, secret, confidential, et cetera) according to which documents are graded to establish the degree of sensitivity and the extent of protection required. Once material is classified special requirements as to custody and access come into operation. These rules are designed to ensure that only trustworthy persons who need to see the material for purposes of their official responsibilities have access to it.

In the United States authority for the protection of government records goes back to a number of statutes collectively known as the 'housekeeping statute'. These were combined in one law in 1875 and authorized the head of a government department to prescribe regulations inter alia for the 'custody, use and preservation of the records, papers, and property appertaining to it'.[116] Because of dissatisfaction with the way this section had been interpreted by the executive and the courts to authorize the withholding of records, Congress amended the statute in 1958 by providing that the section in question did not permit withholding records or information from the public.[117]

Formal classification was first introduced by the military in the First World War when a system of special markings ('Secret', 'Confidential' and 'For Official Circulation Only') was adopted to protect war secrets.[118] The system was retained and extended in the Second Word War and at the end of that war was in use by government departments handling national security information.[119] By this time a paper explosion in government departments had taken place and the system of control was inefficient. The result was the first formal and comprehensive attempt to extend classification throughout federal government in the form of an Executive Order issued by President Truman in 1951.[120] And so it was, not for the first or last time, that an exigency of open war became generalized as a peacetime practice.

The Truman classification system allowed any department to classify on a uniform basis[121] and did not even limit the number of persons entitled to classify. Delegation could extend 'to the very bounds of the executive branch itself'.[122] Procedures for downgrading and declassification, and for review of the administration of the Executive Order, were totally inadequate. Not surprisingly criticism grew, especially from the press which charged that the system made it possible to cover up mistakes and intrigues under a national security veil.[123] Dissatisfaction resulted in the replacement of the Truman system with an Executive Order brought in by General Eisenhower on 15 December 1953.[124] The Eisenhower Order reduced the classification categories from four to three (by eliminating the 'restricted' category) limited the agencies entitled to classify and introduced a declassification system. But there remained as defects the vagueness of the classification categories, insufficient reduction of classifying authority and the lack of automatic declassification and oversight procedures.

Ironically, the current and much improved system of classification now in force was introduced by President Nixon. The Nixon Order took effect on 1 June 1972[125] and followed a number of investigations that had revealed major flaws in the previously operating systems. The reports that followed these investigations revealed a massive over-classification problem together with deliberate and unauthorized disclosures. (The dimensions of the problem are strikingly indicated by the finding that 1,5 million government employees were authorized to classify documents.) They also drew attention to the danger of the suppression of information under the classification programme for purposes other than national security and the resultant distortion of the processes of open government.[126] The possible dimensions of that distortion may perhaps be indicated by the revelation that the State Department had estimated that it held 35 million classified documents and that the Archivist of the United States testified that 470 million pages of classified documents were held in the Archives.[127]

The Nixon Executive Order preserves three categories of classified material which are described as Top Secret, Secret and Confidential. The test for assigning a top secret grading is whether disclosure could reasonably be expected to cause exceptionally grave damage to national security as compared with the reasonable expectation of serious damage in the case of secret information and simply damage in the case of confidential material.[128] Specific examples of what might cause both exceptionally grave damage and serious damage to national security are given and the former category includes armed hostilities against the United States, the compromise of vital defence plans or communications intelligence systems and the disclosure of scientific or technological developments vital to national security.[129] Under the present order the categories are more specific than before and incorporate a test of reasonableness which previous orders lacked. A second major improvement is a reduction in both the number of departments and agencies authorized to classify (23 departments, agencies and executive offices as opposed to 34 under the previous system) and in the number of persons with classification authority (a reduction estimated at 63%).[130] Delegation of classifying authority is now limited to certain groups of of persons and must take place in writing. The third significant feature of the Nixon Order is its automatic downgrading and declassifying schedule which applies to all material except exempted material falling into certain defined categories.[131] Top secret, secret and confidential information is all downgraded at fixed intervals and will become declassified at the end of ten years, eight years and six years respectively. Highly sensitive material exempted from automatic declassification will generally become declassified after 30 years. Finally, the order establishes an Interagency Classification Review Committee whose function is to monitor the administration of the order and to review complaints from within or without the government concerning classification problems. This committee will hear appeals from departmental decisions on reviews sought for the release of exempted material.[132] This internal review procedure is additional to any right of action for the production of material that a citizen may bring under the Freedom of Information Act. However, production of material may not be compelled under that Act if it is 'specifically required by Executive

Order to be kept secret in the interest of national defense or foreign policy'.[133]

What is the legal effect of the classification of material under the Nixon Order? Presidential classification is not backed by any direct statutory authority from Congress and is basically a system of rules internal to the executive branch. The sanctions for revelation of classified material, or for other breaches of the order, are initially disciplinary and range between a reprimand by superiors to dismissal of the offending federal employee.[134] While there is no statutory provision which generally criminalizes disclosure or receipt of classified information, punishment is specifically provided for the communication to unauthorized persons of classified information relating to cryptographic systems and communications intelligence; and government officials who transmit classified information to foreign agents or a member of a communist organization are also punishable.[135] The Espionage Statutes, as we have seen, authorize the President to designate vital military installations and equipment as requiring special protection and in a purported exercise of that power he has designated not just 'secret places and hardware' but all classified documents.[136] This is a dubious exercise of the statutory authority but if valid would put the sanctions of criminal law behind the entire classification programme. The classification of material is not in itself an authority to withhold that material from Congress; but to the extent the concealment is backed by a proper exercise of executive privilege Congress may be deprived of information. Though classified information is frequently made available to the legislature on a confidential basis it is also frequently withheld to the possible detriment of the exercise of legislative power.[137] Thus far Congress has left classification to the executive, but there have been proposals for legislative intervention and there seems little doubt that classification is not constitutionally the exclusive concern of the executive.[138] A final point in relation to the legal effect of classification is that the Nixon Order specifically vests the government Archivist with certain declassification powers in relation to material in the Archives.[139]

Whenever a classification problem has come before the courts the judges have sought to avoid any interference with the executive judgment. As already observed the court declined to enter into the propriety of classification in *Scarbeck* v *United States*[140] in which the accused was convicted of passing classified information to the agent of a foreign government. This judicial abstinence is explicable in terms of the intention of the relevant statute which did not envisage a redetermination of the correctness of classification by the courts. The 'hands off' policy of the Supreme Court in *Environmental Protection Agency* v *Mink*[141] was also essentially one based on assumed statutory intention. However, in *United States* v *Marchetti*[142] the court, in confirming an injunction preventing an ex CIA agent from publishing classified information in breach of an agreement and oath of secrecy, declared categorically that 'the process of classification is part of the executive function beyond the scope of judicial review'.[143] The Supreme Court denied certiorari in this case. One may justifiably conclude that failing congressional authority, the courts will avoid entanglement in classification issues. As we shall see below, amendments to the Freedom of Information Act may have given the courts wider powers of review.

Because neither Congress nor the public, in the nature of things, can expect much assistance from the courts in securing more information about governmental activities and decisions, there have been many proposals for Congressional action designed to increase the flow of information without at the same time jeopardizing vital security interests.[144] Most of these proposals envisage legislation by Congress to achieve the desired goals, the key feature of such legislation being the participation of the legislative branch in the operation and control of classification. Abuse of classification is probably in large measure due to the exclusive power which the executive branch has hitherto been permitted to exercise in this field. Examples of the misuse of that power have been frequent in recent times[145] and point to the need for congressional participation and ultimately a judicial barrier to arbitrary executive suppression of information. The legislative reversal[146] of the *Mink* judgment is a step in that direction but it does not affect directly Congressional access to executive materials.

The issues that underlie the debate over classification reform are too momentous to permit complacency about the undoubted improvements incorporated in the Nixon Executive Order. Classification brings into conflict the right and need of Congress and the public to exercise informed participation in government and the executive's duty to guard against the harmful disclosure of sensitive security information. While no one will dispute the importance of that duty, it has too often become a pretext for concealment of ill-conceived and even corrupt actions in the administrative branch. Classification has become a ready method of shielding the executive from criticism and for enlarging its powers at the cost of other branches of government.[147] This in turn lowers the quality of participation in decision-making and weakens the democratic controls that are both explicit and implicit in the American system of government. An excessive reliance on classification may harm the executive branch itself by depriving its officers of information relevant to recommendations and decisions[148] and of the policy alternatives that wider participation inevitably brings. Obsessive secrecy may encourage an executive to develop and implement policies that will not carry legislative or public approval when the full facts are known, with the disastrous consequences that Vietnam involvement brought about. Over-protection of executive material may also harm the executive (and the nation) more directly since if too much material is classified as sensitive the programme loses credibility and increases the tendency to 'instant declassification' by means of deliberate leaks.

The balancing of all these interests is a delicate and complex problem to which there can never be a simple or final solution. If one important truth does emerge from this brief survey it is that it is dangerous to allow one arm of government the exclusive right to draw lines and set limits. Congress, perhaps at the price of tightening its own security arrangements, needs a larger share in the framing and operation of the classification system. The role of the courts will always be marginal but adjudication, with all its problems, should not be rejected as an ultimate device for the resolution of some classification disputes. Because classification has the potential to neutralize the informed participation that is basic to the principle of self-government it would be dangerous to let it become a subject of undivided control and determination.

NOTES

[1] 18 USCA ¶¶ 793–8.

[2] The provisions referred to here are 18 USCA ¶ 952 and 50 USCA ¶ 783(b).

[3] 40 Stat 217 et seq (1917).

[4] 18 USCA ¶ 794(a) and (b).

[5] 18 USCA ¶ 793.

[6] The most impressive analysis is by Harold Edgar and Benno C Schmidt Jr 'The Espionage Statutes and Publication of Defense Information' 73 *Colum L Rev* 929 (1973). There is a shorter version by Benno C Schmidt Jr entitled 'The American Espionage Statutes and Publication of Defense Information' in *Secrecy and Foreign Policy* 179 et seq.

[7] 18 USCA ¶ 794(a).

[8] 312 US 19 (1941), 85 L Ed 488.

[9] It is not clear whether the accused has 'reason to believe' within the wording of the statute where he is in possession of facts from which a reasonable man would infer the probability (possibility?) of injury or advantage (as the trial court held in *Gorin's* case: 111 F 2nd at 717) or whether as Edgar and Schmidt argue (loc cit 989–90) he is guilty only when proved to be consciously aware of the risk.

[10] 151 F 2nd 813 (2nd Cir, 1945).

[11] At 29–30.

[12] At 28.

[13] At 816. Cf *Gros* v *United States* 138 F 2nd 261 (9th Cir, 1943). Edgar & Schmidt loc cit 982 criticize the principle of making criminality depend on whether 'spreading' is lawful in the United States.

[14] 301 F 2nd 236 (2nd Cir, 1962).

[15] At 239.

[16] See *Gorin* v *United States* (*supra*) at 31–2.

[17] 'The American Espionage Statutes and Publication of Defense Information' 977.

[18] Professor Benno C Schmidt believes that there is no doubt that Congress intended to exclude public discussion from the scope of the prohibition even if the information conveyed thereby is certain to reach a foreign power: See 'The American Espionage Statutes and Publication of Defense Information' 187.

[19] 195 F 2nd 583 (2nd Cir, 1952).

[20] 18 USCA ¶ 794(b).

[21] It seems that the attempt to activate ¶ 794(b) in periods of national emergency when no war has been declared will not be legally effective: Benno C Schmidt Jr loc cit 188–9.

[22] 'The American Espionage Statutes and the Publication of Defense Information' 190.

[23] All the crimes discussed in this section fall under 18 USCA ¶ 793.

[24] 18 USCA ¶ 793(a) and (b).

[25] *Supra.*

[26] Edgar & Schmidt loc cit 974–86 survey the problems created by court findings as to the meaning of 'related to the national defense'.

[27] See, particularly, the articles cited in footnote 6 above.

[28] 18 USCA ¶ 793(c).

[29] The actual words of the section read 'contrary to the provisions of this chapter', a reference to ¶¶ 792–9.

[30] Edgar & Schmidt loc cit 1058–60.

[31] Ibid.

[32] 18 USCA ¶ 793(d) and (e).

[33] See, for example, Leonard B Boudin 'The Ellsberg Case: Citizen Disclosure' in *Secrecy and Foreign Policy* 296–303.

[34] See the sophisticated analysis of Edgar & Schmidt loc cit 1038–46.

[35] *United States* v *Coplon* 88 F Supp 910 (SD NY, 1950) and *Dubin* v *United States*, 289 F 2nd 651 (US Court of Claims, 1961). In the former case the court said of the count framed under the section in question that 'it merely requires that the defendant Coplon obtained possession of the documents and attempted to transmit them to her co-defendant, who was not entitled to receive them' (at 911). In the latter the court declared that mere retention of defence information after demand would be a crime (at 654).

[36] 403 US 713 (1971), 29 L Ed 2nd 822.

[37] *Departmental Committee on Section 2 of the Official Secrets Act 1911*; Cmnd 5104 (1972) ¶ 216.

[38] See Edgar & Schmidt loc cit 1052–7.

[39] Ibid 1032 et seq.

[40] 18 USCA ¶ 793(f).

[41] 18 USCA ¶ 798.

[42] Cf Edgar & Schmidt loc cit 1065–6.

[43] 18 USCA ¶ 798(c).

[44] 50 USCA ¶ 783(b).

[45] 317 F 2nd 546 (DC Cir, 1963).

[46] At 560.

[47] At 559.

[48] 18 USCA ¶ 952.

[49] 18 USCA ¶ 795. Photographic or other representations of defence property is forbidden also by 50 USCA App ¶ 781, but there is no provision related to this section dealing with transmission or publication of such photographs or representations.

[50] Ibid.

[51] 18 USCA ¶ 797.

[52] Exec Order No 10104, 15 Fed Reg 597 (1950).

[53] See Edgar & Schmidt loc cit 1069–73.

[54] See Project: 'Government Information and the Rights of Citizens' (1975) 73 *Mich L Rev* 971 at 1055.

[55] 5 USCA ¶ 552(b)(3).

[56] The cases are reviewed in Project: 'Government Information and the Rights of Citizens' 1055–61. See also 'Developments under the Freedom of Information Act—1974' (1975) *Duke LJ* 416 at 432–441.

[57] 45 L Ed 2nd 164.

[58] Certainly in respect of pre-FOIA statutes: see article by James S Gorski 'Access to Information: Exemptions from Disclosure under the Freedom of Information Act and the Privacy Act of 1974' (1976) 13 *Willamette L Rev* 135 at 146.

[59] At 175.

[60] *California* v *Weinberger* 505 F 2nd 767 (1974) 768.

[61] 5 USCA ¶ 552(b)(3) (May 1977 Suppl). The new exemption was applied in *Seymour* v *Barabba* 45 LW 2061 where a statute imposed 'a flat barrier to disclosure without exercise of discretion permitted'.

[62] 18 USCA ¶ 1905.

[63] See Project: 'Government Information and the Rights of Citizens' 1056–7.

[64] *Supra*.

[65] However, in *FAA Administrator* v *Robertson*, the court did not specifically overrule decisions like *Frankel* v *SEC* 336 F Supp 675 (SD NY 1971) in which the court held that

penal statutes do not establish exemptions under the Act but merely penalize the disclosure of non-exempt materials.

[66] 42 USCA ¶ 2014(y).

[67] 42 USCA ¶ 2201(i).

[68] 42 USCA ¶ 2162. This power must be exercised in accordance with the requirements of common defence and security and, where atomic weapons are concerned, in collaboration with the Department of Defense.

[69] 42 USCA ¶ 2274.

[70] 42 USCA ¶¶ 2275 and 2276.

[71] 42 USCA ¶ 2277.

[72] 42 USCA ¶ 2280. See Edgar & Schmidt, loc cit 1075.

[73] J G Palfrey 'The Problems of Secrecy' (1953) 290 *Annals of the American Academy of Political and Social Science* 90 at 92.

[74] Ibid 96.

[75] The problem is outlined by Robert A Dahl in 'Atomic Energy and the Democratic Process' *Annals of the American Academy of Political and Social Science*, loc cit 1.

[76] 42 USCA ¶ 2252(b). Amendment introduced by 88 Stat 1611.

[77] J G Palfrey loc cit 97 et seq.

[78] 42 USCA ¶ 1306.

[79] 495 F 2nd 639 (3rd Cir, 1974).

[80] See *FAA Administrator* v *Robertson* (*supra*).

[81] In amending exemption three Congress intended to restore the *Stretch* ruling: see R O Berner 'The Effect of the 1976 Amendment to Exemption Three of the Freedom of Information Act' (1976) 76 *Colum L Rev* 1029 at 1043.

[82] Paul A Freund 'The Supreme Court, 1973 Term, Foreword: On Presidential Privilege' (1974) 88 *Harv L Rev* 13 at 19.

[83] Norman Dorsen and John H F Shattuck 'Executive Privilege, the Congress and the Courts' (1974) 35 *Ohio State LJ* 1, 10.

[84] Ibid. 2. Arthur M Schlesinger Jr in *The Imperial Presidency* 158 records that there were 44 instances of refusal to supply information between June 1955 and June 1960— more cases than in the first century of America's history (see also p 247).

[85] Arthur M Schlesinger Jr op cit 156–7.

[86] The US Constitution gives Congress the express power to maintain secrecy in the provision dealing with the publication of journals: See art 1 ¶ 5.

[87] Raoul Berger *Executive Privilege: A Constitutional Myth* 371.

[88] See Dorsen & Shattuck loc. cit. 11–13; Berger op cit *passim*.

[89] Berger op cit 165; Arthur M Schlesinger op cit 157.

[90] 345 US 1 (1953), 97 L Ed 727.

[91] At 735.

[92] As to which, see Berger op cit 116.

[93] 25 Fed Cas 30.

[94] At 34.

[95] At 37.

[96] Paul A Freund loc cit 30–1.

[97] 418 US 683 (1974), 41 L Ed 2nd 1039.

[98] At 1063.   [99] Ibid.

[100] *US* v *American Telephone and Telegraph Co* 45 US LW 2325 (30 December 1976).

[101] *United States* v *Nixon* (*supra*) at 1063.

[102] 45 US LW 4917 (28 June 1977).

[103] Ibid 4924–5.

[104] 498 F 2nd 725 (DC Cir, 1974).

[105] At 730.   [106] At 731.

[107] 'Executive Power and the Control of Information: Practice Under the Framers' by Abraham D Sofaer (1977) *Duke LJ* 1 at 48.

[108] Berger op cit 264.

[109] Dorsen & Shattuck loc cit 29–33.

[110] In this connection *US* v *American Telephone and Telegraph Co* (*supra*) is relevant as the court spoke of the 'suitability of a judicial suggestion of compromise rather than historic confrontation . . .'. The court deferred judgment to allow further efforts at settlement to be made.

[111] Paul A Freund loc cit 38.

[112] See Project: 'Government Information and the Rights of Citizens' 1016.

[113] *Supra* 4923.

[114] Ibid 1022.

[115] Berger op cit 273.

[116] Note: 'Reform in the Classification and Declassification of National Security Information: Nixon's Executive Order 11,652' (1974) 59 *Iowa L Rev* 110 at 112. (Referred to below as Note: 'Reform in Classification'.)

[117] Ibid.

[118] Note: 'Developments in the Law: The National Security Interest and Civil Liberties' (1972) 85 *Harv L Rev* 1130 at 1193. (Referred to below as Note: 'Developments in the Law'.)

[119] Note: 'Reform in Classification' 114. The military classification system received Presidential recognition in the form of an Executive order on 22 March 1940: Arthur M Schlesinger Jr op cit 339.

[120] Executive Order 10290, 16 Fed Reg 9795 (27 September 1951).

[121] William G Phillips 'The Government's Classification System' in *None of Your Business* 61, 63.

[122] Note: 'Reform in Classification' 115.

[123] Ibid.

[124] Executive Order 10501, 18 Fed Reg 7049 (9 November 1953).

[125] Executive Order 11652, 37 Fed Reg 5209 (10 March 1972).

[126] The findings of the reports are briefly summarized by William S Moorhead in 'Operation and Reform of the Classification System in the United States' in *Secrecy and Foreign Policy* 87, 95–8.

[127] Ibid 101.

[128] Executive Order 11652 ¶ 1. The Nixon system has been heavily criticized by Arthur M Schlesinger Jr op cit 349, mainly for expanding the top secret category to include material the disclosure of which would disrupt foreign relations which vitally affect national security. It has also been criticized on the ground that an official who believes that there is some risk of damage, no matter how small, is bound to classify even if there is a compelling contrary interest favouring public knowledge: See Morton H Halperin and Daniel N Hoffman *Top Secret* (New Republic Books, Washington DC, 1977) 33.

[129] Ibid.

[130] Note: 'Reform in Classification' 121.

[131] Executive Order 11652 ¶ 5.

[132] Ibid ¶¶ 5(c) & 7.

[133] 5 USCA ¶ 552(b)(i). The court's power to determine whether information has been properly categorized under this provision will be examined in the section dealing with the Freedom of Information Act.

[134] Note: 'Developments in the Law' 1206.

[135] See p 47 above.   [136] See p 48 above.

[137] Note: 'Developments in the Law' 1208 et seq.

[138] See Project: 'Government Information and the Rights of Citizens' 1000–6.

[139] Note: 'Reform in Classification' 139 et seq.

[140] *Supra*.

[141] 410 US 73 (1973), 35 L Ed 2nd 119. This judgment is analysed below in the section dealing with the Freedom of Information Act.

[142] 466 F 2nd 1309 (1972). The judgment in heavily criticized by Halperin and Hoffman op cit 131 et seq.

[143] At 1317. See, however, the dissent on this point at 1318.

[144] See, for example, William G Phillips loc cit 79 et seq and William S Moorhead loc cit 110 et seq.

[145] See Project: 'Government Information and the Rights of Citizens' 788–890; Note: 'Developments in the Law' 1210 et seq, and Arthur M Schlesinger Jr op cit 342.

[146] This will be discussed below in the chapter on the Freedom of Information Act.

[147] See the article by John F Murphy 'Knowledge is Power: Foreign Policy and Information Interchange among Congress, the Executive Branch and the Public' (1975) 49 *Tulane L Rev* 505.

[148] Classification frequently deprives those *within* the executive branch of essential information relating to their function.

CHAPTER V

The United States—
The Positive Right to Information

The United States law considered so far has had a negative effect on access to information, either prohibiting its release or authorizing concealment. We turn now to laws which confer a positive right of access to information about government. In recognizing the principle of the citizen's right to know what his government is doing and in associating with that right vigorous and effective remedies for its enforcement, the United States has put itself into a position of leadership in the Western democracies. This leadership stems not just from the legal provision of rights and remedies but from the sustained seriousness with which Congress has monitored and supervised the legislative programme and brought about the changes necessary for investing the right with real meaning and content. Recognizing that self-government implies informed participation, Congress enacted the Freedom of Information Act (referred to below as the FOIA) in 1966[1] and this act will dominate the ensuing discussion of laws conferring a positive right to information. Most American states have also enacted open records legislation and because the state statutes contain some interesting innovations, particularly on the procedural side, a sample analysis and discussion of one of these laws will be included. Finally, since open records legislation is complemented by open meeting laws which are equally designed to arm the public with the means of knowing about the activities of government, this chapter will conclude with a synoptic analysis of the federal law on open meetings and a brief description of a progressive state statute on the same subject.

Before examining the relevant American legislation, a sense of justness and fidelity to history requires recognition of the fact that Sweden was in fact first in the field in providing a citizen right of access to public documents. The so-called right of publicity of documents was established in Sweden in 1766 as an aspect of press freedom and rested on constitutional authority.[2] The right of access to public documents belongs to all citizens without proof of any special interest and is subject only to the specific exceptions prescribed or authorized by a Secrecy Act.[3] Officials who wrongfully deny access to public documents were formerly subject to punishment through the criminal courts but the citizen has long had the additional remedies of an appeal to the Ombudsman or to administrative courts.[4] Though the right was weakened by limitations on the powers of the Swedish parliament in the late eighteenth century, it was revived in 1810 and has since been set beyond dispute. The Swedish example in open government is the earliest and perhaps most impressive and all democratic systems, including the American, are indebted to it. It remains the best model for societies seeking less cumbersome and litigious schemes than those evolved in the United States and it has been adopted with variations in countries such as Norway, Denmark and Finland.[5]

BRIEF HISTORY OF THE FOIA

The existence of a general right of access to public records prior to the introduction of statutes to regulate disclosure was a matter of dispute. Though a general common-law right of inspection was recognized, according to some courts only persons demonstrating a special interest were entitled to exercise it; while other courts were prepared to concede a right of access to any person without a showing of special interest.[6] The rulings of the latter courts are noteworthy because their interpretation of the common law appears to diverge from that of English courts which have always maintained a special interest requirement as a condition of access.[7] The English common law virtually limited the right to those who could show a litigatory interest. One of the progressive rulings of American law is *Nowack* v *Fuller*[8] in which the Michigan Supreme Court declared that the rule of English common law denying the public access to records 'is repugnant to the spirit of our democratic institutions' and dismissed the requirement of proof of a litigatory interest as 'absurd'. State governments in America began to enact open records laws from early times and today questions of access are likely to turn on the meaning and effect of the relevant state statute. At the federal level of government no general right to inspect records exists and development of the law here has been entirely dependent upon legislative intervention. Federal law had achieved very little until the introduction of the FOIA in 1967. Prior to that a provision of the Administrative Procedure Act had made federal records available to 'persons properly and directly concerned' subject to vague exceptions intended to protect the public interest and without any supporting judicial remedy.[9] Since this provision in effect became a charter to withhold rather than an instrument of disclosure, it was ultimately repealed and replaced by the FOIA.[10]

The FOIA was the result of 'ten years of congressional labour' in the form of extensive hearings and reports. A detailed review of the first five years of the Act's life took place in Congressional hearings in 1972 and one of the results was a wide-ranging report by the House

Committee on Government Operations.[11] This report discloses that while the Committee accepted that the Act 'was milestone legislation that reversed longstanding Government information policies and customs',[12] it found weaknesses in both the law and its administration which had made possible '5 years of foot-dragging by the Federal bureaucracy'.[13] The Committee recommended changes to the Act and it was extensively amended in 1974. These amendments were vetoed by President Ford, but Congress nullified the veto and the amendments became effective in February 1975.[14] The amendments considerably strengthened the citizens' right to information in several important ways,[15] but these improvements are best considered as part of the synoptic analysis of the amended FOIA offered below. Continued oversight by Congress is guaranteed by the requirement that each agency must report annually and in detail on its administration of the Act.[16] While many legislatures might have been content to place a law on the statute book and commit its administration to the vagaries of court rulings and administrative practices, Congress has set an important example by sustained vigilance aimed at ensuring that its intent is accurately reflected in the application and administration of the law.

THE FOIA IN OUTLINE

The Act is a short, complex and highly technical piece of legislation; but it is premised on a broad, not to say grand, purpose or goal expressive of the American philosophy of government. In his statement made on the signing of the Act, President Johnson said that 'a democracy works best when the people have all the information that the security of the Nation permits' and that no one 'should be able to pull curtains of secrecy around decisions which can be revealed without injury to the public interest'.[17] Attorney General Ramsay Clark, in his memorandum on the Act, declared that 'nothing so diminishes democracy as secrecy' and added that self-government 'is meaningful only with an informed public'.[18] In what way does the Act seek to realize such important principles and purposes? The disclosure provisions fall quite neatly into three distinct requirements. The first may be termed a publication requirement and directs every agency subject to the Act to publish in the Federal Register, and keep up to date, 'descriptions of its organization, method of functioning and procedures for making information available'.[19] The purpose is clearly to help the public to locate the custodian of the record sought and the manner of gaining access to it. The second disclosure provision instructs each agency to make available for inspection and copying final opinions and orders, statements of policy and administrative staff manuals and instructions. Indexes of such material have also to be provided.[20] Following Professor Davis, we may term this second provision the 'secret law' requirement. The third disclosure requirement, the identifiable record provision,

directs agencies to make available to any person upon request reasonably described records other than material that has to be published or
made available under the first and second provisions.[21] The purpose in
this case is to enable members of the public to get at the papers and
files of the agency of government concerned and the law places the
burden of justifying refusal on the agency. The three disclosure provisions are qualified by the exemption of nine defined categories of
information which need not be published, disclosed or otherwise made
available.[22] It is in this complex exemption clause that the right to
know is balanced by the power to withhold information in the public
interest, though it should be observed that the exemptions do not
authorize the concealment of information from Congress.[23]

Two features of the FOIA are of cardinal importance. Any person
may request information under the Act and is not required to show
any interest or give any reason. The preclusion of a need to demonstrate standing follows Swedish law and is one of the main reasons
why the Act has become an effective instrument. Second, an expedi-
tious judicial remedy in the form of a *de novo* trial before the ordinary
courts is granted to any person who feels aggrieved by an agency
refusal of information.[24] The Act contains other sanctions and remedies
but the right of recourse to the courts, recently strengthened by explicit
powers of *in camera* inspection, is its key procedural innovation. Apart
from the former criminal responsibility of officers under Swedish law
resort to the ordinary courts is not a feature of that system. The
litigiousness which the American formula has produced in the information field is probably its most controversial aspect.

ANALYSIS OF THE FOIA

SCOPE OF APPLICATION

The FOIA is a federal measure applying at that level of government.
Its provisions therefore affect the federal government but only to the
extent that it falls within the definition of an 'agency' in the Act. The
provisions requiring disclosure apply to 'each agency' of government
and the expression 'agency' was redefined in 1974 amendments to
include 'any executive department, military department, Government
corporation, Government controlled corporation, or other establishment in the executive branch of the government (including the Executive Office of the President), or any independent regulatory agency'.[25]
The thrust of the disclosure requirements is against the federal *executive*
government, Congress and the courts being excluded from the Act's
prescriptions.[26] The probable justifications for putting Congress and
the courts beyond the reach of the FOIA are that the records of public
administration are primarily in the offices of the executive branch, that
considerable openness already characterizes the proceedings of these
other branches of federal government and that, in the case of Congress,

the information held is controlled by representatives of the people.

The most serious problem that has arisen over the meaning of 'agency' relates to the possibility that there may be agencies within agencies. Large departments of government frequently have units or sub-departments and the question can arise whether these are agencies for purposes of disclosure. The question was submitted for adjudication prior to the 1974 amendments and the courts concluded that the question depended on whether the subdivision possessed 'an independent function of evaluating federal programs';[27] or, as the leading case of *Grumman Aircraft Engineering Corporation* v *Renegotiation Board*[28] decided, a subdivision or unit will be an agency for purposes of the Act if it serves as 'a discrete, decision-producing layer' in the administrative process involved. The decisions therefore establish the test of whether constituent parts of an agency function independently and hold that if they do they are subject to the disclosure requirements of the law. Though the test is clear a possible complicating factor is that the determination could be made 'differently for purposes of various provisions of the Act'[29] and might also depend on whether the independent authority of the subdivision is related to the type of disclosure sought by the plaintiff.[30] Another problem that has presented itself for court determination is the extent to which the Act applies to quasi-government entities. A recent ruling makes the question depend largely on the degree and intensity of federal control over the agency.[31] The court took account of such matters as close governmental supervision, the obligation of the agency to report to government, the status of its staff as federal employees and the fact that its directors were federally appointed.

Though the definition of 'agency' includes the 'Executive Office of the President' the legislative history demonstrates that the President, and his immediate staff whose sole function is to advise and assist him, are not subject to the terms of the Act.[32] Though disclosure cannot be compelled against them under the FOIA, it does not follow that executive privilege will automatically afford protection where the production of information is sought under court subpoena powers or the congressional enquiry power.

THE PUBLICATION AND SECRET LAW REQUIREMENTS

We observed in an outline of the FOIA that its provisions require agencies to publish certain information in the Federal Register and to make available for inspection and copying the 'secret law' of the agency. We shall now examine these two requirements closely, postponing for later the production of records at the instance of a member of the public.

It is mandatory for all agencies to publish in the Federal Register (the official United States 'Gazette')

(i)   descriptions of their central and field organizations and the persons from whom and the methods by which the public can make requests or obtain information,

(ii) explanations of the general course and channelling of functions and responsibilities,

(iii) rules of procedure, available forms and instructions as to the content and scope of papers, reports and examinations, and,

(iv) rules enacted by the agency and statements of general policy adopted by it.[33]

All this information has to be kept up to date by the publication of changes or amendments in the Federal Register. The information must be made available promptly and the court will condone only those delays that are occasioned by the normal publication process.[34] A specific sanction for non-compliance has been enacted and has the effect of precluding agency reliance, to the prejudice of a person, on unpublished matter falling under the mandatory publication requirement unless the person in question had timely notice of the matter.[35] The effect of the sanction is to prevent the agency from imposing an obligation or withholding a benefit under an unpublished rule of which the affected person had no notice.[36]

Even to a trained lawyer but *a fortiori* to the average citizen, major departments of government are confusing and impenetrable labyrinths. The enforced publication of the organizational structure, of the general functions and of the rules and policy determinations of each agency of government will do much to increase understanding of the work of major branches of the administration. The compulsory designation of the persons from whom, the places at which and the methods by which information can be obtained removes a traditional barrier between citizen and the bureaucracy and nullifies the old bureaucratic technique of frustrating enquirers by the process of 'shunting' the ignorant citizen between different officials and places. Enforced publication also facilitates the ability of the citizen to locate material which he wishes to demand under the secret law and identifiable record provisions of the Act described below.

In an early assessment of the FOIA Professor Davis argued that its most impressive accomplishment would be the opening up of secret law.[37] He also said it should be a fundamental principle of interpretation of the Act that 'secret law is an abomination'.[38] Professor Davis was referring to the provision of the FOIA which confers a right of public inspection and copying of final opinions and orders made in the adjudication of cases, statements of policy and interpretations adopted by the agency (and not published in the Federal Register) and administrative staff manuals and instructions to staff that affect a member of the public.[39] The 1974 amendments added to this legal obligation to make material available for copying and inspection, the duty to maintain indexes of such material generated after 4 July 1967 and to publish such indexes at least quarterly. (Index publication which is too burdensome may be dispensed with by notice in the Federal Register but in that case copies of the index have to be provided on request.) Giving the citizen access to the internal law of departments and agencies—a body of law which had previously and regularly affected their rights and obligations without knowledge on their part—is a legislative advance of manifest importance.

Three categories of internal law must be made available. The first refers to final opinions and also to orders made in the adjudication of cases. That this requirement for making agency decisions accessible may be an onerous burden on the government is graphically illustrated by one commentator's observation on its effect:

> 'Each of the million licences issued annually by the F.C.C. is an adjudication, even if automatically issued. Every one of the Immigration Service's 700 000 dispositions of applications annually is clearly an order; when an officer checks one of thirty reasons on a printed card, the check-mark is an opinion.'[40]

The helpfulness of the legal obligation to make accessible final opinions and orders may be diminished in two ways. First, the contextual material (for example prior recommendations, identifying details, et cetera) if not the orders or opinions themselves, may be exempt from disclosure under the Act's exemption clause.[41] Second, where an order is made without accompanying reasons, the general public will gain little by the right to inspect the order itself. Opinions or recommendations which led up to the naked ruling are not disclosable unless they are final, and they will generally fall under the exemption protecting predecisional deliberations. The Supreme Court so held in *Renegotiation Board* v *Grumman Aircraft Engineering Corporation*,[42] a case in which Justice White said:

> 'If the public interest suffers by reason of the failure of the Board to explain some of its decisions, the remedy is for Congress to require it to do so. It is not for us to require disclosure of documents, under the purported authority of the Act, which are not final opinions, which do not accurately set forth the reasons for the Board's decisions, and the disclosure of which would impinge on the Board's predecisional processes.'[43]

Nevertheless, the obligation to make orders available is a clear advance in the search for open government and it will more obviously be so where the authority in question is statutorily obliged to give reasons. If the agency does give a 'final opinion' this must be made available for inspection and copying; but not all opinions are final and the question will depend on whether the material sought expresses the 'working law' of the agency as opposed to its 'group thinking in the process of working out its policy and determining what its law ought to be'.[44]

The second category of internal law that must be made available covers statements of policy and interpretations adopted by the agency and not published in the Federal Register. The publication provision discussed earlier required agencies to publish in the Federal Register 'statements of general policy' or interpretations of general applicability; and what is required to be made available under the provision now being analysed are policy statements and interpretations which lack the broad generality that makes them eligible for publication in the Register. This means that the agencies must allow access to (and index) the numerous rulings on specific cases which they make in the course of their duties. A judicial decision has determined, for example, that 'letter rulings' (a letter to a taxpayer interpreting tax law on specific facts) made by the Internal Revenue Service constitute the case law of the Department if they are adopted as the effective law on the point.[45] If the agency contemplates the use of the ruling as a precedent it becomes a statement of policy or interpretation which has been 'adopted' and must then be made available.[46] But acceptance of the ruling as a precedent for future use is not a necessary condition of its being adopted so long as, it seems, the agency intended to rely on it at the time.[47] Contemplated use as a precedent is a strong form of adoption; but a weaker mode of adoption may suffice.[48]

The final category of internal law to which access must be permitted refers to 'administrative staff manuals and instructions to staff that affect members of the public'. The legislative history shows that Congress did not intend to include law enforcement manuals and that these are exempt from disclosure.[49] Manuals which clarify 'substantive or procedural' law will be administrative whereas those that, for example, reveal techniques of investigation and law enforcement will be protected from disclosure.[50] It seems highly desirable that citizens should have access to documents which explain how an agency understands and applies the law that governs them so long as disclosure will not frustrate law enforcement.

The specific sanction behind the secret law provision of the FOIA is that no such law (whether in the form of an order, final opinion, interpretation, staff manual, et cetera) may be relied on or used against a party unless it has been indexed and made available or the party in question had actual and timely notice of its terms. The availability of this special sanction does not preclude reliance on the judicial remedy discussed below in connection with identifiable records to enforce production of material wrongfully withheld by the agency. Of course, both the publication requirement and the secret law requirement of the Act are qualified by the clause exempting certain categories of information from production. This exemption clause will be examined in the course of considering the obligation of agencies to produce identifiable records at the request of a person.

THE PRODUCTION OF IDENTIFIABLE RECORDS

Over and above the information published or made available under the provisions just discussed, each agency, upon the request of any person who reasonably describes records required by him, is required to make them promptly available to such person.[51] This provision of the FOIA opens up to public inspection the files, papers and documents of government departments and agencies unless the material falls into the categories of information protected by the exemption clause. There are few countries, even in the democratic West, in which government files may be inspected as a legal right as opposed to a special privilege accorded in their absolute discretion by the authorities to 'trustworthy' persons. The sections of the Act which create this right and make it judicially enforceable together constitute the citizens' open record charter.

Actually the right is available not just to citizens but to any 'individual, partnership, corporation, association or public and private organization other than an agency'.[52] The records which may be demanded are not confined to papers and documents but include sound recordings, tapes, films and so on.[53] But an attempt to obtain the rifle, ammunition, clothing and other articles connected with the assassination of President Kennedy failed because tangible objects such as these are not records for purposes of the FOIA.[54] It does not follow that materials of a non-tangible kind are necessarily records within the meaning of the law. Information stored in the computerized data bank of the National Library of Medicine and available generally only to subscribers has been held not to constitute records available under the FOIA.[55] Raw scientific data collected by the recipient of a grant from an agency is also not within the concept of agency records.[56] The requestor is required by the Act to provide the agency with a reasonably specific description of what he requires so that it can identify the records. The request must not be too vague; and an overbroad request for all 'unpublished manuscript decisions' of the Patent Office was rejected by the court as not being reasonably specific.[57]

Upon receipt of a request for a reasonably described record, the agency has ten days (excluding Saturdays, Sundays and legal holidays) to decide whether to comply with the request and must then immediately notify the person who made it of its determination (and reasons therefor) and simultaneously advise the requestor of a right of appeal to the agency head.[58] If an appeal is lodged the agency is required to reach a decision in a further twenty days (excluding Saturdays, Sundays and legal holidays) and notify the person affected of its finding and of his right to judicial review of an adverse appeal ruling.[59] Though the Act specifies precise circumstances in which these periods may be expanded, no extension can be of longer than ten days and a failure to comply with time limits leads to the presumption that the applicant for records has exhausted his administrative remedies. The court's power to allow an extension of time in exceptional circumstances has been reluctantly exercised even where the request places a heavy administrative burden on the agency.[60] These rigorous time limits and accompanying sanctions constitute new teeth put into the law by the 1974 amendments and were enacted following Congressional findings of long agency delays in responding to requests.[61] The delays affected the press most seriously and explain the small reliance on its provisions by the 'fourth estate' in America.[62] The 1974 amendments also brought about other important reforms such as the limitation of costs for searches and copying, these being now restricted to 'direct' costs.[63] Agencies are authorized and encouraged to waive costs where the provision of information 'can be considered as primarily benefiting the general public'.[64]

A person who has been refused records and who has exhausted the administrative remedies (or who is deemed to have exhausted them) may have the entire question determined *de novo* by the federal district court having jurisdiction.[65] In the court hearing that follows, *the burden is on the agency to justify non-disclosure*—an indication (among others) of the presumption of public accessibility which Congress intended. Various prescriptions of procedure add force to the applicant's rights. The defendant must file pleadings within a shortened period, the court may give the hearing precedence over all cases not considered to be of graver importance and, exceptionally for United States law, costs may be awarded against the United States if the plaintiff has substantially prevailed.[66] The court in cases of arbitrary refusal of records may make a finding that will result in disciplinary proceedings against the official concerned and in the event of non-compliance with any order it makes for production, punish the responsible employee for contempt.[67] The effectiveness of the remedy, and the importance which the legislature attached to it, shine through the language of the FOIA.

The FOIA, it is clear, provides a powerful judicial remedy designed to counter the tendency of public officials to rationalize self-interest as a form of national interest in disclosure decisions. The question has arisen whether this and the other remedies provided by the Act are the sole and exclusive remedies provided for non-compliance with its terms. The judiciary has had to face the problem in the form of an assertion that the courts retain their equity jurisdiction to grant a stay of other proceedings pending fulfilment of an FOIA request; but it could also come up in the context of a request for a declaratory judgment. In *Renegotiation Board* v *Bannercroft Clothing Company*[68] the Supreme Court refused to stay concurrent renegotiation proceedings to determine whether Bannercroft had realized excess profits in defence contracts pending fulfilment by the Board of an FOIA request for documents revealing the facts and assumptions on which the Board had provisionally assessed liability. The decision of the majority was based primarily on the nature of the renegotiation process and the court's reluctance to regard it as being impliedly altered by the FOIA. The court, however, rejected the contention that the Act's remedies were intended to be exclusive and it follows that the stay of concurrent proceedings may theoretically be granted, possibly on a showing of irreparable injury if the relief is not granted.[69] Though the grant of a request for the stay of other proceedings pending compliance with an FOIA demand will be acceded to only in exceptional circumstances, the principle of the retention of other remedies (including the power to grant a declaration of rights) has fortunately been preserved.[70]

The additional remedies which the court may grant under equity jurisdiction are of secondary significance in comparison with the provision in the Act for *de novo* judicial redetermination upon denial of a request for records. What power does the court have under this provision and how will it be exercised? The question posed is best considered in the context of the exemption clause of the FOIA.

THE EXEMPTION CLAUSE

All the disclosure provisions of the Act are qualified by the clause[71] which excepts certain categories of information from mandatory revelation. There are nine such categories and any material falling within their ambit need not be revealed. Since a verbal description of a type or category of information can hardly lead to easy and clear-cut practical decisions on disclosure or non-disclosure, a host of cases already exists on the meaning and scope of specific exemptions. The task of charting the line that divides the right to inspect from the duty to withhold is one of difficulty and complexity; but the American experience does not suggest that the judiciary is an inappropriate body to exercise jurisdiction. The ensuing survey will focus on the major findings and, more importantly, upon the conceptual distinctions which they embody.

(a) *The First Exemption*

As amended in 1974, the first exemption has the effect of excluding matters that are 'specifically authorized under criteria established by an Executive Order to be kept secret in the interest of national defense or foreign policy and are in fact properly classified pursuant to such Executive order'.[72] Prior to the amendment the protected material under this exemption was described simply as that 'specifically required by Executive Order to be kept secret in the interest of national defense or foreign policy', there being no requirement in the earlier version of a 'proper' classification.

The first point to be underlined is that this exemption protects two broad categories of information: classified material falling under the head of *defence* or of *foreign policy*. Defence and foreign policy encompass so much in contemporary government that if classification were uncontrolled almost all of it could be concealed from the general view. (The Act, it must be repeated, does not regulate the right of Congress or of its committees to see executive branch material.) Classification, as we have observed, is an executive operation falling under rules imposed by the President and administered by his executive departments. In 1973 the Supreme Court was required to decide in *Environmental Protection Agency* v *Mink*[73] whether a decision taken in the executive branch that information should be classified as affecting defence or foreign policy was reviewable by the courts. The action was brought by Representative Patsy T Mink for production of documents connected with the then proposed Cannikin atomic test explosion due to take place on Amchitka Island off the coast of Alaska. A news 'leak' had suggested that conflicting recommendations on the desirability and dangers of the test had been received from various government agencies and the plaintiff sought disclosure of a report to the President (who was required to give final authority for the detonation) in which the recommendations of the agencies were incorporated. The government pleaded in defence that the papers had been classified as affecting national defence and foreign policy and were therefore exempted from disclosure by *inter alia* the first exemption of the FOIA.[74] After the district court had refused production and the Court of Appeals had remanded the matter to the district court to separate out the secret from the non-secret components of the documents falling under the first exemption, the Supreme Court set aside this remand and declared firmly in its majority judgment that mere classification put the material beyond the reach of the FOIA and that even *in camera* review of the papers was precluded. On this interpretation the first exemption could become 'a bottomless canyon capable of safeguarding from disclosure virtually all information the government prefers to conceal'.[75] Though the action failed in this respect, it should be noted that the court did not preclude *in camera* inspection to determine whether the fifth exemption was applicable but declared that inspection was not 'a necessary or inevitable tool in every case'.[76] So far as the first exemption was concerned, however, the terms of the FOIA precluded both inspection of documents and review. As Justice Stewart said, Congress has enacted an exemption into the Act that 'provides no means to question an Executive decision to stamp a document "secret" however cynical, myopic, or even corrupt that decision might have been'.[77]

Subsequent lower court decisions did permit adjudication to determine whether the documents denied had actually been classified and whether the correct classification procedure had been followed;[78] but they could not undermine the central finding in *Mink* that the classification itself was beyond review. The undermining was achieved at least in part by the legislature which introduced, as part of the 1974 amendments, the requirement that the material must have been properly classified and gave express authority to the courts to inspect *in camera* and to order production of segregable non-sensitive material. The Congressional reversal of the *Mink* judgment was certainly the most dramatic of the amendments to the FOIA enacted in 1974.

An assessment of the effect of these changes ought not to be characterized by too much euphoria. There will be no impetuous rush by the courts to substitute a judicial for the executive judgment on classification. As one commentator has observed, the 'new law does no more than to require the executive department to hold faithful to its own prescriptions'.[79] While certainly not euphoric this comment may err slightly on the side of understatement. The current Executive Order on classification introduces various tests all of which rest upon the *reasonable expectation* of certain kinds of harm to national security.[80] Information would not be properly classified if this criterion is not met and a court could find that the government has not discharged the onus upon it under the Act of demonstrating the applicability of an exemption. Where the first exemption is at issue, judges are likely to defer to the assumed greater knowledge and experience of executive officers in the field of diplomacy and military affairs, at least where these appear to have some rational connection with the material sought to be suppressed. In the words of a recent commentary on the amended exemption, judicial review can 'eliminate only those classifications which are manifestly erroneous'.[81] Perhaps the real gain of the 1974 amendments is that they will prevent the arbitrary, foolish or capricious non-disclosure of material in the supposed interest of foreign or defence policy.

In camera inspection to determine the relevance of an exemption, and to segregate disclosable from protected information, is now also possible where the government relies on the first exemption. Even under the amended Act, however, resort to inspection will not be automatic and the court will afford the government the opportunity of demonstrating the relevance of an exemption by affidavit evidence. Congressional debate shows that the legislature expected the courts to 'accord substantial weight'[82] to the agency's affidavit especially where first exemption protection is asserted. Nevertheless, the judgment in *Vaughn* v *Rosen*[83] indicates that blind reliance on an assertion of exempt status, even first exemption status, will no longer be the order of the day. Declaring that it was the court's duty to assure that a party's right to information 'is not submerged beneath government obfuscation and mischaracterization',[84] Justice Wilkey announced that 'courts will simply no longer accept conclusory and generalized allegations of exemptions . . . but will require a relatively detailed analysis in manageable segments'.[85] He prescribed a system of indexing and itemizing to assist the court to evaluate the government's claim of exemption in respect of different portions of the material. The *Vaughn* judgment has been welcomed as one which transforms an essentially inquisitorial procedure of inspection into one more consonant with the adversary procedure between government and citizen.[86] It has since been followed in a case in which the CIA declared that the existence or non-existence of an intelligence document claimed was itself a classified secret. The court ordered the CIA to provide a public affidavit to provide a basis for its claim that it could be required neither to confirm nor to deny the existence of the record.[87] The present state of the law on *in camera* inspection can be summarized by the statement that though the courts will not automatically resort to it (especially where defence and foreign policy protection is claimed) the agency will have to put up a detailed and factual justification on oath, which satisfies the court that an inspection is not necessary, in order to avoid judicial scrutiny of the disputed materials. In practical terms, the gain is likely to be the frustration of a dishonest or grossly misconceived reliance on the exemption clause of the FOIA.[88]

In conclusion, the comment seems justified that the first exemption accords adequate protection to the weighty interest of government in keeping secret sensitive foreign policy and military matters. At the same time, the legislature and the courts have together evolved sensible procedures that will check against the abuse or misuse of executive secrecy without intruding upon the executive branch's primary responsibility for policy-making in this field.

(b) The Second Exemption

Matters that are 'related solely to the internal personnel rules and practices of an agency' need not be disclosed under the second exemption.[89] Interpretation of the exemption has been bedevilled by conflicting reports of the Senate and the House. The Senate's view, most favoured by the courts, is that the exemption protects, rules, directives and guidelines concerned with employer–employee relations, working conditions and routine procedures.[90] In short, the information protected is limited to the domestic or internal housekeeping aspects of an agency's life. The House report envisages the protection of agency operating rules and manuals of procedure.[91] The difficulty attending this approach is that such manuals and rules are frequently not internal but relevant to relations with the general public; and the problem then arises of reconciling the exemption with the 'internal law' provisions requiring public access to 'administrative staff manuals and instructions to staff that affect members of the public'.[92] Manuals and instructions must be made available unless they fall into the category of 'law enforcement' material; but as *Cuneo* v *Laird*[93] demonstrates some manuals which are not related to law enforcement need protection, in this case instructions to auditors concerning the methods of auditing Defense contracts. The FOIA would be much clarified if the second exemptions were limited to rules of domestic administration (canteen facilities, tea-breaks, staff relations, et cetera) and the section requiring administrative staff manuals to be accessible were subject to a specific exemption, inserted in the general exemption clause, protecting law enforcement and financial control procedures and techniques. Though this would result in a trivial type of information being covered by the second exemption it does seem legitimate to protect agencies from vexatious prying into their purely domestic affairs. In *Department of the Air Force v Rose*[94] the Supreme Court adopted the Senate report but expressly declared that the House report might be relevant where disclosure might defeat agency attempts at regulation. The court affirmed the narrow construction of the second exemption by the lower court and the decision of that court that summaries of disciplinary proceedings (with identifying details deleted) by the US Air Force Academy were not protected by the second exemption as there was a genuine and significant public interest in the material. The purpose of the exemption is to relieve agencies of the burden of assembling and maintaining for inspection matter in which the public could not reasonably have an interest.

(c) The Third Exemption

Matters 'specifically exempted from disclosure by statute' are protected by this exemption.[95] Its provisions were dealt with incidentally in discussing generally statutes that positively prohibit disclosure or authorize non-disclosure.[96] Here it is necessary to record only the ruling that exemptions from disclosures in other laws will not generally be interpreted as a complete exemption from all the provisions of the FOIA.[97] The court delivered this ruling in relation to a statute which exempts the CIA from 'any other law' that would require disclosure of any 'functions . . . of its personnel'. Total exemption from the FOIA would clearly be undesirable and the agency would then have an uncontrolled discretion to conceal.

(d) The Fourth Exemption

This exemption ensures the protection of 'trade secrets and commercial or financial information obtained from a person and privileged or confidential'.[98] Discussion of this provision has tended to intertwine two issues—(i) what the exemption does protect and (ii) what is outside its ambit but ought to be protected. We shall consider first what the exemption has been held to mean and then whether it goes far enough.

According to *Getman v NLRB*[99] the exemption protects two classes of information:

(i) trade secrets; and
(ii) commercial or financial information which has been obtained from a person and which is privileged or confidential.

The first class—trade secrets—has a relatively settled meaning[100] and has not led to difficulties of interpretation. The expression 'obtained from a person' has led to findings that the source of the information must lie outside an agency and that it is unprotected where it does not.[101] But the real difficulty of interpretation has centred on the meaning of 'privileged or confidential'. The word 'privileged' was intended to refer to common-law privileges such as that between lawyer and client or doctor and patient. As information within these privileges is either protected by the sixth exemption or is in any event confidential, the meaning and scope of the exemption turns on the interpretation of 'confidential'. The most compelling judicial determination of the question rests on the premise that the exemption was designed to preserve the government's ability to obtain information from its subjects and to prevent harm to the competitive position of persons who supply information. Information is confidential if disclosure would prejudice either of these two interests.[102] Where the supplier is compelled by law to provide information, the government's ability to obtain it will not be injured by disclosure and the exemption will then operate only if disclosure would injure the competitive position of the supplier.[103] The latter question is one which can be determined on objective grounds and presents no real obstacle to the disclosure policy required by the FOIA. However, a real difficulty does arise where the supply of information is not compulsory by law and impairment of the government interest in securing the information is alleged. If simple reluctance to provide the government with information unless it is kept confidential is evidence of such impairment, the disclosure function of the Act might be drastically harmed by the subjective and perhaps unreasonable desire of suppliers to keep their information secret.

The most satisfactory solution to these difficulties would be an amendment designed to authorize non-disclosure of commercial or financial information only on the objective ground that the competitive position of the supplier would be damaged by revelation.[104] The government's interest in securing the data appears to be adequately furthered by the combined effect of (a) laws requiring the supply of information, (b) other exemptions protecting personal information from disclosure (exemptions 6 and 7), and (c) specific statutory prohibitions on disclosure of information supplied.

Early criticism of the fourth exemption focused on its reference to commercial and financial information and the lack of protection for non-commercial or non-financial information supplied in confidence.[105] Professor Davis, for example, declared: 'Obviously, the good faith understanding that the information will be kept confidential should be honored.'[106] While court interpretation has confined the protection to commercial and financial information which is confidential, this criticism is not nullified simply by the predictable judicial construction of the language of the exemption. However, it seems that the criticism demands too much by its insistence that all information, regardless of its intrinsic claims to protection, should be covered by an exemption if it is given to government on understanding of confidentiality. This would surely constitute a licence to the supplier, or to the government and supplier in collusion, to shut off large areas of material from disclosure under the Act. The features of current law referred to in (b) and (c) of the preceding paragraph demonstrate that certain data which may be neither commercial nor financial has been deemed by the legislature to be intrinsically worthy of protection. Perhaps there are other classes not specifically covered; but this is an argument for extending the categories, not for transferring the decision as to what deserves protection to the citizen or the agency.

(e) The Fifth Exemption

The material shielded from disclosure under this exemption is described as 'inter-agency or intra-agency memorandums or letters which would not be available by law to a party other than an agency in litigation with the agency'.[107] Executive privilege, we have seen, protects *inter alia* the internal advice and consultations of the executive branch from enforced disclosure; and exemption five was intended to further the same purpose. One of the functions of the convention of collective responsibility in cabinet government, as will appear later, is also to create within government a private area of advice and deliberation. There is no doubt that the need for secret deliberation is recognized in many different societies of varied political and social traditions and that its legitimate justification is the need to secure frank and disinterested advice and the consideration of all possible policy options and perspectives. Officials and politicians who can instantly be identified and called to account for airing and weighing unpopular alternatives, and be harassed for developing such alternatives where they seem desirable, will be less capable of wisely exercising the decision-making powers with which they are vested.[108]

All records which form part of the pre-decisional deliberative process may be withheld under the fifth exemption unless they are of a kind that would in general be subject to disclosure in normal litigation. Though the exemption refers to 'memorandums or letters', it may not be interpreted literally;[109] and if it is so interpreted an invocation of executive privilege could serve to protect other records such as tapes, punch cards, and so on. The qualification of the exemption by reference to documents that would generally be available to parties in litigation has the effect of making available factual material that is incorporated into the deliberative processes.[110] The recommendations of consultants employed by the agency would enjoy protection but not records submitted by interested persons from outside the agency.[111] Recommendations and advice that are explicitly incorporated into the final decision or order of the agency thereby lose their exemption five status and become available under the publication provisions discussed earlier.[112] 'Post-decisional communications' which explain the basis of the decision taken are also subject to disclosure.[113] The Supreme Court justified the availability of such communications in *NLRB* v *Sears, Roebuck & Co*[114] on the ground of limited injury to the decision-making process and the increased public interest in knowing the basis of agency policy.

The facilitation by exemption five of 'candid exchange' prior to decision-making is therefore subject to two main limitations: It may not be used to conceal factual material that would normally be disclosable in litigation and it does not immunize advice that is made part of the final opinion or order or which is incorporated into a post-decisional communication. The necessary right to full and frank discussion may therefore not be abused by making it a pretext for concealing the factual basis or final reasons for decisions of government.

(f) The Sixth Exemption

Protection is afforded by this exemption to 'personnel and medical files and similar files the disclosure of which would constitute a clearly unwarranted invasion of personal privacy'.[115] It is by this section in particular that the disclosure policy of the Act is limited by the important interest in privacy. Since the Privacy Act of 1974[116] provides only limited control over the dissemination of personal information collected by agencies,[117] it is chiefly to this exemption that the citizen must turn for vindication of his interest in closing off general access to personal material. The main objective of the exemption is to preclude access to intimate details of a highly personal nature. The courts have sanctioned the use of 'reverse FOIA suits'—actions brought by the suppliers of information to prevent disclosure under the Act; and such reverse suits are appropriate where a threatened release of information will damage personal privacy.[118] The reader should observe that the FOIA prevails over the Privacy Act and material protected by the latter Act may be made the subject of a disclosure order under the FOIA where the court concludes that the invasion of privacy is not unwarranted.[119]

Though the exemption refers specifically to personnel, medical and similar files, it has been suggested that the legislature intended it to cover 'any documented personal information that the government may have in its possession'.[120] Disciplinary files, customs forms and lists of names and addresses have been the subject of suits under the exemption. Once it is clear that the material is covered by the language it will be protected unless its release would not constitute a clearly unwarranted invasion of privacy. In *Getman* v *NLRB*[121] two university professors sought from the defendant Board the release of names and addresses of voters for purposes of conducting research into the Board's voting regulations. The court ordered production on the ground that the invasion of privacy would be minimal whereas the public advantage of providing the information to the applicants was extensive. In contrast, where a list of names and addresses was sought to advance private commercial interests (the distribution of sale catalogues) the court denied production in *Wine Hobby USA Inc* v *IRS*.[122] In these judgments the courts assumed that they were required to balance the public interest in disclosure against the private interest in the prevention of 'clearly unwarranted' intrusion into privacy. While the other exemptions preclude balancing, the language of the sixth exemption clearly contemplated a weighing of interests. The Supreme Court appears to have favoured the 'balancing' approach in its recent decision in *Department of the Air Force* v *Rose*.[123] A more controversial aspect of the *Getman* and *Wine Hobby* rulings is their emphasis on the interest of the applicant in the requested material. The Act affords the right to information to any person irrespective of his interest or standing; but in respect of this exemption the courts appear to be correct in their conclusion that balancing impliedly qualifies the otherwise strict policy of the Act that the 'interest' of the person seeking information is irrelevant.

(g) The Seventh Exemption

Under this exemption, which was extensively amended in 1974, 'investigatory records compiled for law enforcement purposes' are exempt from disclosure;[124] but they are exempt only if their production will interfere with enforcement proceedings, deprive a person of a fair trial, invade personal privacy, reveal a confidential source (or confidential information where the proceedings are criminal), disclose investigative techniques or endanger the safety of law enforcement personnel.[125] In its original form the exemption had referred simply to 'investigatory files compiled for law enforcement purposes', and in an effort to limit its scope the courts, aided by legislative history, identified some of the harms that are now expressly listed as prerequisites for the invocation of the protection afforded to such records. Court adjudicacation of the exemption was nevertheless characterized by conflicts of view and partial appreciation of the legislative goals. In *Bristol-Myers* v *Federal Trade Commission*[126] the court held that the exemption forced an enquiry as to whether the proceedings were concrete enough to bring it into operation and ordered disclosure after declaring that files could not be protected by 'a suggestion that enforcement proceedings may be launched at some future unspecified date'.[127] But in *Weinberg* v *Department of Justice*,[128] though no proceedings were imminent, the court refused production of spectographic reports of the bullet which killed President Kennedy on the ground that the documents sought (mainly work notes and raw analytical data on which the report was based) were legitimately part of an investigatory file.[129] And in *Aspin* v *Department of Defence*[130] the court declined to force disclosure of the army's four-volume investigation of the My Lai massacre in Vietnam on the ground that this might hamper the ability of future investigatory bodies to conduct proper enquiries. The case of *Ditlow* v *Brineger*[131] produced the ruling that once it appeared that the record was investigatory, 'it is not in the province of the courts to second-guess the Congress by relying on considerations which argue that the government will not actually be injured by revelation in the particular case'.[132]

The 1974 amendments reverse this aspect of the *Ditlow* finding since they clearly contemplate a determination by the courts that production will harm the government in one of the ways indicated above. One commentator has suggested that the chief gain of the 1974 amendments is procedural, and that while it may not achieve a reversal of all or even most of the previous cases, it does mandate a careful finding by the court (after *in camera* inspection, if necessary) that revelation of the records sought will produce the harm which Congress has now specifically prescribed as a basis for refusal.[133] The burden of demonstrating that release of material will result in a prescribed harm is on the agency. Nevertheless, it is at least doubtful that the *Aspin* and *Weinberg* rulings would hold under the amended exemption.

(h) The Eighth and Ninth Exemptions

The reports and examinations of agencies responsible for supervision of financial institutions and geological and geophysical data concerning wells are protected by the last two amendments.[134] The precise purpose of the first is not clear since the fourth exemption already protects (it seems adequately) commercial and financial information. The second was designed to protect data given to government agencies by private oil companies primarily to discourage unfair speculation.[135] The overall significance of these two exemptions is small.[136]

GENERAL COMMENTS

Having directed agencies to publish certain material, to make available its internal law and to produce records on request, the FOIA then proceeds to withdraw a body of information from the scope of the disclosure directives. The courts have the task of determining the limits of the withdrawn or exempt information and once they have declared the material exempt the agency cannot be compelled to disgorge. According to the more persuasive interpretation of the FOIA the agency is not forbidden to release exempted material[137] and except where privacy rights may be seriously jeopardized (in which case the aggrieved party may institute a reverse FOIA action to prevent disclosure)[138] it may decide to disregard the protection afforded by the nine exemptions of the Act. On the other hand, the court has no discretion to withhold once it has determined the material to be non-exempt even if disclosure may be thought harmful. Though the point is controversial, the preponderance of authority is against equity discretion to withhold non-exempt material;[139] and desirable policy (though this is controversial too) is against a discretionary power to broaden the field of exempt material.

A reassessment of the FOIA in 1975 underlined the fact that in approximately 200 decided cases the courts had generally ruled in favour of disclosure.[140] While in the initial period the Act was used extensively to further corporate commercial interests, the pressure of litigation has recently made available such matters as scientific reports on the dangers of atomic reactors and the Peers report on the My Lai massacre.[141] Other striking revelations include a report on CIA domestic activities prepared for President Ford, executive branch studies of the intelligence community and Red Cross reports on POWs in Vietnam.[142] Much of the success in extracting by court proceedings information of general public importance is due to the vigorous advocacy of bodies such as the Civil Liberties Union and the Freedom of Information Clearing House.[143] Notwithstanding the more favourable cost rules in American litigation, legal expenses remain an obstacle under a system of judicial enforcement and are most effectively mitigated by private institutional help of the kind afforded by these bodies. Thus a combination of favourable court response to the philosophy of disclosure of the Act, the less burdensome cost system and the activity of public-spirited private groups has made a substantial success of the judicially managed scheme of disclosure inaugurated by the FOIA.

The frequently dramatic court encounters over the disclosure and exemption provisions of the Act tend to distract attention from vitally important administrative requirements and procedures of the Act. These include stringent time-limits for responses to requests for information, the identification of officials who deny information requested, detailed annual reports to Congress on each agency's administration of the Act and tight control over fees charged for compliance with requests for materials. Recognizing the secretive and defensive attitudes of most bureaucracies, Congress has sought 'by a combination of the whip and the carrot' to infuse the administration with an attitude of openness toward the public. The prim Victorian desire to conceal and cover up is to be modified to some extent at least by a harlot's penchant for revelation, though without the latter's implied promise of access to the ultimate. In short, reformers in the United States have realistically understood that new laws need to be backed by an administratively grounded change of spirit, style and practice.

STATE OPEN RECORDS LEGISLATION

In some American states the development of a right of access to information kept by government agencies had progressed reasonably well under the common law, especially where the narrow English rule making its exercise dependent upon a litigatory interest was abandoned. But even the most generous interpretation of the common-law right left the citizen with serious difficulties such as the inadequacy of procedures and sanctions to enforce it. As part of a broad effort to make government more accountable and to increase public participation and confidence, most states have by now enacted open records legislation. A recent survey[144] of state laws demonstrates the great variety of state schemes—the FOIA model described above is by no means universal. State legislation is frequently more restrictive than the FOIA by reason of the narrow definition of public records to which access is granted or on account of the need to show standing. They vary considerably in the range and effectiveness of sanctions provided. But the restrictive statutes are balanced by progressive and innovative legislation in other states of which the Oregon statute is an outstanding example. The ensuing account of the open records law in Oregon will seek to point up departures from the FOIA model.

THE OREGON OPEN RECORDS LAW

SCOPE OF THE LAW

The Attorney-General's memorandum on public meetings and records neatly indicates the scope of the legislation by the following parenthetical remark under the heading 'Open Records': [Everybody, Practically Everything, Anytime, Except . . .].[145] 'Everybody' indicates that any person is entitled to inspect public records without the need to show a special interest or standing.[146] 'Practically Everything' refers to the broad definition of public records which includes any 'information relating to the conduct of the public's business, prepared, owned, used or retained by a public body regardless of physical form or characteristics'.[147] The public records held in 'every state and local governmental agency' are subject to disclosure.[148] The custodian of these records is directed by the Act to furnish 'proper and reasonable opportunities for inspection and examination . . . to all persons who have occasion to make examination of them'.[149] Where practicable certified copies must be provided.[150] Under such expansive provisions, disclosure has become the rule and secrecy the exception.

As indicated by the Attorney-General's parenthetical 'except', the Oregon law does have an exemption clause. The list of excepted categories corresponds broadly to those of the FOIA; but because states lack the federal government's responsibility for national security and foreign policy, no 'cavernous' exemption covering these areas is necessary. On the other hand, the lack of state jurisdication in these areas does mean that decisions on the exemption lack the critical and momentous quality that characterize many decisions at the federal level. The following are the exempted categories in Oregon:[151]

(a)   the records of a public body pertaining to pending or imminent litigation;
(b)   trade secrets;
(c)   subject to the law of disclosure in trials, investigatory information compiled for criminal-law purposes. The record of the arrest and report of a crime are not protected unless there is a clear need to delay disclosure pending investigation. In *Jensen* v *Schiffman*[152] the Court of Appeals found that the purposes sought to be furthered

by this exemption were similar to those now listed in the current FOIA counterpart[153] and rejected as extreme both the plaintiff's claim that reports of investigations must always be disclosed once the criminal investigation has concluded in a trial or decision not to prosecute, and the defendant's claim that such reports are for ever secret. The plaintiff had sought production of a sheriff's departmental investigation into a police department which had been submitted to the district attorney but from which no prosecutions were likely to result. The court overruled the circuit court decision that the record was exempt and remanded the case for rehearing, declaring that on its own *in camera* inspection of the record it appeared to be 'available for public inspection';[154]

(d) test questions, scoring keys and other examination data used in examinations, prior to the examination and if the examination is to be used again;

(e) certain business information submitted to government agencies by private concerns to the extent that disclosure would permit identification of the concerns;

(f) information relating to appraisal of any real estate prior to its acquisition;

(g) inter/intra agency communications, excluding factual material or final determinations of policy or action. However, the exemption does not apply unless the public body demonstrates that the interest in frank communication outweighs the public interest in disclosure. This permits a court controlled balancing of interests that is not permissible in the federal counterpart. In *Turner* v *Reed*[155] the court held that evaluations and recommendations to a parole board were protected as being of an advisory nature but excluded from the ambit of its ruling both factual material and the actual determination by the board;

(h) personal information kept in personal, medical or similar files if public disclosure would constitute an unreasonable invasion of privacy. The exemption goes on to place the burden of demonstrating that disclosure would not constitute an unreasonable invasion of privacy on the person seeking the material;[156]

(i) information submitted to an agency in confidence without a legal obligation to do so. The agency is required to show both that it obliged itself in good faith to keep the confidence[157] and that the material should reasonably be considered confidential. This second requirement imports an objective test. The legislature has followed the reasoning of the Oregon Court of Appeals in *Papadopoulos* v *State Board of Higher Education*[158] in which Schwab CJ said in relation to the earlier disclosure law: 'If the promise of confidentiality were the end of our enquiry, we would be allowing a state agency official to effectively eliminate the public rights . . .'. The court ordered production of a report on a university department

having found no objectively valid reason in the case for concealment on grounds of confidentiality;
(*j*)   certain prison records, but only to the extent that disclosure would
interfere with rehabilitation or substantially interfere with the
carrying out of the function of the department. Even then, disclosure may be ordered if the public interest in revelation outweighs the interest in confidentiality;
(*k*) information protected from disclosure under specific statutes. This
is similar to the FOIA counterpart except that the statutes are listed
in the Oregon law.

This list of the main categories of exemption is followed by a provision
which gave to public bodies the right to seek from the governor of the
state exemption for any other class of public records on the ground that
unlimited public access would be detrimental. The application had to
be submitted to the governor prior to the 1975 legislative session and
any exemption granted by him would be effective only until the
adjournment of that session.[159] This is a useful device which enables the
legislature, after a period of experience with the administration of the
law, to close off any undesirable gaps in the exemption clause.

The Oregon statute, unlike the FOIA, allows few absolute exemptions to its disclosure requirements. In most cases the court is entitled
on the ground of compelling public interest to order disclosure of
information falling into the exemption clause. The balancing task
entrusted to the courts is complex and may depend on the nature or the
content of the document. Referring to its function under the exemption clause, the court in *Turner* v *Reed*[160] said that 'in applying the
exemptions . . . there will be extremes at either end of a spectrum:
certain categories of documents will always be available for public
inspection, regardless of their contents, and other classes of documents
will never be available for inspection, regardless of their contents.
Between these extremes, decisions may have to be based, in part at
least, on the contents of individual documents.' While the decision to
protect or disclose turns both on type and content, it may be facilitated
by the agency's duty to separate exempt from non-exempt material.[161]
Difficult though the court's task may be, it has thus far had few cases
referred to it—a fact that is probably attributable to the novel enforcement provision of the statute to which we now turn.

THE ENFORCEMENT OF THE LAW

A special feature of the open records law in Oregon is the provision
it makes for an appeal to the Attorney-General. A person denied the
right to inspect or receive a copy of any public record of a state agency
may petition the Attorney-General 'to review the public record to
determine if it may be withheld from public inspection'.[162] The
petition to the Attorney-General is made on a simple form (of which
a specimen is printed in the Act) and on receipt of notice that it has

been received by him, the agency is required to transmit the record to the Attorney-General or, in appropriate cases, a description of the nature or substance of the public record.[163] The agency has the burden of sustaining its case before the Attorney-General who is required to give his decision on disclosure within three business days from the date of appeal.

If the decision is in favour of disclosure, in whole or part, the agency concerned may seek declaratory or injunctive relief before the circuit court. If the Attorney-General decides not to order disclosure, or declines it in part, or if the agency continues to withhold notwithstanding an order against it, the person seeking disclosure may approach the same court for similar relief.[164] While this provision has the effect of throwing the burden of seeking court reversal of an adverse decision on the party aggrieved thereby, agencies are likely to take the initiative where they feel that the order of the Attorney-General to disclose is wrong. The practical result is that in many cases the citizen will be relieved of the burden of instituting court proceedings, especially where the Attorney-General adopts a disclosure-oriented policy.

Where the matter does come before the circuit court for review, the matter is tried *de novo* with the onus again falling on the agency to justify its refusal to produce.[165] The court is authorized to review the documents themselves by *in camera* inspection and directed to give cases under the statute precedence over other hearings which are not considered of greater importance.[166] It may punish disobedience of its order as contempt and is directed to award costs where the person seeking the information is successful. If he is partially successful the court is empowered to award costs, either in full or part.[167]

COMMENT ON THE LAW

The Oregon open records statute favours citizen access to public information by the adoption of a broad definition of the documents subject to it and of the agencies bound by its disclosure terms.[168] While it does create traditional categories of exemption, unlike the FOIA, the court is in general not compelled to declare prima facie protected information as exempt and retains a wide discretion to balance the conflicting interests. The Court of Appeals has so far favoured disclosure except where a clear interest in confidentiality is established.[169] The citizen denied access by an agency is afforded a right of rapid review before the Attorney-General which he may exercise without incurring costs. Being an elected official, the Oregon Attorney-General is unlikely to be hostile to the citizen's interest in securing production of public records. If he succeeds on his petition to the Attorney-General, the agency will normally take the case on review to the circuit court if it still declines to comply; and a citizen who wins at that level will be awarded costs. The weight of the Act, and especially of its procedural provisions, is against the agency which chooses to deny inspection of its records. The chief defects of the Oregon statute are the failure[170] to specify time-limits for anything except the disposition of a petition to the Attorney-General and the absence of specific sanctions against officials who arbitrarily and wrongfully refuse access to persons entitled. Measured against its achievements, these shortcomings are of limited significance. Nothing better characterizes Oregon law than the quotation on the cover page of the Attorney-General's memorandum: 'Freedom of information is now, by statute, the rule and secrecy the exception.'

OPEN MEETING LAWS

Not just records but meetings have to be opened up if the citizen is to have the ability to learn what his government is doing. While access to documentary material is likely to remain the most important source of information, no account of the positive right to know would be complete without some reference to legislation requiring public bodies to afford citizens access to their meetings. Until the passing of the Government in the Sunshine Act[171] in 1976 legislative activity at the federal level was minimal. Many states have long had open meeting laws on their statute books and the pioneering work in this area has clearly been accomplished by state governments.

FEDERAL LEGISLATION

The Federal Advisory Committee Act,[172] first introduced in 1972, requires meetings of advisory committees as defined in the Act to be open to members of the public.[173] An advisory committee is a committee established by statute or reorganization plan, or established or utilized by the President or one or more agencies in order to obtain advice or recommendations for the President, or an agency or officer of the federal government.[174] The definition specifically excludes a committee which is composed wholly of full-time officers or employees of the federal government. Numerous advisory committees have been set up on such diverse matters as the status of women, consumer problems and physical fitness and sports. All formally organized committee meetings have to be open to the public unless the President or the head of the agency to which the committee reports determines that one of the exemptions to the open meeting requirement of the Government in the Sunshine Act is applicable.[175] Casual and informal contacts between outside groups and the President, federal agencies or officers are not within the scope of the Act which was intended to apply only to meetings with an 'established structure' which are formally constituted.[176]

Though the disclosure requirements of the Federal Advisory Committee Act regulate a narrowly circumscribed area of federal government meetings, their enactment represented an important advance in open government which the court in *Gates* v *Schlesinger*[177] characterized as a legislative counter to 'the proliferation of unknown and sometimes secret "interest groups" or "tools" employed to promote or endorse agency policies'. Moreover, by making public the advice which advisory committees give to the President or federal agencies, the legislature has paved the way for open discussion of governmental problems *prior* to decision-making. Previously public discussion frequently took place *ex post facto* when there was no longer any opportunity to influence the persons or bodies with authority to decide. The extension of the principle of open discussion to a wider range of federal agencies has since been achieved by the Government in the Sunshine Act (referred to below as the Sunshine Act).

The definition of 'agency' in the Sunshine Act is broad and corresponds with the FOIA definition.[178] But for the purposes of the Sunshine Act a federal agency or department does not qualify unless it is headed by a collegial body composed of two or more individual members a majority of whom are appointed to such position by the President with the advice and consent of the Senate.[179] Since the Sunshine Act was enacted to open up meetings, and since meetings require more than one person, it seems quite rational to make its provisions applicable only to multiple-member agencies. Congress has not taken up the suggestion that single-member agencies should be covered when they conduct hearings.[180] A subdivision of an agency authorized to act on its behalf falls within the definition and must comply with the Act.

An agency falling under the statutory definition is required to observe the injunction that 'every portion of every meeting of an agency shall be open to public observation'.[181] The term 'meeting' is defined as

'. . . the deliberations of at least the number of individual agency members required to take action on behalf of the agency where such deliberations determine or result in the joint conduct or disposition of official agency business . . .'.[182]

The two elements which convert deliberations into meetings covered by the Act are (i) a quorum limit in respect of the persons taking part and (ii) the actual disposition or conduct of agency business. The definition therefore rules out exploratory discussions among members not constituting a quorum and possibly exploratory talk between members constituting a quorum provided that such talk is purely preliminary and informal. However, it is not clear that prior deliberations towards a decision between members constituting a quorum will not constitute 'joint conduct . . . of official agency business' and thereby fall under the publicity requirements of the Sunshine Act. One of the first authoritative commentaries on the Act expresses the conclusion that all discussion 'leading up to the final decision will be open to the public'.[183] Nonquorate informal discussions are clearly outside the reach of the Act but on this view informal quorate discussions are covered by the law even if they are genuinely exploratory. Judicial interpretation may be needed to resolve this problem of the scope of the law. A final point about the definition of 'meeting' requires underlining: Since there is no requirement that the deliberations must be between persons assembled together, the provisions of the Act cannot be avoided by the disposition of business by telephonic or other forms of indirect communication. This does not apply to disposition of business in writing since the written transaction of an agency's affairs does not fall under the Act and may in any event be exempt under the FOIA as an intra-agency memorandum.[184]

The statutory obligation to hold open meetings does not apply where the agency *properly* determines that the public transaction of its business will result in the disclosure of information falling within ten exemptions listed in the Act.[185] The exemption clause is closely parallel to the FOIA exemptions and incorporates material relating to national defence and foreign policy, internal personnel rules and practices, trade secrets and commercial or financial information, personal affairs, investigatory records, financial institutions and agency adjudication. It also covers material protected from disclosure by other statutes other than the FOIA and information which if disclosed prematurely would hamper the implementation of proposed agency action. This last exclusion has been described as a loosely worded catch-all inserted in the interests of agency efficiency.[186] Its exact contours will be clear only after judicial interpretation.

The invocation of the exemption clause by agencies falling under the Sunshine Act is subject to a number of important rules and procedures. The agency need not invoke an exemption even where applicable since it may decline to do so where the 'public interest requires otherwise'.[187] A majority of the entire membership of the agency must vote in favour of applying any exemption to a meeting or portion of a meeting and the Act requires publicity to be given to the determination, including the vote of each member.[188] The general counsel or chief legal adviser to each agency is required to certify publicly the applicability of a specific exemption for each meeting closed.[189] The application of the exemption clause, and of other provisions of the Act, is subject to review at the instance of 'any person' before the district courts of the United States which have jurisdiction to conduct *in camera* inspection and to grant a declaratory judgment, injunctive relief or other remedy deemed appropriate.[190] The setting aside or invalidation of agency action, other than the decision to close a meeting or withhold information, is not within the power of the reviewing court.[191] A speedy procedure is provided for the reviewing court and the burden is on the agency to sustain its action. The reviewing court has power to award attorney fees against either party but they may be assessed against the plaintiff only where his action was initiated for frivolous or dilatory purposes.[192]

A number of supplemental provisions in the Act are worthy of special mention. Timeous notice (in general, at least one week) has to be given of all agency meetings and any changes in time and venue must also be publicized.[193] Transcripts or recordings of closed meetings, excluding matter that may be withheld under the exemption clause, must be made available to the public at the actual cost of duplication or transcription.[194] The Sunshine Act is not authority to withhold information from Congress or matter that would be available under the Privacy Act.[195] Each agency subject to the Act is required to adopt and publish regulations implementing the provisions of the Act[196] and to report annually to Congress on the implementation of the Act to its meetings.[197]

The Sunshine Act appears to constitute an acceptable compromise between administration in a fish-bowl and closed-door conduct of federal business. Its full impact will have to await experience of its actual administration; but it does promise to minimize the effect of secret pressure groups and to guarantee a measure of public discussion of government actions before they crystallize into decisions.

STATE OPEN MEETINGS LEGISLATION

The range and diversity of state laws preclude a detailed or comprehensive examination of even the leading models in the conservative or progressive tradition.[198] The account that follows is a broad-brush treatment of state statutes with some specific references to the Oregon open meetings legislation. All fifty states have enacted open meeting laws.

Like open records legislation, the state statutes vary considerably in range and effectiveness. At the one end of the spectrum there are laws which, by intent at least, require state and local administration to take place in a fish-bowl. At the other end lie those laws which are ostensibly designed to create a right of citizen access to meetings but which have become charters for secrecy by reason of the exceptions and qualifications incorporated into the statutory text.[199] One clear moral that emerges from the administration of state open meeting (sunshine) laws is that weak laws, with loopholes and broad in-built limitations, are better not enacted at all.

The enactment of a sunshine law involves initially a decision as to what public bodies will be covered. These may be described by listing, or by functional or public-funding criteria, or a combination of any of these methods.[200] The Oregon law on public meetings incorporates a broad definition which declares that 'public body' means 'the state, any regional council, county, city or district, or any municipal or public corporation, or any board, department, commission, council bureau, committee or sub-committee or advisory group or any other agency thereof'.[201] This language discloses an intention to cover governmental bodies at every level.

Once the bodies affected are identified, the more difficult task confronting the legislature arises—that of prescribing what meetings must be open. Narrow definitions limit the statute to meetings at which final decisions are taken or resolutions adopted;[202] but this enables public authorities to transfer effective decision-making to preliminary meetings from which outsiders (including the media) are excluded. This kind of evasion seems precluded by the Oregon definition of 'meeting' which covers meetings for which a quorum is required 'in order to make a decision or *to deliberate toward a decision*'.[203] The Oregon statute also precludes a quorum of a governing body meeting in private for purposes of either decision or deliberation.[204] Where the meetings covered are very broadly defined, it is desirable that the law specifically exempt social or chance meetings at which public business is discussed for otherwise any informal discussion between members would be illegal.

Most statutes recognize by way of special exceptions that the interest in public knowledge and participation has to be counterbalanced in appropriate cases by the interest in insulating some deliberations from 'the intense heat of public pressure'.[205] In a model exception clause prepared by one commentator, public bodies are permitted to hold an executive or private session where they are considering or acting on staff matters (hiring, firing and discipline) or matters that would adversely affect the reputation of any person who is not a member of the body, conducting an official investigation, considering the sale or acquisition of land or negotiating collective bargaining agreements.[206] In addition to these exceptions there would be others authorized by specific statutes. American experience teaches that the right to hold private sessions must be narrowly circumscribed if it is not to become a technique of subverting the purposes of the entire law.

Perhaps the most difficult task in legislating for open meetings will be that of devising appropriate sanctions. Sanctions enacted range from criminal fines for offending officials through mandamus or injunctive proceedings to nullification of decisions taken at meetings wrongfully closed to the public. The difficulties inherent in each of these sanctions cannot be surveyed here;[207] but one solution is worthy of special note. The Oregon statute enables any person affected by a decision to bring a suit for the purpose of requiring compliance or preventing violation of the law. The court is empowered to order such equitable relief as it deems appropriate.[208] This flexibility leaves the court with a discretion to apply the most appropriate remedy to the case before it.

The low level of citizen interest in the meetings of public authorities, and the lack of time and opportunity for minitoring their proceedings, means that the public gain from open meetings will be smaller than the benefit of open records. The activities of private organizations, and especially of the press, radio and television, will be crucial in converting the paper right into an active instrument of knowledge and participation. It has been said that an aggressive and independent newspaper or broadcast station can make the difference between closed and open government.[209] Nevertheless, the first stage of reform is the enactment of a favourable law which public-spirited citizens can turn into an instrument of informed and active government.[210]

NOTES

[1] The Statute, Public Law 89–487, received Presidential signature on 4 July 1966 and became effective one year later on 4 July 1967. It was codified as 5 USC 552.

[2] Nils Herlitz *Elements of Nordic Public Law* (P A Norstedt & Söners Förlag, Stockholm, 1969) 196–200; Nils Herlitz 'Publicity of Official Documents in Sweden' 1958 *Public Law* 50; Stanley V Anderson, 'Public Access to Government Files in Sweden' (1973) 21 *Am J Comp Law* 419 at 421–4.

[3] Nils Herlitz *Elements of Nordic Public Law* 197.

[4] See references cited in footnote 2 above. Individual criminal responsibility for a culpable failure to disclose was abolished in 1976: See *An Official Information Act* (Outer Policy Unit, London, 1977) 39.

[5] Stanley V Anderson loc cit 428–41 and Niels Eilschov Holm, 'The Danish System of Open Files in Public Administration' (1975) 19 *Scandinavian Studies in Law* 153.

[6] *Corpus Juris Secundum* vol 76 ¶ 35; *American Jurisprudence 2nd* vol 66, 349.

[7] *Halsbury's Laws of England* 3 ed vol 11, 88–9.

[8] 60 ALR 1351.

[9] 60 Stat 238.

[10] Note: 'The Freedom of Information Act: A Seven-Year Assessment' 74 *Colum L Rev* 895 at 897; Project: 'Government Information and the Rights of Citizens' (1975) 73 *Mich L Rev* 971 at 1023 (referred to below as Project: 'Government Information').

[11] Freedom of Information Act and Amendments of 1974 (PL 93–502); Sourcebook: Legislative History, Texts and other Documents, 94th Congress, 1st sess, 8–96 (March 1975) (Referred to below as 'Sourcebook').

[12] Ibid 2.

[13] Ibid 8.

[14] Project: 'Government Information' 1025.

[15] The 1974 Amendments are discussed in detail by Elias Clark 'Holding Government Accountable: The Amended Freedom of Information Act' (1975) 84 *Yale LJ* 741 at 751 et seq.

[16] Ibid 766.

[17] 'Sourcebook' 8.

[18] Ibid 12.

[19] This compendious description of 5 USC ¶ 552(a)(1) is by Elias Clark loc cit 743–4.

[20] 5 USCA ¶ 552(a)(2) (Supp 1976).

[21] 5 USCA ¶ 552(a)(3) (Supp 1976).

[22] 5 USCA ¶ 552(b) (Supp 1976).

[23] 5 USCA ¶ 552(c).

[24] 5 USCA ¶ 552(a)(4)(B) (Supp 1976).

[25] 5 USCA ¶ 552(e) (Supp 1977).

[26] Project: 'Government Information' 1029.

[27] *Soucie v David* 448 F 2nd 1067 (DC Cir, 1971) 1075.

[28] 482 F 2nd 710 (DC Cir, 1974) 715.

[29] Attorney General's Memorandum on the 1974 Amendments to the FOIA, US Dept of Justice, February 1975, 26. (Referred to below as 'Attorney General's Memorandum'.)

[30] Project: 'Government Information' 1028.

[31] *Rocap v Indiek* 45 US LW 2019. (21 June 1976.)

[32] Project: 'Government Information' 1029.

[33] This is an abbreviated version of 5 USC ¶ 552(a)(1).

[34] *Merrill v FOMC* 44 US LW 2434 (9 March 1976). An agency policy of delaying for 45 days was held violative of the Act.

[35] 5 USCA ¶ 552(a)(1).

[36] Project 'Government Information' 1033. The sanction is not enforced where the party in question is not adversely affected.

[37] Kenneth Culp Davis, 'The Information Act: A Preliminary Analysis' (1967) 34 *Univ of Chicago L Rev* 761 at 804.

[38] Ibid 779.

[39] 5 USCA ¶ 552(a)(2).

[40] Kenneth Culp Davis loc cit 721–2.

[41] Ibid 805. The Agency is specifically authorized, moreover, to delete identifying details that would constitute a clearly unwarranted invasion of privacy: ¶ 552(a)(2).

[42] 44 L Ed 2nd 57 (1975).

[43] At 75.

[44] *NRLB* v *Sears, Roebuck & Co* 44 L Ed 2nd 29 (1975) 48–9. The meaning of a 'final opinion' is canvassed in 'Developments Under the Freedom of Information Act—1975' (1976) *Duke LJ* 366 at 377.

[45] *Tax Analysts & Advocates* v *Internal Revenue Service* 362 F Supp 1298 (DDC 1973). The ruling on this point was sustained on appeal: 505 F 2nd 350 (DC Cir, 1974).

[46] Ibid 1305.

[47] Ibid 1303.

[48] This view may help to reconcile the conflicting interpretations of the judgment cited in footnote 45 above: See Project: 'Government Information' 1036, and compare 'The Freedom of Information Act: A Seven-Year Assessment' 901–2.

[49] Project: 'Government Information' 1036 et seq.

[50] 'The Freedom of Information Act: A Seven-Year Assessment' 903–4.

[51] 5 USCA ¶ 552(a)(3).

[52] 5 USCA ¶ 551(2).

[53] Project: 'Government Information' 1042.

[54] *Nichols* v *United States* 325 F Supp 130 (D Kan, 1971). The case was confirmed on appeal (460 F 2nd 671 (10th Cir, 1972)) and the Supreme Court denied *certiorari*. The district court decided the question on the basis that even if it constituted a record, which it did not decide, the material was exempt.

[55] *SDC Development Corp* v *Mathews* 45 US LW 2221 (29 September 1976).

[56] *Ciba-Geigy Corp* v *Mathews* 45 US LW 2456 (8 March 1977).

[57] *Irons* v *Schuyler* 465 F 2nd 608 (DC Cir, 1972). The decision is criticized in 'The Freedom of Information Act: A Seven-Year Assessment' 905–6 but it seems that it was not unreasonable for the court to take the view that sweeping requests are unspecific.

[58] 5 USCA ¶ 552(a)(6)(A).

[59] Ibid.

[60] The FBI, which has been inundated with FOIA requests since the law was enacted, failed in *Hayden* v *US Department of Justice*, 44 US LW 2558 (21 May 1976) and in *Hamlin* v *Kelley* 45 US LW 2595 (2 June 1977) to secure extensions; but in *Open America* v *Watergate Special Prosecution Force* 45 US LW 2035 (7 July 1976) the court treated a heavy volume of requests as justifying an extension of time. The court took into account the overall costs to the FBI in complying with a heavy volume of requests and decided that a very sharp rise in expenditure could constitute an 'exceptional circumstance' justifying delay. The decision has been criticized in a Note in 71 *Nw Un L Rev* 805 (1977).

[61] See, for example, 'Sourcebook' 29 where the finding is recorded that most agencies took a month to respond to requests and two months to determine appeals.

[62] Ibid 45.

[63] 5 USCA ¶ 552(a)(4)(A).

[64] Ibid.

[65] 5 USCA ¶ 552(a)(4)(B).

[66] Ibid ¶ 552(a)(4)(C), (D) and (E). A court order directing production is not a precondition of the award of fees so long as the suit was necessary and had a substantial causative effect on the delivery of information: *Vermont Low Income Advocacy Council* v *Usery* 45 US LW 2306 (9 December 1976).

[67] Ibid ¶ 552(a)(4)(F) and (G).

[68] 415 US 1 (1974).

[69] *Sears, Roebuck & Co* v *NLRB* 473 F 2nd 91 (DC Cir, 1972) and *Lennon* v *Richardson* 378 F Supp 39 (1974).

[70] For a review of more recent cases in which the power to enjoin was assumed, the reader should consult 'Developments Under the Freedom of Information Act—1975' (1976) *Duke LJ* 366 at 367.

[71] 5 USCA ¶ 552(b).

[72] 5 USCA ¶ 552(b)(1).
[73] 410 US 73 (1973), 35 L Ed 2nd 119.
[74] A detailed account of the events leading up to the suit has been given by Patsy T Mink in 'The Cannikin Papers: A Case Study in Freedom of Information' *Secrecy and Foreign Policy* 114 et seq.
[75] Ibid 124.
[76] At 135 (L Ed 2nd).
[77] At 136.
[78] See Elias Clark loc cit 753.
[79] Ibid 758.
[80] Morton Halperin 'Judicial Review of National Security Classifications by the Executive Branch after the 1974 Amendments to the Freedom of Information Act' (1975) 25 *Am UL Rev* 27 at 30–2.
[81] The same commentary proposes congressional action to specify more exact criteria for classification in order to give courts greater power of review: see Note: 'National Security and the Amended Freedom of Information Act' (1976) 85 *Yale LJ* 401 at 416 and 421.
[82] Elias Clark loc cit 758.
[83] 484 F 2nd 820 (DC Cir, 1973).
[84] At 826.
[85] At 827.
[86] Note: 'Vaughn v Rosen: Toward True Freedom of Information' (1974) 122 *U Pa L Rev* 731. See also the note in (1974) 87 *Harv L Rev* 854.
[87] *Phillippi v CIA* 45 US LW 2274 (16 November 1976). In *Halperin v Department of State* 46 US LW 2088 (16 August 1977) the Court of Appeals referred the case back to the district court for *in camera* inspection where the first exemption was invoked by the government.
[88] Professor Elias Clark has noted certain more specific gains: 'It will keep agencies from classifying material after a request for disclosure of that material has been made, from claiming the exemption for material because it is classifiable although it has not in fact been classified, and from withholding the whole because some of the parts are classified': loc cit 758. Reliance on classification where the declassification procedure should have operated will also be precluded: Morton Halperin loc cit 29.
[89] 5 USCA ¶ 552(b)(2).
[90] Project: 'Government Information' 1051.
[91] Ibid.
[92] See pp 70–2 above.
[93] 338 F Supp 504 (DD C, 1972).
[94] 425 US 352 (1976).
[95] 5 USCA ¶ 552(b)(3).
[96] See pp 49–50 above.
[97] *Phillippi v CIA (supra)*.
[98] 5 USCA ¶ 552(b)(4).
[99] 450 F 2nd 670 (DC Cir, 1971).
[100] Project: 'Government Information' 1063n619. See, however, *Washington Research Project Inc v Dept of Health, Education and Welfare* 504 F 2nd 238 (DC Cir, 1974).
[101] Ibid 1064. It is suggested here that an amendment may be necessary to protect information of a commercial or financial kind which would normally be regarded at confidential but which is not supplied by a person outside the agency.
[102] *National Parks & Conservation Association v Morton* 498 F 2nd 765 (DC Cir, 1974); *National Parks and Conservation Association v Kleppe* 45 US LW 2273 (15 November 1976).
[103] Ibid 770.
[104] As held in *Continental Oil Co v Federal Power Commission* 519 F 2nd 31 (5th Cir, 1975).
[105] Kenneth Culp Davis loc cit 787–93.
[106] Ibid 787.
[107] 5 USCA ¶ 552(b)(5).
[108] The policy functions of exemption five are outlined in Note: 'The Freedom of Information Act: A Seven-Year Assessment' 938.
[109] Project: 'Government Information' 1070. *Aviation Consumer Action Project v*

Washburn 535 F 2nd 101 (DC Cir, 1976) extended the exemption to non-written materials. Decisions on the meaning of 'memorandums or letters' are reviewed in 'Developments Under the Freedom of Information Act—1975' (1976) *Duke LJ* 366 at 389–95.

[110] Ibid 1072–3. (See also *Environmental Protection Agency* v *Mink (supra)* 132 et seq.) But if the factual material is inextricably intertwined with the deliberative process, it is exempt: *Soucie* v *David* 448 F 2nd 1067 (DC Cir, 1971). It will also be suppressed if disclosure would hinder the ability of an agency to gather the facts themselves: 'Developments under the Freedom of Information Act—1975' (1976) *Duke LJ* 366 at 386–8.

[111] Ibid 1071.

[112] See pp 69–72 above. Thus exemption five status may be lost by incorporation of the material into a final opinion: See 'Developments Under the Freedom of Information Act—1975' (1976) *Duke LJ* 366 at 373.

[113] Note: 'The Freedom of Information Act: A Seven-Year Assessment' 938 et seq.

[114] *Supra* at 48.

[115] 5 USCA ¶ 552(b)(6).

[116] 5 USCA ¶ 552(a).

[117] 'Non-routine' transfers of information by the agency require the written consent of the subject: See ¶ 552(a), (b) and the discussion in Project :'Government Information' 1324 et seq.

[118] Project: 'Government Information' 1157 et seq. The court in *Sonderegger* v *US Dept of the Interior* 45 US LW 2327 (17 December 1976) enjoined the release of details of amounts paid to flood victims as an unwarranted invasion of privacy.

[119] James M Gorski loc cit 140; Jerome J Hanus & Harold C Relyea 'A Policy Assessment of the Privacy Act of 1974' (1976) 25 *Am Un L Rev* 555 at 581 and 590.

[120] Project: 'Government Information' 1079–80.

[121] 450 F 2nd 670 (DC Cir, 1971).

[122] 502 F 2nd 133 (3rd Cir, 1974).

[123] *Supra*. The interests to be balanced are the general public's interest in the information sought as opposed to the individual interest in protecting his privacy: See 'Developments under the Freedom of Information Act—1976' (1977) *Duke LJ* 532 at 543.

[124] 5 USCA ¶ 552(b)(7). (The exemption applies to all law enforcement proceedings, whether civil, criminal or administrative: Project: 'Government Information' 1089.)

[125] Ibid. The effect of the changes introduced by the 1974 amendments is discussed in detail by Larry P Ellsworth in 'Amended Exemption 7 of the Freedom of Information Act' (1975) 25 *Am UL Rev* 37. Recent judicial interpretation of the exemptions is outlined in 'Developments under the Freedom of Information Act—1976' 547.

[126] 424 F 2nd 935 (DC Cir, 1970).

[127] At 939.

[128] 489 F 2nd 1195 (DC Cir, 1973).

[129] The substitution of 'records' for 'files' in the amended Act will force a closer analysis of separate documents in investigatory files to determine whether they have protected status.

[130] 491 F 2nd 24 (DC Cir, 1974).

[131] 494 F 2nd 1073 (DC Cir, 1974).

[132] At 1074.

[133] Elias Clark loc cit 759–63. In *Deering Milliken Inc* v *Nash* 44 USLW 2252 (12 November 1975) the court concluded that production of the material in issue would benefit rather than harm enforcement proceedings but refused an order to disclose on the ground that personal privacy would be invaded. In *Title Guarantee Co* v *NLRB* 534 F 2nd 484 (2nd Cir, 1976) the judge dispensed with proof of specific harm and was prepared to presume it in the circumstances of the case; but the court limited its ruling narrowly to NLRB proceedings. On the implications of this judgment see 'Developments under the Freedom of Information Act—1976' 547.

[134] 5 USCA ¶ 552(b)(8) and (9).

[135] Project: 'Government Information' 1103.

[136] These two exemptions have so far generated only one decision each; James M Gorski loc cit 158–9.

[137] Note: 'Protection from Dislcosure—The Reverse—FOIA Suit' (1976) *Duke LJ* 330 at 333 et seq. The most recent decision at the time of writing, *Chrysler Corp* v *Schlesinger* 46 US LW 2202 (25 October 1977), has ruled that disclosure of exempt material is generally permissive.

[138] Ibid.

[139] Project: 'Government Information' 1150–6; 'Developments Under the Freedom of Information Act—1975' (1976) *Duke LJ* 366 at 370.

[140] Elias Clark loc cit 748.

[141] Ibid 750–1.

[142] Morton H Halperin & Daniel N Hoffman *Top Secret: National Security and the Right to Know* (New Republic Books, Washington DC, 1977) 50.

[143] The writer personally investigated the work that these bodies are doing in further-ance of the private citizens' right to secure information during a visit to the United States in 1976.

[144] Project: 'Government Information' 1163–87.

[145] Attorney General's Public Meetings and Records Manual, 1 February 1976 (Att Gen's Opinion ¶ 7252) (Referred to below as 'Attorney General's Manual'.).

[146] ORS 192.420. The current law on open records was enacted in 1973. Legislation on the subject was in existence much earlier: See the leading case of *MacEwan v Holm* 359 P 2nd 413 (1961) and also *Papadopoulos v State Board of Higher Education* Or App 494 P 2nd 260 (1972). The latter case (at 263) shows that the state's first 'right to know' statute was passed in 1862, that the right was expanded in 1909 and that a total revision of the laws was brought about in 1961.

[147] See ORS 192.410(4) and (5).

[148] ORS 192.410 and 'Attorney General's Manual' 6.

[149] ORS 192.430.

[150] ORS 192.440.

[151] The exemptions are contained in ORS 192.500. The individual sub-paragraphs will not be cited in this account. Certain exemptions of small general interest have been omitted.

[152] Or App 544 P 2nd 1048 (1976).

[153] 5 USCA ¶ 552(b)(7).

[154] At 1052.

[155] Or App 538 P 2nd 373 (1975).

[156] In *Turner v Reed (supra)* at 376 the court noted that this provision appears to conflict with the general burden of sustaining its action which the statute places upon the agency in ORS 192.490(1).

[157] In *Sadler v Oregon State Bar* 275 Or 279 (1976) the court declined to apply the exemption to complaints about the conduct of a member of the Bar on the ground that there was no evidence that the complaints had been submitted in confidence. That being so, the Oregon State Bar could not oblige itself in good faith not to disclose the informa-tion. For this reason the court did not decide the more difficult question of whether disclosure or non-disclosure would best serve the public interest.

[158] *Supra* at 267.

[159] ORS 192.500(4).

[160] *Supra* at 378.

[161] ORS 192.500(3).

[162] ORS 192.450. If the report is not in the custody of a state agency, but of some other public body, the petition is made to the district attorney having jurisdiction.

[163] ORS 192.470.

[164] ORS 192.450(2).

[165] However, the onus appears to be reversed in cases in which disclosure would injure privacy.

[166] ORS 192.490.

[167] Ibid.

[168] Project: 'Government Information' 1165–70 indicates that many states define records much more restrictively.

[169] *Turner v Reed (supra)* and *Jensen v Schiffman (supra)*.

[170] Project: 'Government Information' 1184.

[171] 5 USCA 552(b).

[172] 5 USCA Ap.

[173] 5 USCA Ap ¶ 10(a)(1).

[174] 5 USCA Ap ¶ 3(2). The statutory definition has been paraphrased in the text.

[175] 5 USCA ¶ 552b(c). Before this Act was introduced, the meeting could be closed on the basis of the FOIA exemptions which correspond closely to those listed in the

Government in the Sunshine Act. The FOIA exemptions were not entirely appropriate and the courts were required, in particular, to construe narrowly the inter/intra agency memorandum exemption in *Nader* v *Dunlop*, 370 F Supp 177 (DD C, 1973).

[176] *Nader* v *Baroody* 44 USLW 2031 (DD C, 23 June 1975). This decision is criticized in Project: 'Government Information' 1213.

[177] 366 F Supp 797 (DD C, 1973).

[178] 5 USCA ¶ 552b(a)(1).

[179] Ibid. A subdivision of an agency authorized to act on the agency's behalf also falls under the law.

[180] See, for example, Project: 'Government Information' 1215. Single-member agencies may be dealt with in separate legislation to be introduced later: see Note: 'The Government in the Sunshine Act—An Overview' (1977) *Duke LJ* 565 at 568n18.

[181] 5 USCA ¶ 552b(b) (May 1977 Supp).

[182] 5 USCA ¶ 552b(a)(2). Deliberations to determine the time and place of a meeting or decide whether a meeting should be closed in terms of the exemption clause do not fall under the definition.

[183] Note: 'The Government in the Sunshine Act—An Overview' 569.

[184] Ibid 570.

[185] 5 USCA ¶ 552b(c).

[186] Note: 'The Government in the Sunshine Act—An Overview' 580.

[187] See the opening words of 5 USCA ¶ 552b(c). Presumably a reverse suit will be available to a party whose privacy interests may be jeopardized.

[188] 5 USCA ¶ 552b(d). Agencies whose business will regularly involve certain of the exemptions may resolve to close meetings by regulation in which case the decision need not be publicized each time.

[189] 5 USCA ¶ 552b(f). Transcripts or recordings of closed meetings have to be kept.

[190] 5 USCA ¶ 552b(h)(1).

[191] 5 USCA ¶ 552b(h)(2).

[192] 5 USCA ¶ 552b(i)

[193] 5 USCA ¶ 552b(e)(1) and (2).

[194] 5 USCA ¶ 552b(f)(2).

[195] 5 USCA ¶ 552b(l) and (m).

[196] 5 USCA ¶ 552b(g).

[197] 5 USCA ¶ 552b(j).

[198] For a comprehensive survey of state legislation, the reader should consult William R Wright 'Open Meeting Laws: An Analysis and a Proposal' (1974) 45 *Miss LJ* 1151.

[199] M L Stein 'The Secrets of Local Government' in *None of Your Business: Government Secrecy in America* 151, 156 et seq.

[200] Douglas Q Wickham 'Let the Sunshine In' (1973) 68 *NW UL Rev* 480, 482–3.

[201] ORS 192.610(4).

[202] Douglas Q Wickham loc cit 483.

[203] ORS 192.610(4) (Emphasis supplied.)

[204] ORS 192.630(2).

[205] Douglas Q Wickham loc cit 482.

[206] Ibid 500.

[207] For a good discussion, see Project: 'Government Information' 1204 et seq.

[208] ORS 192.680.

[209] M L Stein loc cit 162.

[210] For an early assessment of the success of open meeting laws in achieving this purpose, see Note: 'Open Meeting Statutes: The Press Fights for the "Right to Know" ' (1962) 75 *Harv L Rev* 1199. This assessment was cautiously optimistic and concluded that while many past practices had been broken down, the legislation 'has neither revolutionized the conduct of state and local government nor brought it to a grinding halt' (at 1219).

CHAPTER VI

United Kingdom Law

The current law regulating the citizen's access to information about public affairs in the United Kingdom is almost exclusively negative in effect. There is no statute which confers a general right to information, and the common law is totally underdeveloped in the direction of providing either rights or remedies to that end.[1] The Public Bodies (Admission to Meetings) Act 1960,[2] which provides the public with a qualified right to attend meetings of local authorities and other scheduled public bodies,[3] is a partial exception to the generally benighted condition of British law in this sphere. The Franks Committee[4] declared that proposals to reform the law by granting subjects a positive right of access were beyond its terms of reference. Enthusiasm for change of that kind has been practically non-existent within government circles, whether Conservative or Labour,[5] and even outside government the impetus for the introduction of a citizen's information charter has remained feeble at best.[6] In contrast, British laws that have a negative impact on access to information are impressive in scope, number and effectiveness. This body of law is headed by the Official Secrets Acts which remain unchanged despite much political noise about the need for change following the publication of the Franks Report.[7] Their comprehensiveness renders specific provisions prohibiting access to information almost unnecessary; but there is, nevertheless, a body of statutes which supplement the protection afforded by the Official Secrets Acts. As a kind of British counterpart to executive privilege in America, the doctrine of breach of confidence has recently been elevated to the area of public law where it threatens to be serviceable as a device for protecting state secrets. Contempt of court has been used, on at least one major occasion, to prevent newspapers from publishing matters of general interest though on this occasion the information did not relate to public administration. Finally, although not yet employed for the purpose, the law of copyright deserves analysis for its possible use in the protection of secrecy.

101

THE OFFICIAL SECRETS ACTS

BRIEF HISTORY OF THE OFFICIAL SECRETS ACTS

The first Official Secrets Act[8] in Britain was passed in 1889 and stood as law until 1911 when it was repealed and replaced. It seems to have been a response to leaks of official documents relating to foreign affairs, one of which disclosed the terms of a secret treaty between the United Kingdom and Russia entered into in 1878.[9] The 1889 law was aimed at persons who disclosed government secrets rather than at spies[10] and subjects to punishment the disclosure of both military and non-military information contrary to the interests of the state. Where the communication is to a foreign state the crime is elevated to the status of a felony with higher penalties; however, the basic crime is com-munication of official information, not espionage. Inability to convict persons thought to be spies of the more serious offence under the 1889 Act seems to have led to its replacement in 1911.[11] The new Act opens with an espionage provision which criminalizes the communication of information useful to an enemy for a purpose prejudicial to the safety or interests of the state but immediately weakens the impression of its concern with espionage by some sweeping presumptions designed to facilitate proof of the required purpose. The second main provision of the Act reintroduces the crime of the communication of official information but without the earlier requirement that disclosure had to be contrary to the interests of the state. While the framers of the 1911 law may have had espionage in view, the overriding objective remained the punishment of those who merely disclosed official information. Parliament appears to have been lulled into a mood of complacency by the protestations of the movers of the measure that espionage was the object of the whole exercise. In 1920 there was less complacency when an amending Act[12] was introduced—but not sufficiently less to prevent the government from beefing up an already broad and tough measure. This Act introduced a number of new crimes of which the most notorious were the failure to give information on demand of an offence or suspected offence under the Act[13] and the statutory equation of 'any act preparatory to the commission of an offence' with the substantive offence itself.[14] These and other new crimes introduced by the 1920 Act were accompanied by further presumptions to facilitate conviction of persons charged.[15] In 1939 Parliament again turned its attention to official secrets but chiefly to limit the crime of failing to give informa-tion to the espionage provision of the 1911 Act.[16]

The Official Secrets Acts 1911–1939 today constitute the British law on this subject and, as analysis will demonstrate, conflate and confuse acts of spying with the simple disclosure of official information. They achieve this by provisions that must be the broadest in United Kingdom criminal law and which abrogate some of the most basic principles of both substantive criminal law and procedure. Unlike the position in the United States there is no constitutional limitation upon such derogations from due process, either procedural or substantive.

DETAILED ANALYSIS OF THE OFFICIAL SECRETS ACTS 1911–1939

(a) The crime of spying

The crime misleadingly called spying in the relevant marginal note is committed by any person who 'for any purpose prejudicial to the safety or interests of the state' does any single act falling into one of three groups of activities specified by the statute.[17] The three groups of activities which are criminalized if done with the prescribed purpose are the following:

(i) approaching, inspecting, passing over, entering or being in the neighbourhood of a prohibited place;

(ii) making a sketch, plan, model or note which might be or is intended to be useful to an enemy;

(iii) obtaining, collecting, recording, publishing or communicating to any other person documentary or other information which might be directly or indirectly useful to an enemy.[18]

The great breadth of these prohibitions is underlined by (a) the definition of 'prohibited place' which ranges far beyond military places and installations to include inter alia any office 'belonging to or occupied by or on behalf of Her Majesty';[19] (b) the finding that 'enemy' includes a potential enemy;[20] and (c) the fact that information includes all kinds of information, whether military or non-military, official or non-official, which might be useful to an enemy. In addition, either the breadth or the severity of the crime is aggravated by a number of other provisions which declare (d) that proof of a purpose prejudicial to the safety or interests of the state need not depend upon proof of an act having that tendency but may be inferred from the circumstances of the case or the conduct or known character of the accused;[21] (e) that if information relating to a prohibited place has been made, recorded or communicated by a person other than one acting on lawful authority, the onus of disproving a purpose prejudicial to the safety or interest of the state falls upon the accused;[22] (f) that communication or attempted communication with a foreign agent is evidence that the accused has for a prejudicial purpose obtained or attempted to obtain information which might be useful to the enemy;[23] and (g) that the performance of an act preparatory to the commission of the crime is equivalent to the crime itself.[24] The legislature clearly intended to leave nothing to chance and in the process violated some basic principles normally associated with British criminal justice such as the rule excluding character evidence to prove a crime, the responsibility of the prosecution to prove the case against the accused and of course nullum crimen sine lege.

Is the sweeping nature of the crime of spying not to some extent mitigated by the *mens rea* requirement—the need, in addition to proving only one of an incredibly broad range of acts, to show that this particular act was done with the intention of prejudicing the safety or interests of the state? The problem with such an argument is that 'safety' and 'interests' are disjunctively linked with the result that the prosecution need show only an injury to the interests of the state. 'Interests' lacks the connotation of national security which 'safety' carries and could therefore refer to any interest of the state whether military, economic or otherwise. Nevertheless, a court could restrict 'interests' to those touching upon defence or national security by reason of the primary (though not exclusive) reference in the definition of 'prohibited places' to military places and installations and the requirement where information is communicated that it should be useful to an enemy. This would have the effect, for instance, of excluding industrial spying in the purely economic interests of another nation from the compass of the crime.

The meaning of a 'purpose prejudicial to the safety or interests of the state' has been the subject of an authoritative pronouncement by the House of Lords in *Chandler* v *Director of Public Prosecutions*.[25] The accused, members of the Committee of 100,[26] were charged with conspiracy to violate the provision under analysis[27] by making and attempting to implement plans to enter and immobilize a RAF station as a protest against the deployment of nuclear weapons. They sought unsuccessfully to avoid guilt by arguing that their purpose was not prejudicial because they believed that unilateral nuclear disarmament, the objective of the campaign, furthered rather than prejudiced the interests and safety of the state. The judgments handed down in this case distinguish between immediate (or primary) purposes and secondary (remote or ultimate) purposes. Though the accuseds' ultimate purpose, in their belief at least, might well have been to benefit and not injure the state, their immediate purpose (the immobilization of the base) was prejudicial and this was held sufficient to constitute *mens rea*. The Act does not require as a condition of guilt that the accused's ultimate purpose or goal be prejudicial—but is met if an immediate purpose is so characterized. Perhaps less convincingly the court went on to accept the interests of the state as determined by the policy of the government of the day. On this interpretation of the House of Lords *mens rea* is satisfied if the accused knowingly performs a prejudicial act, the question of its prejudicial nature being determined not by his state of mind but by investigation of current state policies.[28]

Even though the *Chandler* judgments are unanimous on the conclusion that sabotage (or acts akin to it) is covered by the statutory crime of spying, there is small reason to quarrrel with the finding of the court on the facts.[29] The act of knowingly entering a military base to immobilize aircraft is clearly within the statutory prohibition on being within a prohibited place for a prejudicial purpose, whether the crime be described as spying or otherwise. The accuseds' objective was to immobilize the aircraft at the base and, whatever ultimate goal this was intended to further, it disclosed a purpose prejudicial to the interests of the state. It seems far-fetched to argue that the paralysis (albeit temporarily) of a section of the nation's military forces is in the interests of the state or not opposed to the interests of the state. What does seem open to objection is the readiness of the court to allow the policy of the day to determine conclusively the interests of the state, at least in respect of defence matters. Lord Pearce unashamedly equated the interests of the state with those of the ruling authorities:

'In such a context the interests of the state must in my judgment mean the interests of the state according to the policies laid down for it by its recognized organs of government and authority, the policies of the state as they are, not as they ought, in the opinion of a jury, to be. Anything which prejudices those policies is within the meaning of the Act "prejudicial to the interests of the State".'[30]

This identification of state and government interests did not produce a disturbing result in *Chandler's* case but its lack of wisdom will readily become apparent in other cases. Assume that a newspaper editor comes into possession of classified information revealing disastrous weaknesses in the nation's defence system. Knowing that the governing party believes it to be expedient to tolerate the situation because of its spending priorities, he decides that publication of the information is the only effective way to force a reconsideration of defence plans and strategies. With that objective in mind he publishes in his newspaper information which he knows the government of the day is unwilling to release. His action is literally within the definition of spying since he has communicated information which might be useful to an enemy. Suppose that he argues as in *Chandler's* case that his real purpose was to benefit the state by provoking the correction of serious errors in its defence plan. The reasoning in that case requires court rejection of his defence since publication of classified information, a primary purpose corresponding to the immobilization of aircraft at a military base, was a knowing act violating the government's policy decision to keep the information in question secret. The House of Lords might have been wiser if it had kept open the possibility of a judicial finding that the interests of the state, as conceived in the statutory definition of spying, might not always be found in the policies of the ruling party. Lord Devlin alone envisaged such a possibility when he declared that while there was a presumption that current defence policy (the disposition of the armed forces) was in the interests of the state, 'the presumption is not irrebuttable'.[31] He added

'The servants of the Crown, like other men animated by the highest motives, are capable of formulating a policy *ad hoc* so as to prevent the citizen from doing something that the Crown does not want him to do. It is the duty of the courts to be as alert now as they have always been to prevent abuse of the prerogative.'[32]

Keeping open the possibility of a divergence between the interests of state and the government of the day does not imply that every editor who publishes secret information is entitled to an acquittal. A court might well decide as in *Chandler's* case that the two sets of interests do not diverge. But they surely subject themselves too slavishly to current political interests by adopting a self-imposed prohibition on the possibility of a contrary finding. By so doing they ensure that citizens performing a service for their society, even if they thereby incidentally benefit an enemy, must be condemned as spies.[33] This would be an unjust and incongruous result.

Criticism of the crime of spying has frequently focused on the finding in *Chandler's* case that sabotage and related offences fall within the ambit of the crime notwithstanding explicit statements to the contrary in Parliament at the time of enactment.[34] It certainly is odd to find the crime of sabotage in a section purportedly dealing with spying. However, sabotage is a serious offence and criticism which points up its illogical inclusion in an espionage law tends to deflect attention from more objectionable features of the law. One such feature, and it is one which simultaneously accounts for sabotage being within the reach of the crime, is the failure of Parliament to specify communication (or attempted communication) with a foreign nation as an essential requirement of the crime of spying. Such communication is logically implied by the concept of spying or espionage and its omission as an element of the offence is surprising. This omission draws attention to a second undesirable feature—the desire of the legislature to punish acts which are usually preliminary to the crime of spying (for example, collecting sensitive information) as the substantive crime itself. The legislative desire is implicit in the language of the section, the related presumptions referred to previously and the statutory declaration that a preparatory act is equivalent to the substantive crime. Frustration at being unable to prove a case against real spies[35] has led the government to the unwarranted conclusion that acts which might be preliminary to spying are necessarily the forerunners to that offence. This is manifestly not so. A newspaper reporter who persuades a government servant to pass on sensitive information without authority is within the wording of the statute. He has obtained information which might be 'directly or indirectly useful to an enemy'. Since he got the information without authority he is presumed to have intended to prejudice the safety or interests of the state unless he proves the contrary. If it was his intention to publish because he thought that the public ought to be informed he will probably be unable to rebut the presumption because non-publication was the policy of the government of the day and this is presumed to coincide with the interests of the state. The information need not relate to military matters as long as it might be useful to an enemy. This single example makes it obvious that a whole range of legitimate political activities falls within the potential reach of the crime of spying—surely a more serious state of affairs than the misplacing of the crime of sabotage. That this is not a fanciful suggestion is illustrated by the threatened use of the Act against Mr Duncan Sandys who in 1938 had raised with the Secretary of State for War the inadequacies of the air-defences around London which he had learnt of while an officer in the Territorial Army.[36] Mr Sandys was threatened with prosecution[37] for failure to reveal his sources and was probably saved only by his parliamentary privilege.

We may conclude with the observation that the crime of spying is objectionable not because it could be used to persecute political radicals as a recent author has suggested in his statement that 'a known activist seen approaching Her Majesty's stationery office . . . a prohibited place under the 1911 Act . . . could be sent to prison for between three and seven years'.[38] Such bizarre uses of the Acts are imaginable but scarcely likely. The prime source of concern is that spying, as defined in the Act, inhibits legitimate speech and debate activities which are central to the proper functioning of democratic institutions.

(b) Crimes analogous to spying

The offence of spying[39] is supplemented by a number of analogous provisions. The first makes it criminal to use 'official'[40] information 'for the benefit of any foreign power or in any other manner prejudicial to the safety or interests of the State'.[41] As later analysis of official information will demonstrate, all information irrespective of whether it is defence-related is covered. Communication or attempted communication with a foreign power is not an element of the crime. The prosecution of an accused will succeed if it is shown that the use of the information benefited a foreign power in any conceivable way *or* prejudiced the safety or interests of the United Kingdom.[42] The second analogous provision declares that it is a crime for a person who has possession or control of information[43] which 'relates to munitions of war' to communicate it directly or indirectly to any foreign power or in any other manner prejudicial to the safety or interests of the state.[44] By reason of the reference to communication with a foreign power and the restriction of information to that affecting 'munitions of war'[45] this crime comes closest of all to a true concept of espionage. Nevertheless, the crime is committed by an accused who is shown to have communicated the information in a manner prejudicial to the safety or interests of the state even without attempted or successful communication to a foreign power. Finally, it is a crime to retain for any purpose prejudicial to the safety or interests of the state any 'official document' when the accused has no right to retain it or when it is contrary to his duty to retain it.[46] Official document is narrowly defined in this case as 'any passport or any naval, military, air-force, police, or official pass, permit, certificate, licence or other document of a similar character'.[47] Despite the affinity which each of these three crimes has with spying, by reason mainly of the requirement of a prejudicial purpose, their application to non-spying activities (for example, communication to a journalist to further public debate) is certainly possible.

THE CRIME OF COMMUNICATING OFFICIAL INFORMATION

The notoriety of the Official Secrets Acts is due almost exclusively to the central notion to which they have given legitimacy—that the mere communication of information in the possession or control of government is a criminal offence. It must certainly be one of the conundrums of comparative politics that this notion was adopted in democracy's mother country as late as 1911 and that it is still currently in force there. Disputes about whether to introduce or retain an official secrets law are in essence arguments about whether the simple act of disclosing official information without authority ought to be a crime. The provision which makes it a crime in the United Kingdom is a complex measure which criminalizes several activities other than unauthorized disclosure.[48] While such other punishable activities will be referred to in passing, the emphasis will fall on the unauthorized disclosure by Crown servants and contractors with government of information acquired during the course of their work; and on the criminal responsibility of others who pass on such information or, in some circumstances, simply receive it.

The section in question[49] makes it criminal to deal in various ways with four classes of documentary or other information.[50] These are (in summary):

 (i) information relating to prohibited places;[51]
 (ii) information obtained in contravention of the Official Secrets Acts;
 (iii) information entrusted to a person in confidence by a Crown servant;
 (iv) information obtained by a person by virtue of government office or contract with government.

As the Franks Committee observed there is no limitation of subject-matter[52]—every imaginable kind of information is protected so long as it is possessed or controlled by the central government.[53] A convenient shorthand description for all such protected information is the expression 'official information'.

It is a crime to deal with official information in various ways specified by the statute. Two forms of unauthorized dealing analogous to spying have already been discussed—using information for the benefit of a foreign power and, where it relates to munitions of war, communicating it to a foreign power or in a manner that is prejudicial to the state. The other forms of prohibited dealing are (a) unauthorized retention of documentary or similar kinds of information; (b) failure to take reasonable care of official information; (c) communication of the information to unauthorized persons; and (d) receipt of information communicated in contravention of the Act. Each offence requires separate treatment.

Retention of official information of the documentary type is a crime where the person in possession had no right to retain it or where it was contrary to his duty to retain it.[54] It is also an offence to fail to comply with directions given by lawful authority for its return or disposal.[55] 'Retention' is defined so as to include the act of copying the document or causing it to be copied.[56] Though there have been some prosecutions[57] for the retention offence there are no reported cases and therefore no indication of whether *mens rea* is an element of the crime and, if so, in what form. Presumably the offence is absolute[58] and guilt will be established by proof that the accused knowingly retained a document that objectively speaking he had no right to keep. But knowledge of the wrongfulness of the retention is probably a requirement where there is nothing to indicate to the possessor that the document is official. Failure to take care of official information or acting so as to endanger its safety is another form of prohibited dealing which constitutes an offence.[59] This crime must be applicable mainly to state servants and obviously requires *mens rea* in the form of carelessness.[60]

The act of communicating official information to unauthorized persons is the form of prohibited dealing that is most sweeping and it is this provision, more than any other, which can be used to shroud government activities in secrecy. The offence is committed by a person who communicates to any other person information falling into any of the classes of protected information,[61] the recipient not being a person to whom he is authorized to communicate it or to whom it is his duty in the interests of the state to communicate it.[62] Of the classes of information affected (relating to prohibited places, entrusted to the accused in confidence, obtained in contravention of the Act or obtained by virtue of government office) the broadest is information which the accused has obtained by virtue of his office in government or as a contractor with government, or as a servant of either such person. In reference to this offence, the Franks Committee has said: 'In ordinary language, it is an offence under section 2(1)(*a*) for a Crown servant or a government contractor to make an unauthorized disclosure of information which he has learnt in the course of his job'.[63] The statutory net is virtually impenetrable and catches up all information including, according to one commentator, the number of cups of tea drunk in government offices.[64]

The Court of Criminal Appeals has held that the crime of communicating official information is absolute. It reached this conclusion in *R v Fell*,[65] a case in which the accused had passed confidential documents to an employee of a foreign embassy in order to influence him in favour of British policies. The crime is committed, the court declared, whatever the accused's motive and whether or not disclosure is prejudicial to the state. Nevertheless, the statement that the crime is absolute may be too broad. *Mens rea* must be required, at least in the limited sense that the accused is aware that the information transmitted is official. In *Fell's* case the accused, an employee of the Central Office of Information, was aware of the fact that she was handing over documents which were officially regarded as confidential. In different circumstances an employee might legitimately believe, contrary to fact, that he is authorized to communicate information. This should be a defence at least where his mistake is not one of law. In the *Sunday Telegraph* case,[66] where the charge was against persons who had published material subsequent to its release by a government official, it was assumed that *mens rea* was an ingredient of the crime and the accused were acquitted because of its absence. (The editor of the *Sunday Telegraph*, before publishing a confidential assessment on the Nigerian Civil War, had checked to see whether the report was covered by the D-Notice system and was assured that it was not.) In respect of communications subsequent to disclosure of information by an official, it must surely be a requirement of guilt that the accused knew, or had reasonable grounds for knowing, that the information was official and confidential. But even in respect of communications by an official, a reasonable mistake as to the existence of authority[67] to communicate should exonerate him from liability. If this is correct, it would follow that a stronger form of *mens rea* is required than Smith & Hogan's formulation of it as 'an intention to cause the *actus reus*'.[68] The stronger form of *mens rea* will not protect a person who knows that the disclosure is unauthorized but who genuinely and reasonably believes that revelation is in the public interest. But the interpretation of the *mens rea* requirement should be liberal enough to free from criminal liability a person who on reasonable grounds believed either that the information was not official or that, if official, its release was authorized.[69]

The accused is not guilty of the crime of communicating official information if the recipient is 'a person to whom he is authorized to communicate it, or a person to whom it is in the interests of the state his duty to communicate it'.[70] There is no more cloudy concept in the law than that of authorization or duty to communicate. The Franks Committee findings on the concept appear to be (*a*) that authorization does not imply a formal process, (*b*) that some officials are impliedly authorized to communicate information,[71] and (*c*) that all official material is protected from disclosure unless release is validly authorized.[72] While these findings do mean that in practice citizens learn about government activities and decisions where officials are willing to talk, they also point up the fact that the citizen's right to know depends entirely upon official discretion and that the criteria for authorization— and consequentially of criminal liability for passing on information— are extremely hazy. The parameters of the defence that the accused communicated to a person to whom it was his duty in the interests of the state to divulge are not explored at all by the Franks Committee.

If 'interests of the state' is interpreted in this context to mean no more than the interests of the government,[73] then the defence has limited scope and the accused will be required to establish an affirmative duty to hand the material to the person who in fact received it. The wishes and practices of the government of the day will be determinative of this question. However, the statute does not speak of the 'interests of the government' and there is no need for the courts to rewrite Parliament's prescriptions in this way. The Australian High Court, interpreting the crime of inciting disaffection against the government, has declined to equate 'government' with the persons actually in office and considered it to be an organized entity apart from the persons of whom it consists.[74] 'State' is a conception more abstract than 'government', and *a fortiori* its interests may not coincide with the policies of those who operate its machinery. There would be nothing absurd or illogical in a court finding that the revelation of confidential information revealing mismanagement or inefficiency, while not in the interests of the government, *is* in the interests of the state. In short, the phrase 'in the interests of the state' gives the British courts the opportunity (so far neglected) of weighing the interests in concealment against those favouring disclosure in prosecutions for communicating official information.[75]

Conjecture as to how courts could interpret the statutory offence of communicating official information must not be permitted to distract attention too much from the actual application of the law. This is an area in which the law that *is* tends to be very different from the law that *ought to be*. Convictions have been secured for the releases of the most trivial or at least harmless kinds of information and the courts have either said or assumed that the nature of the official material or the purposes for which it was released are entirely irrelevant. Prosecutions for disclosure of trivial information are exemplified by *R v Crisp & Humewood*[76] in which information about contracts for army officers' clothing was disclosed to a firm of tailors and the unreported case in which disclosure of the wills of three prominent persons a few hours before they were officially released by Somerset House led to conviction and a sentence of two months' imprisonment.[77] Convictions for the disclosure of information that might have served a legitimate public purpose (and therefore been in the interests of the state) are exemplified in particular by the sentencing in 1958 of two Oxford undergraduates who had written an article published in the university publication *Isis* revealing that the British military authorities had engaged in provocative incidents on the frontiers of communist countries.[78] The students had acquired the information during their national service and were jailed for three months for the disclosure. A commentator on the case has remarked that '. . . this information was of a kind that it was in the public interest for it to be made known, for how else can public opinion play a part in restraining the lunacies to which governments are so partial'.[79] So far as the British courts are concerned, the mere act of disclosing official information is enough.

On the settled and authoritative interpretation of the law a Crown servant who discloses official information without authority is guilty of a crime. Persons other than Crown servants (called 'private persons' for convenience) may also incur liability for the transmission of information that is unauthorized. Private persons are criminally responsible if information acquired in their capacity as government contractors (or employees of such contractors) is communicated without authority. They are equally responsible where they pass on information which was received in confidence from a Crown servant or information (however obtained) relating to a 'prohibited place'. Finally, the private person is liable if he has information 'which has been made or obtained in contravention of this Act'[80] and he communicates it without authority. The effect of this last provision is that the information becomes 'quarantined' and subsequent disclosures which are unauthorized, whether by officials or private persons, constitute crimes. Therefore the editor who receives unauthorized information from a Crown servant, or from someone who received it without authority from such a person, commits an offence by publishing the material. However, the court in the *Sunday Telegraph* case appears to have assumed correctly that liability depends on the editor knowing or having reason to believe that the information was official and communication unauthorized.

If the publication of information disclosed without authority by a servant of government is an offence, why did the Attorney-General in the Crossman Diaries case[81] not claim the desired injunction on the basis of threatened violations of the Official Secrets Acts? It may also appear to be something of a puzzle that the *Sunday Times*, which published a serialized version of the Diaries, was not prosecuted under the Acts. The information revealed in the Diaries included detailed accounts of cabinet deliberations which on any test constituted official information the disclosure of which was certainly not authorized. We now know from Mr Hugo Young's book that the government lawyers concluded that there had been no breach of the Acts and that this was why the proceedings were founded upon breach of confidence.[82] At the date of Richard Crossman's death, the Diaries were unpublished and were in fact in the hands of his literary executors who were preparing to submit them to the Secretary of the Cabinet in accordance with the convention governing publication of ministerial memoirs. When he died Crossman had therefore not communicated the information contained in the Diaries without authority and in breach of the Official Secrets Acts. It is difficult to categorize transmission of them to his literary editors for submission to the cabinet secretary as a form of unauthorized communication. Since he could not have communicated them unlawfully after his death it follows that the publishers were not guilty of communicating information 'made or obtained in contravention of this Act', there having been no such illegal act prior to his death.[83] Had Richard Crossman lived to authorize publication, the Attorney-General might have gained the injunction that he failed to secure in the breach of confidence suit and he could have authorized criminal proceedings with high hopes of success. In effect the Crossman case affirms the criminal liability of private persons who disclose information communicated to them without authority by government servants; only the untimely death of the chief actor in the affair left the state without its usual remedies.

The final form of prohibited dealing with official information is its receipt by a person who knows, or has reasonable grounds to believe, that it is communicated to him in contravention of the Acts.[84] A person who so receives information is guilty unless he proves that the communication to him was contrary to his desire.[85] It seems likely that the accused will escape only if he can demonstrate an active expression of a desire at the relevant time not to receive the material wrongfully communicated. Where information is accepted without protest the fact that the accused did not solicit it will not exonerate him. But for a prosecution to succeed the accused must have known or had grounds to believe at the time of receipt of the material that communication to him was in contravention of the Act. It appears to follow that if, for example, a Crown servant mails a confidential document to an unsuspecting journalist who discovers after reading it that the transmission to him was an offence, he will not be guilty because he did not know the nature of the document at the time of receipt.[86] A journalist who actually seeks to provoke a leak of official information will clearly be in difficulty unless the leak was authorized.

OTHER CRIMES UNDER THE OFFICIAL SECRETS ACTS

The Acts create a number of other criminal offences of which some are only indirectly concerned with the punishment of persons seeking information about governmental activities. A broad section introduced in 1920[87] provides for the punishment of those who wear uniforms without authority, make false declarations, impersonate officers of government, forge documents or wrongfully possess dies, seals or stamps for the purpose of gaining access to a prohibited place or for any other purpose prejudicial to the safety or interests of the state. Another provision declares it a crime to obstruct officers near prohibited places[88] while other sections dealing with the production of telegrams upon official demand and the registration of accommodation addresses create incidental offences for non-compliance with their terms.[89] Because of their remoteness from the general theme of this work—legal access to information—these crimes do not require detailed analysis.

Two offences do, however, call for more than passing reference.

The first subjects to criminal punishment a person who after demand fails to give information about an offence or suspected offence of spying, or who gives false information about such offence or suspected offence.[90] When first enacted this crime was not limited to information about the offence of spying but to any offence under the Official Secrets Acts. It was the case of Mr Duncan Sandys, discussed earlier in this chapter, which led Parliament in 1939 to restrict the scope of the offence to a failure to supply information about an actual or suspected spying offence, or the giving of false information in that connection.

A chief officer of the police duly sanctioned by the Secretary of State (in cases of emergency, only a subsequent report to the Secretary of State is required) may require a police officer not below the rank of inspector to order any person whom he believes able to furnish information about the actual or suspected offence to attend at a reasonable time and place for the purpose of furnishing the information.[91] A person who fails to attend or who upon attendance knowingly gives false information is guilty of an offence.[92] The crime is one degree removed from misprision of treason since it punishes not mere failure to give information but the omission to do so after official demand.

Notwithstanding the requirement of prior demand and the limitation of the provision to information about spying, there are features of the crime which make it undesirable in a society that values civil liberties. Spying, we have observed, is limited not just to classic espionage but encompasses such actions as the publication of information in order to stimulate debate about the adequacy of defence policy. The power to harass journalists by demanding that they reveal the sources of their information on penalty of imprisonment or a fine is certainly one that could be used to stifle unwelcome debate as well as to uncover persons guilty of espionage. If a threat of this kind could be directed against a member of Parliament seeking to remedy a believed inadequacy in the defence system,[93] a journalist who lacks the status and privileges of a parliamentary representative will be more vulnerable to political misuse of the law. The danger is more than theoretical and will remain so as long as spying is defined in broad terms. It is a danger not just to persons but also the possibility of free enquiry and free debate.

The second crime requiring special mention is that of knowingly harbouring a person whom the accused knew or had reason to believe had committed any offence under the Official Secrets Acts or was about to commit such an offence.[94] The crime also covers the acts of allowing such persons to meet or assemble in premises in the occupation or control of the accused or, having harboured such persons or permitted them to assemble, failing to disclose to a superintendent of police information relating to such persons.[95] When one considers what activities constitute offences under the Acts (including those of simple communication of official information) the astonishing nature and breadth of the crime becomes manifest. No one can legitimately cavil at the punishment of those who knowingly harbour a true spy; but why the crime should extend to the act of permitting a team of investigative reporters who have wheedled some confidential information out of government to meet in one's home or office, is almost beyond comprehension.

PROCEDURAL PROVISIONS OF THE OFFICIAL SECRETS ACTS

Prosecutions under the Official Secrets Acts cannot be brought unless authorized by the Attorney-General.[96] Though this requirement could be circumvented by prosecuting the accused for conspiracy to commit a crime under the Acts instead of charging them with a breach of a provision of the Acts themselves, the loophole has apparently never been used.[97] One of the reasons for the introduction of the requirement of the Attorney-General's consent is that the Acts were deliberately framed in broad terms and the device of special consent to prosecutions was intended to preclude misuse of a dragnet law. Evidence given by Home Office representatives to the Franks Committee included mention of the need to secure consistency of practice in prosecutions.[98] This seems spurious as a rationale for the consent requirement which is designed to discriminate between different offenders under the Acts; and even if the Attorney-General acts for sound reasons a policy of differentiated treatment of offenders excludes consistency by definition. The real vice of the provision is the assumption on which it rests—the assumption that the overbroad definition of a crime is cured by vesting a discretion to prosecute in the Attorney-General. In fact all that the provision does is to add another imponderable to a grievously obscure law. Moreover it conflicts with a requirement of the rule of law to define broadly and to narrow by a rule of discretion. The role into which this casts the Attorney-General is unfortunate as the Franks Committee acknowledged, and it is one which has led one writer to the conclusion that the judgment of attorneys-general in official secrets prosecutions indicate 'more evidence of prejudice than of principle'.[99] This may not be true and in any event is incapable of verification. What seems certain is that it brings respect neither to the law nor to the office to make the Attorney-General Parliament's agent for the purpose of narrowing down a broad law.

The Franks Committee, which has proposed some narrowing down of the most undesirable provision of the Acts,[100] nevertheless wishes to retain the requirement of the Attorney-General's consent where the prosecution relates to information in the field of defence, internal security, foreign relations, the currency and reserves, cabinet documents or confidences of the citizen.[101] The committee stressed a more valid reason for the consent provision—the delicate political and international implications that might be involved in an official secrets prosecution.

A prosecution could force the disclosure of information that would seriously embarrass a friendly power and this is the kind of factor which a person in the position of Attorney-General[102] is competent to weigh against the factors favouring prosecution. Such a power could legitimately be entrusted to the Attorney-General under a more tightly drawn law.

The court in an official secrets case, on application of the prosecutor, may order an *in camera* hearing on the ground that public proceedings could endanger national safety.[103] So long as the requirement of injury to national safety is adhered to, this is an acceptable provision for official secrets prosecutions. Less desirable is the provision that the offence is for purposes of trial deemed to have been committed either where actually committed or where the defendant is found in the United Kingdom.[104] This may be acceptable for crimes committed abroad but could be harsh on an accused who is charged for acts committed in the United Kingdom. Finally, in respect of procedure, there are provisions for arrest without warrant of offenders or suspected offenders and for search by warrant (or without warrant in cases of emergency) of places or premises for evidence of suspected offences.[105]

CLASSIFICATION OF INFORMATION

The classification of documentary information in the United Kingdom is an administrative procedure internal to the departments of government. Little was known about the classification system until it was brought into the light by the Franks Committee which has described its main features[106] and published the Civil Service Department memoranda to the committee on classification practices and procedures.[107] The committee has also recommended changes[108] to the system which, like its recommendations for amendments to the Official Secrets Acts, have as yet gone unheeded.

There is no direct legal relation between the Official Secrets Acts and the classification system operated by departments of government. Whether material has been classified or not does not affect its protection under the Acts, and persons may be punished under them for dealing with information which is unclassified. Nevertheless, the declaration of the Franks Committee that security classification 'is a purely administrative system, unrelated to the criminal law'[109] is an overstatement. While classification lacks statutory authority and is without effect on the range of material protected by the criminal law, it might influence liability under the law in at least two possible ways. The offence of wrongfully communicating official information[110] takes place when the information is passed to someone who is not authorized to receive it, and classification could have a bearing on whether there was authority to communicate to the person to whom the information was given. In the second place, where *mens rea* is an element of the offence, the presence or absence of a security marking might have a determinative influence on the question whether the person accused knew, or had reason to believe, that the communication had been authorized or that the information had been 'made or obtained in contravention of the Official Secrets Acts'.[111] Subject to these exceptions, it is generally true that classification in the United Kingdom lacks both statutory backing and general legal significance.[112]

The classification system disclosed by the Franks Committee Report is in many respects a traditional one. It employs a four-tier scheme of classification with conventional criteria for the identification of each category. The categories, with the appropriate criteria in brackets, are Top Secret (exceptionally grave damage to the nation), Secret (serious injury to the interests of the nation), Confidential (prejudicial to the interests of the nation), and Restricted (undesirable in the interests of the nation). In addition, confidential information in the hands of government requiring protection in the interests of privacy is identified by the label 'In Confidence'. Responsibility for classification generally lies with the originator of a document and there are Civil Service guidelines for review of classification and for declassification. The main consequence of classification is that strict rules for the physical protection of the material and access to it come into operation.

The evidence to the Franks Committee naturally does not reveal what information (or examples of what information) is actually classified under the system but the published 'Aids to Correct Classification and Regrading'[113] certainly justifies some apprehension. One of the examples given of legitimate top secret classification is 'Higher defence *policy* and strategy'.[114] Allowing for difficulties of separating policy from strategy, it is yet arguable that defence policy ought to be a matter of public information and debate. Under the 'secret' category, the following appears as an example of proper classification: 'Forecasts of future economic developments or economic policies which might damage confidence at home or abroad.'[115] An example given under the heading 'confidential' reads: 'Assumptions used in economic forecasting . . . where unauthorized publication might prejudice the Government's ability to develop suitable policies.'[116] What might equally be prejudiced by concealment in the last two examples is the ability of the public to understand government policy and to develop suitable alternatives to the programmes officially adopted or proposed. Apprehension about classification criteria has certainly not been minimized by the few classification decisions that have become public knowledge. Dr Williams has recorded that a memorandum giving information about a RAF anniversary concert in 1964 was given a restricted stamp;[117] and, more recently, a *Sunday Times* report to the effect that rail services were to be reduced by 40% was said by the authorities to refer to a classified secret.[118]

The security classification system also has other unsatisfactory features, not the least of which is the following directive: 'Emphasis should be placed more on the recipient destroying classified material, or returning it to the point of origin, than on seeking the originator's authority to downgrade it.'[119] This instruction adds credibility, if any be needed, to the recent assertion of the historian, Professor A J P Taylor, that considerable 'weeding out' and 'doctoring' of official records has taken place when they are released after the 30-year period specified by the Public Records Act.[120] Of the other unsatisfactory features of the system of classification, two are of central importance:

(a) The absence of any independent review committee to scrutinize the operation of classification and (b) the failure to make automatic downgrading or declassification mandatory after certain periods of time.[121]

The recommendations of the Franks Committee incorporate suggested revisions of the classification system.[122] One of the suggestions is that a classifications committee should be set up by the government but with the limited function of being consulted prior to the adoption of new classification regulations and of assisting the citizens to understand the operation of the system.[123] The most far-reaching and significant suggestion relating to classification is that it should be directly linked with the criminal law by making prosecutions for wrongful dealing with official information[124] relating to defence, foreign relations, the currency and the reserves dependent upon the information having been classified,[125] and upon a certificate by the relevant Minister that it was correctly so classified at the date of disclosure.[126] Under this proposal an accused could not be found guilty of wrongful dealing with information relating to the categories specified unless the information was correctly classified and remained so, according to the Minister's certificate, at the time of the disclosure. The apparent advantage of this legislative connection between classification and the criminal law is deceptive, at least in part. Without some control over the criteria used by the government in classification, the citizen could be in almost as poor a position as he is under present law. The Franks Report does not recommend a review committee with 'teeth' and it rejects a review of the Minister's certificate by the courts. The Minister's word is to be final so far as the courts are concerned. Without any check, administrative or judicial, over decisions to impose and maintain a classification on material a strong possibility remains that as in the past the revelation of politically embarrassing information will be a crime under the law. The reasons given in the Franks Report[127] for rejection of any form of judicial control are not persuasive. The question of classification need not (and should not) be a matter within the jury's power of decision but could be entrusted to the judge trying the case. The task of the reviewing court need not be an *ab initio* review of the classification decision, as the Committee appears to have assumed; it could be limited to the power to set aside manifestly unreasonable classifications.[128] The danger of disclosure in adjudication of the very information the government wishes to protect will be avoidable if the courts exercise the power of *in camera* inspection only when affidavit evidence leaves it dissatisfied with the government's arguments for concealment. These considerations suggest that court involvement need not be as unsuitable and impracticable as the Franks Committee assumed. It certainly seems necessary to protect public servants and citizens against prosecution for revealing classified information which should not have been embargoed because revelation is in the public interest.

THE 'D NOTICE' PROCEDURE

Another institution which is related in an unofficial sense to Official Secrets, but which lacks statutory sanction or direct legal relevance to the criminal law, is the 'D Notice' procedure. D Notices (D stands for 'Defence') have been described as 'formal letters sent to editors of newspapers, TV and radio news programmes, certain periodicals concerned with defence matters and, occasionally, book publishers'.[129] The letters are sent on the authority of a committee representative of both government and the media which is called the Services, Press and Broadcasting Committee. The notices issued by the committee are intended to prevent the publication of information relating to defence or security on the ground that disclosure would be harmful to the nation. The D Notice, it has aptly been said, constitutes both a warning and a request—a warning that publication may infringe the Official Secrets Acts and a request not to publish in any event.[130] Failure to respond to a D Notice is not itself a crime.

The origin of the Services, Press and Broadcasting Committee and its D Notice procedure has been traced to the enactment of the Official Secrets Act 1911.[131] Because the prohibitions of that Act were so sweeping, the press was in an impossible situation and required guidance on what it could or could not safely publish in its columns. However, because the system, both then and now, is entirely without legal basis the guidance has neither binding effect on the Crown nor exculpatory effect on the press. Professor Street has described the arrangement as an 'unofficial assurance' to the press and broadcasting authorities that action would not be taken if they complied.[132]

Though D Notices were meant to operate in conjunction with the Official Secrets Acts and to mitigate some of their consequences, it is clear that they have no legal standing. The Crown is in no sense dependent upon the issue of a D Notice for the successful prosecution of a member of the communications industry; and that member is in no sense assisted in his defence by the absence of a D Notice covering the information in question. Nevertheless, as happened in the *Sunday Telegraph* case, reliance on the D Notice system could affect the *mens rea* aspect of a trial. In that case, an assurance given to an editor by the secretary to the Services, Press and Broadcasting Committee that a document was not covered by any standing D Notice, was accepted as evidence tending to disprove *mens rea*. Unlike classification, however, D Notices will have no effect upon authority to communicate official information.

The D Notice procedure has been described as a form of self-censorship and even castigated as an instrument facilitating the suppression of non-secret information embarrassing to the government of the day.[133] The attempt in 1967 to employ the D Notice machinery to prevent publication of a story of security service vetting of cables and telegrams does illustrate a danger of abuse.[134] Occasional abuses are probably not sufficient to outweigh the advantages of a properly conducted D Notice system.[135] One thing may be said with confidence—the system is a poor way of alleviating the ill-effects of an overbroad law. It might serve a more acceptable and legitimate function if it operated against the background of tightly limited secrecy laws.

OTHER LAWS CONTROLLING ACCESS TO INFORMATION

The comprehensiveness of the Official Secrets Acts has rendered unnecessary the enactment of a large number of laws to protect specific kinds of information held by government departments or officials in the United Kingdom. Of the few such statutes currently in force, those protecting nuclear secrets are perhaps the most important group. Some of these provisions merely bring the Official Secrets Acts into play, as for example the designation of certain sites under the Nuclear Installations Act and the Atomic Energy Authority Act as prohibited places for purposes of the former Acts.[136] In similar fashion, legislation has declared that the holding of office under the United Kingdom Atomic Energy Authority is deemed to be the holding of office 'under Her Majesty' for purposes of section 2 of the Official Secrets Act 1911.[137] The result is that persons who acquire information by virtue of their position as office holders or employees of the Atomic Energy Authority may not disclose such information to any unauthorized person. In other cases the laws governing nuclear energy contain their own substantive prohibitions on the transmission of information, as, for example, the prohibition under the Atomic Energy Act of the disclosure without authority of information relating to existing or proposed atomic energy 'plants'.[138] Members or employees of Euratom (the European Atomic Energy Community) are guilty of a crime if they communicate without authority any classified information which they acquired by virtue of their office or position.[139] The Radioactive Substances Act also contains a prohibition on the disclosure without authority of 'any relevant process or trade secret' obtained by a person in the course of the execution of the Act.[140]

Another important category of specific prohibitions on disclosure of information is intended to protect private information obtained by government officials in the course of their duties. Examples are contained in the Health and Safety at Work Act, which prohibits the disclosure, without the consent of the person who furnished it, of information gathered except for certain prescribed purposes;[141] and in the Control of Pollution Act[142] and the Sex Discrimination Act,[143] which have similar prohibitions protecting respectively trade secrets and information connected with formal investigations. Another provision that comes under the heading of privacy will be found in the Rehabilitation of Offenders Act. This declares that subject to certain specified exceptions, officials or ex-officials may not disclose information about the 'spent convictions'[144] of any person unless this is done in the course of official duties.[145] The laudable purpose behind this measure is that of enabling a person to bury an unfortunate past and of protecting him against prying enquiries by others.

The defence forces in the United Kingdom have their own official secrets legislation in the form of provisions[146] which subject members of the forces to criminal punishment if they disclose without lawful authority information which might be useful to an enemy. It is specifically declared to be a defence that the accused did not know and had no reason to believe that the information might be useful to an enemy. This defence mitigates to some extent the broadness of the prohibition which encompasses any information that might assist an enemy. Since the punishment of a member of the defence force for disclosing information might be achieved by reliance on the provisions of the Official Secrets Acts analysed above,[147] it is not clear why the military counterparts appear on the statute book. The question is dealt with somewhat confusedly in a memorandum[148] submitted by the Ministry of Defence to the Franks Committee from which it appears that the sections in question were enacted and have been retained 'to provide a ready means of dealing with relatively minor disclosures in a service environment'.[149] The sections have the effect of making the law of official secrets a little more obscure since they straddle the crime of espionage (which requires a purpose prejudicial to the safety or interests of the state) and the crime of disclosing official information (which does not require that the information disclosed be useful to an enemy). This offence of 'half-spying' could be abolished without serious inconvenience.

BREACH OF CONFIDENCE

The use of the breach of confidence action to protect what Lord Widgery has somewhat Irishly called 'public secrets' is a new development. Though the employment of the action in cases that concern non-private information was contemplated in *Fraser* v *Evans*[150] in

1968, the origin of the doctrine's elevation into the field of public law is *Attorney-General* v *Jonathan Cape Ltd*[151]—the Crossman Diaries case—which was decided late in 1975. In the former action, a public relations firm, in a contract with the then military government in Greece apparently aimed at improving its image abroad, had bound itself never to reveal any information related to its duties under the contract. The *Sunday Times* obtained a copy of one of its confidential reports to the Greek government and was planning to publish excerpts from it. The injunction against publication obtained in a lower court by the firm was discharged by the Court of Appeal on the ground that the contractual obligation of confidence was owed by the plaintiff to the Greek government, and not vice versa. Though an action might be brought by the Greek government, the plaintiff had to fail since no obligation of confidence was owed to him. While Denning MR rested his judgment squarely on the plaintiff's lack of standing,[152] Davies LJ expressed no qualms about a possible action by the Greek government, declaring that 'the government might well have the right to ask the court to prevent the publication of the document or the facts therein contained . . .'.[153] This almost unqualified recognition that a right of action vested in the other party to the contract is surprising since the information in question, while originating in a private contract, concerned matters of general public interest. Nevertheless, the court in *Fraser* v *Evans* did not actually allow an action however incautious one of its members might have been as to its availability. The momentous jump there contemplated was taken some seven years later in the Crossman Diaries case.

Prior to *Attorney-General* v *Jonathan Cape Ltd*, the 'developing equitable doctrine' of breach of confidence had flourished only in the realm of private law. There it was used to protect commercial secrets (industrial and trade secrets), at first on the basis of a contractually imposed obligation of confidence but later on other variously designated grounds ('property', 'trust' or simply 'confidence').[154] Subsequently in *Duchess of Argyle* v *Duke of Argyle*[155] the action was extended to the protection of domestic secrets (in this case marital confidences) thus adding a privacy function to the hitherto commercial role of the remedy. Examples of confidences which the courts in Britain had protected either against the confidant or some other person guilty of threatened or actual revelation include the privately printed etchings of Prince Albert and Queen Victoria, an unpatented secret recipe, the drawings of dies for leather punches and personal information confided by one marriage partner to the other. According to a recent authoritative pronouncement, the legal requirements for an action based on breach of confidence are (1) that the information in question must be characterized by a 'quality of confidence'; (2) that it must have been imparted in circumstances which import an obligation of confidence and (3) there must be unlawful use (or presumably threatened use) of

the information to the detriment of the party who imparted it.[156] The
Law Commission, after extensive review of the current law (but without reference to problems that arise in the area of public law) has
proposed a new statutory tort of breach of confidence.[157] The general
requirements for liability would be similar under these proposals but
a somewhat broader defence of public interest is suggested by the
Commission.[158]

In extending the law of breach of confidence to the affairs of government (which may conveniently be called public information) Lord
Widgery broadened the requirements of the action in his exposition
of the law in *Attorney-General* v *Jonathan Cape Ltd*.[159] He declared that
the Attorney-General, in addition to proving a breach of confidence,
carried the burden of demonstrating to the court that the public
interest required suppression of the publication and that there was no
other more compelling public interest which favoured disclosure.
Public interest was previously relevant in breach of confidence actions
but only as a defence, and in a form much narrower than the concept
adumbrated by Lord Widgery.[160] This broadening out of the requirements, according to a commentator on the judgment, 'has not left
newspaper publishers groaning under the weight of the nascent law of
breach of confidence, but may actually have lightened their load a little
in this sphere'.[161] This mildly euphoric statement assumes that the
action for breach of confidence should be available against newspapers
who publish public information. This is a highly debatable assumption.

The Crossman case was brought by the Attorney-General to secure
an injunction against the publishers of his diaries and against Times
Newspapers Ltd which had by then already serialized and published
extracts from the diaries. The Diaries had been kept by Richard
Crossman while he was a cabinet minister during the period 1964–70,
and contained detailed references to cabinet and cabinet committee
discussions which revealed the positions taken up by members on
various issues. Information about discussions between Richard Crossman
and senior civil servants, and criticisms of these advisers, were also
included in the diaries. Volume 1 of the Diaries, which the Attorney-
General sought to interdict and from which the serialized extracts
were drawn, was submitted by Crossman's literary editors (Richard
Crossman having died some time before) to the cabinet secretary for
vetting but neither the *Sunday Times* nor these editors were prepared
to accept all the deletions sought by the cabinet secretary. Objection
was taken by the secretary to 'blow by blow' accounts of cabinet
discussions which revealed the actual differences between ministers and
to disclosure of advice given by civil servants and discussions of their
suitability for appointment. He expressed the view that publication
would seriously weaken, and would in fact be opposed to, the conventions of collective and individual ministerial responsibility upon
which modern cabinet government was dependent. When the *Sunday*

Times published extracts which included particulars of the matters objected to by the cabinet secretary, the Attorney-General moved to enjoin any further publication in which similar revelations were included.[162]

The defendants conceded the right of the Attorney-General to approach the court for suppression, in the public interest, of information that would jeopardize national security,[163] an issue which, it was agreed, did not arise in the case. They joined issue with the plaintiff's claim that the courts are empowered to prohibit the disclosure or publication of cabinet secrets on the basis of the doctrine of collective responsibility or of individual ministerial responsibility.[164] This claim of the plaintiff has a delusive simplicity since it coalesces at least three major issues which are frequently not distinguished from each other with the needed sharpness. The first issue raises the principle and practice of cabinet confidentiality and of the confidentiality between ministers and their civil service advisers. It is beyond dispute that in the freest of societies confidentiality is maintained and is desirable 'at the inner centre of the government'. While there may be arguments about the extent of the secrecy which should prevail (should factual material discussed in the inner circles of government and the decisions which are there taken also be secret?) few would dispute that some measure of confidentiality is necessary and desirable for effective and wise policy formation. As Lord Salisbury, the nineteenth-century statesman, said 'members must feel themselves untrammelled by any consideration of consistency with the past or self-justification in the future'.[165] The second issue is the relationship of this rule and practice of confidentiality to the constitutional conventions of collective and individual ministerial responsibility. The Radcliffe Committee on Ministerial Memoirs believes that collective responsibility, at least, is unworkable without a concurrent rule of secrecy,[166] and this was the view accepted by Lord Widgery in the Crossman case.[167] In total opposition to this viewpoint, a commentator has said:

> 'Essentially collective responsibility means that the Government stand or fall together, that the administration speaks formally to Parliament with one voice and that ministers resign if defeated on a Commons vote of confidence. None of these practices would be substantially impeded by the publication of the views of individual members of the administration.'[168]

It might be argued with equal force that the rule of individual ministerial responsibility which makes the minister answerable for the decisions of his department is workable without the need to keep secret the advice he has received from civil servants. The third issue implicit in the Attorney-General's claim in the Crossman case concerns the existence and desirability of a *legally* enforceable right of action to protect confidentiality at the inner centre of government. This issue was glossed over by Lord Widgery and is overlooked by commentators who assert that his judgment, by imposing stricter preconditions for the enforcement of the action, has conferred an advantage on the press. The question that needs a serious answer is whether the press is (and should be) burdened by such an action at all. 'The Government's right', it has been forcefully asserted, 'is not matched by a directly correlative Hohfeldian duty on everybody else to submit to, or facilitate conceal-ment.'[169] Many pronouncements on breach of confidence take the existence of a correlative duty for granted and by perpetuating the old myth that courts 'find' the law rather than create it, effectively conceal the legislative role of the judiciary on the frontiers of case law. The Crossman judgment, in brief, assumed the applicability of a rule the very existence of which was the subject of dispute between the parties to the action.

By separating the three issues that discussion has tended to merge and confuse, we can see that it is perfectly logical and sensible to believe in and support cabinet confidentiality and collective responsibility whilst simultaneously opposing the notion of the government having a legal right to suppress the publication of secrets that have leaked out. Cabinet business, unlike sensitive military information (for, example, the design of new weapons) is not per se unfit for public discussion. The business of a cabinet may range over the entire spectrum of public affairs and the stultifying effect of a legal right and remedy to protect confiden-tiality ought to be obvious to any supporter of self-government. The recent leaks of cabinet discussions leading up to the ditching of the child benefit scheme constitute a case in point. A Labour government commitment to the child benefit plan[170] which carried the support of the TUC was abandoned by announcement to Parliament in May 1976. The decision was subsequently shown to have been taken for reasons which, as Professor Dworkin has said, 'have nothing in com-mon with the justifications provided'[171] in the cabinet report to the House. The revelation of this fact, even if accomplished by unautho-rized access to cabinet minutes and discussions, does not seem to have harmed an important governmental interest worthy of protection by a legal action. On the contrary, this is precisely the kind of case which demonstrates that legal backing for cabinet confidentiality could help to produce a general public that is substantially misinformed on an important question of general policy. If the subject-matter of the dis-closures is as non-sensitive as child benefits, the potential distortion of informed self-government implicit in the legal protection of secrecy makes it a dubious and even dangerous policy for the legislature or courts to adopt.

Lord Widgery in the Crossman judgment decided that an action for breach of confidence lies to restrain the publication of cabinet material which discloses the 'expression of individual opinions by cabinet ministers'.[172] Somewhat inconsistently, he declined to extend the action to advice given to ministers by 'senior civil servants'.[173] But the Attorney-General's action failed because the Diaries (volume I) referred to discussions that were ten years old and which he therefore felt had lost their power to inhibit the free expression of views.[174] Does the narrow reach of his judgment not rescue it from the foregoing criticisms of the legal protection of confidentiality since it would permit cabinet business to be disclosed so long as individual positions are not? Moreover, even 'blow by blow' accounts become permissible after a decent interval of silence. An action to prohibit publication as a breach of confidence is certainly less fearsome than an injunction based on a projected breach of the Official Secrets Acts which for a substantially technical reason could not be brought to suppress the Crossman Diaries. All cabinet business, not just individual attitudes, is covered by the Acts and their operation is not limited to a ten-year period.[175] Yet the application of the doctrine of breach of confidence to public information remains unfortunate. If the Official Secrets Acts were narrowed[176] the action for breach of confidence would remain to inhibit disclosures of at least recent cabinet business. While the law at present limits an injunction to 'blow by blow' descriptions, there is no guarantee that courts might not extend the action to other cabinet business[177] and to the advice given to ministers by civil servants. While executive policy-making clearly requires secrecy, there are disadvantages in turning a principle or convention of politics into an enforceable legal rule. Secrecy at the inner centre of government has both advantages, which are generally well understood, and disadvantages which are but faintly appreciated. A weakness in the Radcliffe report is its failure to explore the negative effects of secrecy such as the power of misinformation that it confers (as in the child benefit case) and the opportunities it creates for under-cover pressure and interest groups to affect and distort decision-making. It seems unwise to encourage such tendencies by putting the force of law behind cabinet confidentiality.

The Crossman Diaries judgment has added to the law that needs to be reformed in the interests of open government. Even aside from the fact that its effect 'could be to confine quite substantially the already restricted information about the business of government',[178] it has produced other serious problems. It has increased the potential range of litigants aiming to suppress information about public affairs since presumably individual cabinet ministers and even ex-ministers who relied on the confidentiality of discussions could move to prohibit embarrassing revelations. Secondly, the elevation of the action to the sphere of public law has required the recognition of new pre-conditions and defences designed to give some effect to the general public interest in knowing about the affairs of government. The criteria which the courts will apply in this balancing of interests were only vaguely articulated in the Crossman case[179] with the result that a new dimension of uncertainty has been added to an already hazy branch of the law. These two factors, and the others already considered, almost force the conclusion that the court would have done better to avoid what has been called the extreme of compulsory secrecy[180] and to accept the proposition 'that governments have a right or liberty to protect their secrets whilst others have a right to find them out'.[181]

CONTEMPT OF COURT

The thalidomide affair in the United Kingdom has provided a vivid illustration of the potential of contempt of court for inhibiting the free discussion of important public issues. In two cases arising out of the thalidomide tragedy and the litigation against the drug company responsible for its distribution in the United Kingdom, injunctions were granted restraining the publication or use of material on the ground that such actions would constitute contempt of court either because they constituted public pre-judgments of issues in pending litigation or because they tended to subject litigants seeking to vindicate their legal rights to undesirable pressure. In the first case, *Attorney-General* v *Times Newspapers Ltd*,[182] the court restored an injunction granted by the divisional court (and set aside by the Court of Appeal) to restrain publication by Times Newspapers Ltd of an article 'tracing in considerable detail the history of the development, marketing and testing of thalidomide from the early stages of its discovery until it caused the terrible deformities in children where mothers took it during pregnancy'.[183] The article charged Distillers (the company responsible for marketing the drug in the United Kingdom) 'with neglect in regard to their own failure to test the product, or their failure to react sufficiently sharply to warning signs obtained from the tests by others'[184] and was to be published during protracted litigation between claimants and the company that was pending though dormant at the particular time. In the second case, *The Distillers Co (Biochemicals) Ltd* v *Times Newspapers Ltd*,[185] the court allowed an action to restrain the defendant company from using or publishing material which had been disclosed by way of discovery in litigation to recover damages from Distillers and which had come into the hands of Times Newspapers Ltd.

In both cases the courts recognized that two public interests were brought into conflict by the actions for orders to prohibit publication. The first was characterized by Lord Simon as that of 'freedom of discussion in democratic society'.[186] In describing this interest he said that '[p]eople cannot adequately influence the decisions which affect their lives unless they can be adequately informed on the facts and arguments relevant to the decisions'.[187] The second public interest which the law of contempt sought to vindicate is the interest 'in the resolution of disputes, not by force or by private or public influence, but by independent adjudication in courts of law according to an objective code'.[188] It was accepted that the courts were required to hold these two interests in balance but in each case the interest in securing the fair and objective adjudication of pending litigation (even if temporarily dormant) was held to prevail over the general interest in an informed public. This was so because in the first case the comment constituted prejudgment of 'the case or . . . the specific issues in it',[189] and in the second because disclosure would jeopardize the discovery procedure and thereby the administration of justice. However, where the proposed comment constitutes a prejudgment on the issues in a pending case, the House of Lords held that the balance is conclusively struck in favour of protection of the administration of justice until the litigation is concluded.[190]

The judgments in the two cases present a freedom of speech rather than a freedom of information issue since in both the defendants proposed not merely the release of information but critical comment and argumentation on the factual material. Though the findings were adverse to the free speech interest, the courts recognized the need for a balancing of interests and for some limitation on the 'gagging' effect of the contempt of court rule. In *Attorney-General* v *Times Newspapers Ltd* Lord Simon indicated that public debate that was in progress when litigation commenced could continue so long as the issues in the matter were discussed incidentally and without the intent to cause injury to a litigant.[191] Moreover, not all manner of pressure on litigants was to be suppressed and particularly not where the comment was fair and temperate. The form of comment that the courts condemned most strongly and were prepared to protect almost absolutely was pre-judgment of the specific case before the courts. Finally, it was recognized in *The Distillers Co (Biochemicals) Ltd* v *Times Newspapers Ltd* that the defence of public interest would be available to a defendant who proposed to publish information about

'matters carried out or contemplated, in breach of the country's security, or in breach of law, including statutory duty, fraud, or otherwise destructive of the country or its people, including matters medically dangerous to the public; and doubtless other misdeeds of similar gravity'.[192]

Clearly, then, there are limits to the suppressive power of the contempt rule though it has been argued that the limitations do not go far enough.[193]

Whether the courts would strike a balance more favourable to public knowledge where an injunction is sought to prohibit publication of purely factual material related to the issues in a pending suit is not at all clear. Since disclosure of factual material does not constitute an express or overt prejudgment of issues or pressurizing of litigants there ought to be far more latitude to publish, but it would perhaps be too strong to say that such disclosures should never be treated as a contempt. The courts should certainly give more weight to the defence that publication will be in the public interest and to the principle that incidental debate on issues before the courts in pending litigation may proceed without risk of contempt. Such an attitude is all the more important where the information in question relates to some aspect of public administration in which the public by definition have a right to be informed and the suppression of which, even in the interest of protecting the adjudicatory process, should not be lightly undertaken.

COPYRIGHT LAW

Copyright law in the United Kingdom provides yet another weapon available to the government to suppress information about public affairs. This is because the copyright in every original 'literary'[194] work 'made by or under the direction or control of Her Majesty or a Government Department' is vested in Her Majesty.[195] While it is arguable that the state, like any private person or group, should be entitled to restrain the commercial exploitation of its papers, since its officials transact public business the principle of American federal law that copyright may not subsist in publications of the United States Government[196] is clearly preferable to the British rule. However that may be, the law now in force in the United Kingdom confers copyright upon the state in government publications and papers, including statutes and subsidiary legislation, parliamentary papers and reports and the papers of government departments.[197] In practice the copyright is not enforced in respect of Acts, bills, parliamentary papers and reports[198] but in theory even these most public of government documents are covered by copyright. In both theory and practice, government papers in departments of state are protected.

Though the law of copyright is potentially available to limit access to information, this weapon may be less effective than others at the disposal of government. Copyright applies to papers and documents, not to verbal discussions. As Lord Denning said in *Fraser* v *Evans*,[199] copyright does not subsist in information but 'in the literary form in which the information is dressed'. Moreover, since an infringement will take place only where the paper or document is substantially reproduced, references to it in newspaper discussions or radio or television broadcasts might not necessarily ground an action.[200] Despite these limitations copyright confers a useful option on the government which in the United Kingdom would be available, for example, to prohibit revelations based on government reports and papers. A Pentagon Papers exercise in Britain must be viewed as a still-born possibility at best, in view *inter alia* of the law on copyright. Where the government does rely on copyright protection it has the advantage of a statute affording the triple remedy of injunction, damages and criminal penalties.[201] These remedies will become more significant if the Official Secrets Acts are narrowed and the law on state copyright is left unchanged.

At first sight the rule that copyright is not infringed unless a substantial reproduction of the protected material takes place, limits the possibility of its misuse through the denial of information to which the public should be entitled. However, the question whether there has been substantial borrowing depends not just on the quantity that is published but also on the quality of the material that is taken over. Reproduction of a vital part of the protected documents may be an infringement even if it represents only a small portion of it in quantity.[202] The defence of fair dealing 'for the purpose of reporting current events' is of questionable value to the publisher of material from government papers since it is not available in respect of papers that have not been published or widely circulated.[203] Since it is primarily in relation to government papers that have not been published or widely circulated that the communications industry may wish to exercise its responsibility to inform the public, the defence of fair dealing offers no real escape. Finally, the defence that publication was in the public interest appears to have been narrowly circumscribed by the courts to the disclosure of misdeeds of a serious nature.[204] In *Initial Services Ltd* v *Putterill*[205] Lord Denning declared that the defence would encompass 'crimes, frauds and misdeeds', but even this approach appears to exclude reports drawing attention to inefficiency, mismanagement or ill-advised policies in government. Unless the publisher of protected material can show that the government papers which he discloses contain evidence of crimes and misdeeds in a fairly strict and technical sense, he is guilty of a copyright infringement, though arguably there is room for judicial creativity where matters of general public interest are concerned.[206]

This brief survey of copyright law as a possible instrument of limiting knowledge of public affairs suggests strongly that the copyright concept, designed as it was to prevent the misappropriation of another's labours, has unfortunate and undesirable results in the realm of public information.

BRIEF EVALUATION OF UNITED KINGDOM LAWS

The feature of the laws examined in this section that stands out most conspicuously is their cosmic coverage. Whatever the position may be in practice, the government is legally in a position to enforce a total blackout on public affairs. A second prominent feature is the antiquarian nature of some of the laws, not just in the sense of their ill comportance with modern democracy but also in their dependence on ancient customs and conventions. The information that cabinet secrecy rests in part upon the oath taken by Privy Counsellors[207] and upon the rule that cabinet decisions are formal advice to the Queen[208] must strike the modern reader as evidence of a quaint national belief in ancient relics or in a grotesquely outmoded conception of politics. The attitude of the courts to secrecy which Professor De Smith characterized as displaying 'a keen sense of obligation to serve the interests of the state ...'[209] constitutes a third feature worthy of mention. While British courts admittedly lack the constitutional authority of their American counterparts, they appear to have taken an unnecessarily restricted view of their competence in administering secrecy laws.

Faced with the limited reforms proposed by the Franks Committee and the tendency in government circles to treat these proposals as unbearably radical, many commentators advocate retention of current laws on the principle that 'the fact that the Act looks so bad may have a reverse—"chilling effect"—on prosecution'.[210] Admittedly, half-hearted reform which merely makes the law more respectable and enforceable is undesirable. Nevertheless, for several reasons acceptance of the current law, even on grounds of expediency, seems unwise. The Franks Committee generally played down the effect of the law[211] but it undoubtedly creates 'psychological barriers'[212] to desirable disclosures about government administration; and though prosecutions (for offences other than spying) have not been numerous in recent years, there is evidence that official thinking is much influenced by the law and that it is not infrequently used as a threat to prevent disclosures.[213] More enlightened laws seem necessary to lead the society away from such practices towards a more modern condition of open government.

Programmes for reform will necessarily have as their main emphasis the amendment of the Official Secrets Acts. The broad objectives of such a programme should be (1) the restriction of the crime of espionage to cases of classic espionage by limiting it to the communication or attempted communication to a foreign power of information connected with the safety or defence of the country; and (2) the restriction of the crime of communication *simpliciter* to a narrow range of highly sensitive information in the nature of codes, cryptographic materials, new weapons designs, military strategies and the like. Professor Harry Street's proposal to limit the Official Secrets Acts to espionage[214] is unrealistic in the failure to recognize that there are some secrets so vital to a nation's safety that their simple disclosure ought to be an offence. The changes to the Official Secrets Acts will require reform of the law on breach of confidence and copyright if these concepts are not to acquire a new and unfortunate prominence by the narrowing of the Acts. Piecemeal reform of the kind envisaged in the Franks Report will fall a long way short of desirable change. But all these recommended changes are 'negative' and need to be complemented by the creation of a positive right to information.[215]

NOTES

[1] The British common law is briefly reviewed by Enid Campbell in 'Public Access to Government Documents' (1967) 41 *ALJ* 73 at 77–8. She demonstrates that the common law has even been used to limit statutes granting a right to inspect records.

[2] 8 & 9 Eliz II c 67. The statute requires bodies subject to its provisions to open their proceedings to the press and public unless by resolution specifying the reasons the

body in question decides to close the meeting. Though the Act specifies certain reasons which will justify closure (e g the confidential nature of the business) the body may rely on any other reason so long as the resolution specifies it and it arises from the nature of the business or proceedings. The provision was extended to local authority committees by section 100 of the Local Government Act 1972. Another limited exception to the absence of laws conferring positive rights to information is section 159 of the Local Government Act 1972, which gives to 'any person interested' the right to inspect accounts and related papers at the time of audit.

[3] The bodies scheduled in the Act include local authorities, rural parishes, certain water boards and education committees and bodies constituted under specified provisions of the National Health Service Act, 1946: see Schedule to the Act. There is power to add to or subtract from the bodies listed in the schedule: See section 2.

[4] Departmental Committee on Section 2 of the Official Secrets Act 1911 Cmnd 5104 (1972) § 85 (referred to below as the 'Franks Committee' or the 'Franks Report').

[5] Even Mr Roy Jenkins, who favours drastic amendment of the Official Secrets Acts in Britain, is unwilling to promote the idea of a Freedom of Information Act on the ground that its operation is 'costly, cumbersome and legalistic': Granada Lecture of 10 March 1975, 10–11 (unpublished manuscript).

[6] Examples of academic appeals for such legislation are those of William Birtles in 'Big Brother Knows Best: The Franks Report on Section 2 of the Official Secrets Act' in 1973 *Public Law* 100 and H W R Wade in his evidence to the Franks Committee (Vol II 418–22). More recently The Outer Circle Policy Unit has called for extensive changes in a booklet entitled *An Official Information Act* (London, 1977).

[7] In November 1976 the Home Secretary announced the Government's intention of introducing legislation to give effect to the Franks Report. The approach of the Franks Committee would be liberalized, he said, in two respects and made more restrictive in one respect: see Ronald Wraith *Open Government: The British Interpretation* (Royal Inst of Public Adm, London 1977) 63.

[8] Official Secrets Act 1889 (52 & 53 Vic c 52).

[9] David Williams *Not in the Public Interest* (Hutchinson, London, 1965) 15–20.

[10] Ibid 23.

[11] Official Secrets Act 1911 (1 & 2 Geo V c 28).

[12] Official Secrets Act 1920 (10 & 11 Geo V c 75). For a summary of the changes introduced see David Williams op cit 35–6.

[13] Section 6.

[14] Section 7.

[15] Section 2.

[16] Official Secrets Act 1939 (2 & 3 Geo VI c 121).

[17] Section 1 of the Official Secrets Act 1911. The maximum penalty is imprisonment for a period of fourteen years.

[18] The relevant provisions of section 1 have been somewhat paraphrased in this account.

[19] For the full extent of 'prohibited place' see Halsbury 4 ed vol 11 § 900.

[20] *R v Parrott* (1913) 8 Cr App Rep 186 (CCA).

[21] Section 1(2).

[22] Ibid.

[23] Section 2 of the Official Secrets Act 1920. This section incorporates further presumptions to facilitate proof of the crime; for example, a person is deemed, unless the contrary is proved, to have been in communication with a foreign agent if he has visited such a person or associated with him, or if information about the foreign agent is in his possession. 'Foreign agent' includes persons employed by a foreign power to commit acts prejudicial to the safety or interests of the state or reasonably suspected of having been so employed. It seems that almost all elements of the crime could be established by the prosecution, at least prima facie, by reliance on statutory presumptions.

[24] Section 7 of the Official Secrets Act 1920. Other inchoate offences such as those of attempt and incitement are also deemed equivalent to the crime of spying.

[25] [1964] AC 763, [1962] 3 All ER 142 (HL).

[26] Though Bertrand Russell was prominently associated with this committee and its anti-nuclear weapons campaign, he was not one of those selected for prosecution.

[27] That is, section 1 of the Act of 1911.

[28] Smith & Hogan *Criminal Law* 3 ed (Butterworths, London, 1973) 652–3.

[29] The case is subjected to vigorous criticisms by Donald Thompson in 'The Committee of 100 and the Official Secrets Act 1911' 1963 *Public Law* 201. His critique is more impressive in respect of the decision to prosecute and the sentence than in its reference to the court's interpretation of the statutory language.

[30] *Chandler* v *Director of Public Prosecutions* [1964] AC 763 (HL) at 813.

[31] *Chandler* v *Director of Public Prosecutions (supra)* at 811.

[32] Ibid. The reference to the prerogative is due to the fact that the disposition of the armed forces is a matter within crown prerogative.

[33] The liability of such citizens under other provisions of the Official Secrets Acts is considered below.

[34] Donald Thompson loc cit 203.

[35] David Williams op cit 24, 27.

[36] For a detailed account see David Williams op cit 73–4.

[37] Under section 6 of the Official Secrets Act 1920.

[38] Tony Bunyon *The Political Police in Britain* (Julian Friedmann, London, 1976) 11.

[39] Section 1 of the Official Secrets Act 1911.

[40] That is, information protected by section 2(1) of the Official Secrets Act 1911. From the analysis of section 2(1) presented below, it will be seen that official information covers in the main material in the possession of officials of the central government in the United Kingdom.

[41] Section 2(1)(aa).

[42] 'Safety or interests of the state' will no doubt carry the same meaning as it was given in *Chandler* v *Director of Public Prosecutions (supra)*.

[43] The information may be documentary or otherwise and includes sketches, plans, models and articles.

[44] Section 2(1A) of the Official Secrets Act 1911.

[45] Which are, however, widely defined: see section 12 of the Official Secrets Act 1911.

[46] Section 1(2)(a) of the Official Secrets Act 1920. The section also punishes, apparently without proof of a prejudicial purpose, failure to comply with official directions for return or disposal of an official document.

[47] Section 1(c) of the Official Secrets Act 1920.

[48] Section 2(1) of the Official Secrets Act 1911. The maximum penalty on conviction after indictment is imprisonment for two years. On summary conviction the penalties are a maximum of three months imprisonment or a fine of £50, or both.

[49] Ibid.

[50] The material protected is described as 'any secret official code word, or pass word, or any sketch, plan, model, article, note, document or information . . .'. The words 'model' and 'article' suggest that the material protected is not limited to that of an informational type but includes 'hardware'.

[51] As already observed this covers military installations and places but is not limited to them.

[52] Franks Report vol I 112–13 (Appendix I). An attempt to persuade the courts to limit the provision to information related to prohibited places failed in *R* v *Simmington* [1921] 1 KB 451 (CCA).

[53] The relevant words are 'holds . . . office under Her Majesty' and these indicate both the inclusion of central government and the exclusion, for example, of local government. Certain independent authorities such as the Post Office and the Atomic Energy Authority have been specifically included by statute. For a general discussion of the levels of authority included, see the Frank's Report vol I 113 (Appendix I) and Halsbury 4 ed vol 11 § 901n7. In *Lewis* v *Cattle* [1938] 2 All ER 368 the court decided that police officers are subject to the statute.

[54] Section 2(1)(b). Retention for a prejudicial purpose has been dealt with above under 'Crimes Analogous to Spying'.

[55] Ibid.   [56] Section 12 Official Secrets Act 1911.

[57] See, for example, David Williams op cit 98 and Tony Bunyon op cit 20.

[58] Communication of official information without authority has been held to be an absolute offence.

[59] Section 2(1)(c). An analagous offence in the form of allowing unauthorized persons to have possession of official documents of the narrow class defined in section 1(1)(c) of the Official Secrets Act 1920 is created by section 1(2)(b) of that Act.

⁶⁰ For an instance of a successful prosecution see Tony Bunyon op cit 20.

⁶¹ See above p 108.

⁶² Section 2(1)(a).

⁶³ Franks Report vol 1 112 (Appendix I).

⁶⁴ Unless, of course, the communication of this vital information is 'authorized'.

⁶⁵ [1963] Crim LR 207 (CCA).

⁶⁶ This case is not reported. The fullest account is by Jonathan Aitken in *Officially Secret* (Weidenfeld & Nicolson, London, 1971).

⁶⁷ Authority to communicate is discussed below.

⁶⁸ Smith & Hogan op cit 654.

⁶⁹ The position where the accused acts on a supposed duty to communicate in the interests of the state is analysed below.

⁷⁰ Section 2(1)(a).

⁷¹ Ministers of the Crown are said to be 'self-authorizing'. In the case of other Crown servants, the nature of their job will determine whether they have authority to disclose. Ministers are presumably self-authorizing only in respect of their own departments and not, for example, in respect of all cabinet business.

⁷² Franks Report vol I §§ 18 & 216.

⁷³ As Lord Pearce interpreted the phrase in *Chandler* v *Director of Public Prosecution* (*supra*).

⁷⁴ *Burns* v *Ransley* (1949) 79 CLR 101 at 115.

⁷⁵ If the court did adopt this approach, the requirement of *mens rea* would necessarily be different. A reasonable belief that disclosure would advance state interests might then afford an escape from criminal liability.

⁷⁶ (1919) 83 JP 121.

⁷⁷ David Williams op cit 94–5.

⁷⁸ The facts are outlined by David Williams op cit 76.

⁷⁹ Paul O'Higgins *Censorship in Britain* (Thomas Nelson & Sons Ltd, London, 1972) 39.

⁸⁰ The reference to 'this Act' appears to incorporate a reference to section 2(1) of the Act in which these words appear with the result that information communicated by an official without authority may not be passed on by anyone else.

⁸¹ *Attorney-General* v *Jonathan Cape Ltd* [1975] 3 WLR 606.

⁸² Hugo Young *The Crossman Affair* (Hamish Hamilton Ltd, London, 1976) 33.

⁸³ Unless the state could prove that the intention was to publish irrespective of the cabinet secretary's decision, it is doubtful that a prosecution would have succeeded on the ground that Crossman had offended against section 7 of the Official Secrets Act 1920 by committing an act 'preparatory to the commission of an offence under the principal Act or this Act . . .'.

⁸⁴ Section 2(2) of the Official Secrets Act 1911 as amended by section 10 of the Official Secrets Act 1920.

⁸⁵ Ibid.

⁸⁶ His retention of the document would not be an offence unless a prejudicial purpose is proved but failure to comply with lawful directions for its return or disposal would constitute a crime: see above p 107. These offences apply only to the narrow class of documents there indicated.

⁸⁷ Section 1 of the Official Secrets Act 1920.

⁸⁸ Section 3 of the Official Secrets Act 1920.

⁸⁹ Sections 4 and 5 of the Official Secrets Act 1920.

⁹⁰ Section 6 of the Official Secrets Act 1920 as amended by section 1 of the Official Secrets Act 1939.

⁹¹ Reasonable expenses must be tendered.

⁹² The punishment provided is imprisonment for a period not exceeding three months or a fine not exceeding £50, or both.

⁹³ David Williams op cit 73.

⁹⁴ Section 7 of the Official Secrets Act 1911 as amended by sections 10 and 11 of the Act of 1920. The maximum applicable penalty is imprisonment for two years.

⁹⁵ Ibid.

⁹⁶ Section 8 of the Official Secret Acts 1911. The reference to the Attorney-General includes the Solicitor-General for England and means the Lord Advocate for Scotland: see section 12 of the same Act.

[97] David Williams op cit 104.

[98] Franks Report vol 1 § 243.

[99] Jonathan Aitken op cit 72.

[100] That is, of section 2 of the 1911 Act dealing with the communication of official information.

[101] Franks Report vol 1 § 255.

[102] A member of the cabinet in the United Kingdom.

[103] Section 8(4) of the Official Secrets Act 1920. The sentence of the court must be pronounced in public.

[104] Section 8(3) of the Official Secrets Act 1920.

[105] Sections 6 and 9(1) of the Official Secrets Act 1911.

[106] Franks Report vol 1 §§ 61–64.

[107] Franks Report vol 2, 15–23.

[108] Franks Report vol 1 §§ 144–161.

[109] Franks Report vol 1 § 61.

[110] Section 2 of the Official Secrets Act 1911.

[111] Ibid.

[112] Of course, it might be relevant in enquiries as to whether civil servants have been in breach of their official duties and responsibilities.

[113] Franks Report vol 2, 18–23.

[114] Ibid 21 (emphasis supplied).

[115] Ibid 22.

[116] Ibid 23.

[117] David Williams op cit 185.

[118] J A G Griffith 'Government Secrecy in the United Kingdom' in *None of Your Business: Government Secrecy in America* 331.

[119] Franks Report vol 2, 20.

[120] *Daily News* report of 4 August 1975.

[121] Exceptions to automatic declassification might be specified as in American law. The 30-year rule of the Public Records Act 1967 is far too long for much of the information that is classified.

[122] Franks Report vol 1 §§ 144–169.

[123] Franks Report vol 1 § 165.

[124] Which the Committee would define more narrowly than in section 2 of the Official Secrets Act 1911.

[125] Or, if it is non-documentary information, of a kind that would be classified were it documentary.

[126] Franks Report vol 1 §§ 157, 161.

[127] Vol 1 § 146.

[128] Cf Harry Street 'Secrecy and the Citizen's Right to Know: A British Civil Libertarian Perspective' in *None of Your Business: Government Secrecy in America* 353.

[129] T C Hartley & J A G Griffith *Government and Law* (Weidenfeld & Nicolson, London, 1975) 268.

[130] Ibid 270.

[131] Harry Street *Freedom, the Individual and the Law* (Penguin, 1973) 218.

[132] Ibid 219.

[133] See, for example, Paul O'Higgins op cit 58–9, Jonathan Aitken op cit 45 and Anthony Sampson in 'Secrecy, News Management and the British Press' published in *Secrecy and Foreign Policy* 225.

[134] For an account of this episode, see Hartley & Griffith op cit 272–3.

[135] On the advantages see David Williams op cit 86–7.

[136] Nuclear Installations Act 1965 section 2(1)–(1B) and the Atomic Energy Authority Act 1971 section 17 and Sch.

[137] Atomic Energy Authority Act 1954 sections 6(1), 6(4) and Sch 3.

[138] Section 11 of the Atomic Energy Act 1946. Section 13 prohibits disclosure without authority of information obtained by a person in the exercise of powers under the Act.

[139] European Communities Act 1972 section 11. The Official Secrets Acts have application and 'classified information' means information subject to the security rules of a member state or a Euratom institution.

[140] Section 13(3) of the Radioactive Substances Act 1960.

[141] Section 28 of the Health and Safety at Work Act 1974. The information will have

been obtained by inspectors acting under section 20 or after notice served upon the person required to give it under section 27.

[142] Section 94 of the Control of Pollution Act 1974.

[143] Section 61 of the Sex Discrimination Act 1975.

[144] A person is regarded as rehabilitated and his sentence 'spent' when he has served the sentence imposed upon him, but certain grave sentences are excluded from rehabilitation and do not therefore become 'spent' under the Act: sections 1 and 5.

[145] Section 9 of the Rehabilitation of Offenders Act 1974. The exception allows disclosure at the request of the convicted person.

[146] See, for example, section 24 of the Armed Forces Act 1971, inserting a new section 60 into the Army Act 1955 and into the Airforce Act 1955. The provisions correspond to section 34 of the Naval Discipline Act 1957. The maximum penalty on conviction is imprisonment for two years.

[147] Notably under the espionage provisions (section 1) and the section dealing with disclosure of official information (section 2).

[148] Franks Report vol 2, 36–8.

[149] Ibid 38.

[150] [1969] 1 All ER 8, [1969] 1 QB 349.

[151] [1975] 3 All ER 484.

[152] At 11.

[153] At 12.

[154] For a brief historical review, the reader is referred to *Breach of Confidence*, Law Commission Working Paper No 58 (HMSO, London, 1974).

[155] [1965] 1 All ER 611, [1967] Ch 302.

[156] *Coco v A N Clark (Engineers) Ltd* (1969) RPC 41 at 47.

[157] See *Breach of Confidence* above. The absence of reference to the kind of issues that arose in the Crossman Diaries case was probably due, apart from the *sub judice* rule, to the limitation of the statutory tort to three categories of information which appear to exclude information connected with the affairs of government: See 48–9 of the Working Paper.

[158] At 68–70.

[159] *Supra* at 495.

[160] M W Bryan 'The Crossman Diaries—Developments in the Law of Breach of Confidence' (1976) 92 *LQR* 180 at 181–2.

[161] Ibid 183–4.

[162] The reason for the decision to proceed for breach of confidence rather than by way of action to restrain contraventions of the Official Secrets Act is described above at pp 112–13.

[163] *Attorney-General v Jonathan Cape Ltd (supra)* at 491. It is not clear whether the defendants conceded that a breach of confidence could be the basis of an action brought to protect national security.

[164] Details of the case for the plaintiff are described in chapter 3 of Hugo Young's *The Crossman Affair*.

[165] Quoted in Report of the Committee of Privy Counsellors on Ministerial Memoirs (Cmnd 6386, January 1976) 13. This report is referred to below as the 'Radcliffe Report'.

[166] Radcliffe Report § 33.

[167] *Attorney-General v Jonathan Cape Ltd (supra)* at 495–6.

[168] See 'Comment' in 1975 *Public Law* 277 at 279.

[169] Ibid.

[170] The details of the child benefit plan are summarized in the 17 June 1976 issue of *New Society*. The essence of the scheme was a merger of child tax reliefs and family allowances into a tax-free cash benefit for each child payable to the mother.

[171] Ronald Dworkin 'Open Government—or Closed' *The New Society* 24 June 1976.

[172] *Attorney-General v Jonathan Cape (supra)* at 495.

[173] Ibid 496.

[174] The suggestion that the importance of confidentiality diminishes in time is challenged in 1975 *Public Law* 277 at 278.

[175] Release of papers after 30 years under the Public Records Act would render the Official Secrets Acts inoperative in respect of the released material.

[176] The Franks Committee proposed that the communication of cabinet documents should be an offence but not disclosure of cabinet discussions: Franks Report § 190.

[177] The Radcliffe Committee found that the rule of confidentiality attached to all cabinet business. The courts are not bound, of course, to extend *legal* protection that far.

[178] Hugo Young op cit 197.

[179] See criticism along these lines in the Radcliffe Report § 65, Hugo Young op cit 200–3 and (1976) 92 *LQR* 180 at 182.

[180] Ronald Dworking loc cit 679.

[181] 1975 *Public Law* 279. This rule could not be applied to intrinsically sensitive material such as military secrets.

[182] [1973] 3 All ER 54 (HL).

[183] Antony Whitaker 'The Sunday Times and the Thalidomide and Crossman Diaries Affairs' (1976) 10 *The Law Teacher* 74.

[184] Ibid.

[185] [1975] 1 All ER 41 (QBD).

[186] *Attorney-General* v *Times Newspapers Ltd (supra)* at 77.

[187] Ibid.

[188] *Attorney-General* v *Times Newspapers Ltd (supra)* at 78.

[189] Ibid 65.

[190] In so doing, the court extended the scope of the contempt rule: C J Miller 'The Sunday Times Case' (1974) 37 *Modern Law Rev* 96. The Phillimore report on contempt has also rejected the notion of balancing where the comment constitutes a prejudgment but it does recommend that comment should only constitute contempt if it creates a risk that the course of justice will be seriously impeded or prejudiced: Stephen J Sauvaign 'The Report of the Committee on Contempt of Court' (1975) 38 *Modern Law Rev* 311 at 312.

[191] At 82.   [192] At 50.

[193] Antony Whitaker loc cit 79.

[194] Dramatic, musical and artistic works are excluded from this discussion since, although equally protected, they are not likely to be relevant to the citizen's right of access to information about public affairs.

[195] Section 39 of the Copyright Act 1956.

[196] 17 USCA § 105 (May 1977 Supp).

[197] Copinger and Skone James on *Copyright* 11 ed (Sweet & Maxwell, London, 1971) § 871 et seq.

[198] Ibid § 886.   [199] *Supra* 12.

[200] On the acts restricted where copyright is held in a literary work see Halsbury 4 ed §§ 909–23.

[201] A useful survey of remedies will be found in Halsbury 4 ed §§ 940 58.

[202] Halsbury 4 ed § 921 and authorities there cited.

[203] *Hubbard* v *Vosper* [1972] 1 All ER 1023 (CA) at 1028. An earlier decision limited the defence of fair dealing to published works but the court here extended it to works which are widely distributed.

[204] Halsbury 4 ed § 939 and authorities there cited.

[205] [1967] 3 All ER 145 (CA) at 148. In *Beloff* v *Pressdram Ltd* [1973] 1 All ER 241 at 260 the court held that the defence of public interest does not extend beyond misdeeds of a serious nature . . . clearly recognizable as such'.

[206] 'Misdeeds' could be extended to cover serious inefficiency or mismanagement in government and perhaps even questionable or contentious policy-making.

[207] Radcliffe Report § 21.

[208] David Williams op cit 44.

[209] Stanley de Smith 'Official Secrecy and External Relations in Great Britain: The Law and its Context' in *Secrecy and Foreign Policy* 325.

[210] Thomas M Franck and Edward Weisband 'Dissemblement, Secrecy and Executive Privilege in the Foreign Relations of Three Democracies: A Comparative Analysis' in *Secrecy and Foreign Policy* 438–9.

[211] Notably, of section 2 of the Official Secrets Act 1911: see, for example, the conclusion in Franks Report vol 1 § 67.

[212] Jonathan Aitken op cit 218.

[213] See, for example, Paul O'Higgins op cit 147–8; Jonathan Aitken op cit 37 st seq.

[214] Harry Street 'Secrecy and the Citizen's Right to Know: A British Civil, Libertarian Prospective' in *Secrecy and Foreign Policy* 345.

[215] See Part IV chapter XI below.

CHAPTER VII

South African Law

Denial of access to information is carried to its logical extreme by the relevant laws in South Africa. These laws are so negative in terms both of number and impact that it is impossible to conceive of anything on the positive side. This is true even at the level of local government where provisions requiring council meetings to be open are subject to the uncontrolled discretion of councils to resolve themselves into closed committee sessions.[1] Local government documents other than council minutes[2] may not be inspected unless permission is given, either because of specific provisions in local government ordinances[3] or because no such right is available at common law. In *Visser* v *Minister of Justice*[4] the court declared that '[t]he ordinary rule seems to be that every owner of a document is entitled to keep it private, except in so far as he is specifically required by law to disclose it'.[5] No glimmering of hope appears to radiate even from the common law of the land.

Legislation restricting access to official information is dominated by the Official Secrets Act of 1956.[6] Though the comprehensiveness of this law appears to render other legislation superfluous, there is a body of statutes in which specific restrictions on information flow are included. Among this group there are some unusual statutory prescriptions which are designed to further ideological control or the maintenance of 'security'; and these have no counterparts in either United States or United Kingdom legislation. Special features of South African common law, especially in the field of tort, deprive breach of confidence of any real relevance to the control of public information; but copyright law in South Africa is favourable to use (or abuse) for that purpose.

THE OFFICIAL SECRETS ACT

BRIEF HISTORY

Prior to 1956 when the Act currently in force was enacted by Parliament,[7] the English law in the form of the Official Secrets Act

1911 was in force in South Africa.[8] Amendments to that law in the
United Kingdom were not taken over with the result that the law
remained unchanged[9] until it was repealed and replaced in 1956.
However, the Act introduced in 1956 is substantially a re-enactment
of the British Acts of 1911 and 1920 with, if that is conceivable, some
broadening of the terms of the statutes of the mother country. The
law now in force is therefore essentially a British law fortified by some
local innovations.

The 1911 Act received its most extensive application during the
Second World War when its use in South Africa survived constitutional
challenge in the courts.[10] The reported prosecutions of that time relate
to the espionage provision of the law, and since the war only one
decision features in the reports.[11] It is against this background of virtual
non-use of the law that Parliament substituted a local enactment in
1956 with the consent of almost the entire opposition, who were
lulled into a mood of complacency by the British origin of the
measure.[12]

In the analysis of the Official Secrets Act of 1956 that follows,
emphasis will fall upon those features that are different from the law
currently in force in the United Kingdom. Offences that are identical
in the South African law will not be analysed, and in general only the
significant departures will be discussed.

ANALYSIS OF THE OFFICIAL SECRETS ACT

Espionage

Espionage in the South African Act is defined in almost identical
terms to its British counterpart,[13] thus making it unnecessary to repeat
the analysis in the chapter on United Kingdom laws.[14] However, there
are two South African judgments in which the courts had to interpret
and apply the crime of espionage as defined in the Official Secrets Act
1911, which was at the time applicable in South Africa. In R v *Wentzel*[15]
the accused was charged with having written and placed in an envelope
ready for posting to an address outside the country information which
might have assisted the foreign powers with whom South Africa was
then at war. The court accepted as not inherently improbable the
accused's explanation that he never intended to post the letter but had
written it to protect himself as a German national against the vengeance
that would have been taken against him for his work in the Censor's
Department by the seemingly victorious (at that time) Nazi government. The court accordingly acquitted him on the basis that the
state had not proved that it was his purpose to communicate the letter
or its contents to the enemy. The relevant words in the statutory crime
of espionage[16] refer to the making of a note 'which is calculated to be
or might be or is intended to be' useful to an enemy. Notwithstanding
the presence in the section of the words 'or might be' the court inter-

preted the crime restrictively by requiring proof of an intention to advantage an enemy. The espionage provision now in force[17] penalizes the making of a note 'likely . . . to be useful to an enemy', a wording which appears to preclude a repetition of the generous approach to the requirements of the crime adopted in *Wentzel's* case.[18] Yet the court's interpretation was a sensible view of what constitutes espionage even if a literal reading of the law suggests that an intention to advantage the enemy is not a requirement.

In the second case, *R v Vorster*,[19] the accused was charged with an act of espionage for having collected *inter alia* information concerning the number and calibre of guns at the naval base in Simonstown and the reliability of its personnel. The Appellate Division confirmed the conviction of the accused and in doing so held that the fact that information about a prohibited place had been obtained from a person unauthorized to communicate it brought into play the presumption[20] that an accused who had so obtained information was acting for a purpose prejudicial to the safety or interests of the state. Since the accused had not rebutted this presumption the court found that he had been correctly convicted of espionage. The establishment of guilt by means of a presumption in *R v Vorster* is perhaps only slightly disturbing in view of the fact that he had gathered highly sensitive defence material during a period of actual war. But the presumption could convert more innocent acts into criminal espionage and it is clearly undesirable that, in an offence as broadly framed as the crime of spying, proof of a vital element of the offence can be secured through a statutory deeming clause. The presumption would be more acceptable if espionage were limited to the communication or attempted communication of defence-related information to a foreign power. In that case it would not be unreasonable to require the communicator to establish an innocent purpose.[21]

Communication of Official Information

The South African offence of the unauthorized communication of official information[22] is a repetition of its British counterpart with minor and immaterial variations of wording. As there are no reported cases[23] dealing with this crime, it is unclear whether the courts will follow English authority to the effect that the offence is an absolute one. For reasons advanced in the chapter on the United Kingdom law,[24] the courts should require proof that the accused either knew or had grounds to believe that the information was official and that its communication was unauthorized. Furthermore, as suggested in the same chapter,[25] the courts, by a creative interpretation of the Act, could hold that the communication of information of government inefficiency, maladministration or corruption is 'in the interests of the Republic' and therefore not a crime.

Communication of Information with a Prejudicial Purpose

The chapter on United Kingdom law, in the section headed *Crimes Analogous to Spying*, dealt with the offence committed by a person who is in possession or control of information relating to 'munitions of war' and who communicates it to a foreign power (either directly or indirectly) or in any other manner prejudicial to the safety or interests of the State.[26] South African law has taken over and extended this offence.[27] In its extended form the provision refers not just to documentary or other information relating to 'munitions of war' but also to 'any military, police or security matter'. The offence in South Africa is therefore committed by any person who has in his possession or control any information relating to munitions of war or to *any military, police or security matter* and who publishes it or directly or indirectly communicates it to any person in any manner or for any purpose prejudicial to the safety or interests of the Republic.[28] A 'police matter' means any matter relating to the preservation of internal security or the maintenance of law and order by the police; and a 'security matter' means any matter relating to the security of the Republic, including matters dealt with by the Bureau for State Security (BOSS).[29] Whereas a statutory definition might normally be expected to pinpoint a matter described in general terms in the provision creating the crime, these definitions have the effect of broadening the generality and heightening the obscurity of the terms to which they refer. All that one can say with certainty is that all military, police and security matters are covered.

No offence is committed unless the publication or communication took place in a manner or for a purpose prejudicial to the safety or interests of the Republic. But a statutory presumption declares that if the communication appears prejudicial 'from the circumstances of the case or the conduct of the accused' the court may so accept it unless the accused proves the contrary.[30] Moreover, if the information was made, obtained, communicated et cetera by an unauthorized person a similar presumption of prejudicial purpose arises.[31] In *S v Marais*[32] the court accepted the finding in *Chandler v Director of Public Prosecutions*[33] that whatever the ultimate goal of an accused person it is sufficient for the purposes of guilt that he has committed towards the realization of his purpose any intermediate act which objectively speaking is prejudicial to the interests or safety of the Republic. *Mens rea*, the court said, may consist either of knowledge of the prejudicial consequence of such an act or of a culpable failure to appreciate the prejudicial result.[34] After this judgment and the publication of the Potgieter Report[35] into matters relating to state security, this approach to *mens rea* was made an explicit part of the crime and the statute now reads that the accused at the time of communication must either have known or had reason to believe that the information related to munitions of war, or a military, police or security matter.[36] A culpable failure to appreciate that it is so related coupled with the knowing commission of an act that is prejudicial in the objective sense satisfies the *mens rea* requirement of the crime.[37]

The accused in *S v Marais* was charged with communicating the contents of a government document sent to him anonymously which apparently revealed the existence of a secret section of the security police entrusted among other things with the duty of monitoring the telephone calls of certain opposition politicians. The accused believed that public knowledge of such activities was in the interests of the state rather than being prejudicial to them as claimed by the prosecution, and the act of communication alleged in the charge sheet was the transmission of a press statement on the subject to a journalist. The trial court had convicted him in a judgment which is itself a state secret and which is known only to the extent that the Appellate Division quoted short extracts in its judgment acquitting the accused. The basis of the acquittal was on the sole ground that the matters alluded to in the press statement were already general public knowledge and that communication could therefore not be regarded as prejudicial to the interests or safety of the state. An ironic consequence of this judgment is that those who first reveal the activities which the accused had communicated will be guilty but not those who publish them after they are known.[38] It is a pity that the court did not reach the question whether a first release of the material was not in the interests of the state as it purported to disclose misuse of police powers. The judgment in *Chandler* v *Director of Public Prosecutions* equating the interests of the state with those of the government of the day promises little comfort to an accused who has made such revelations; but it is primarily in a case of this kind that the authority of that case needs to be called into question.

The civil case of *Minister of Police* v *Marais*[39] in which the court granted an interdict prohibiting publication of what was apparently the same material[40] that led to Marais's prosecution, demonstrates the danger to civil liberty of the sweeping criminal prohibition on the communication of military, police and security matters. Though Marais was acquitted in the criminal case, the narrow basis of the court's judgment forces the conclusion that the two cases (the criminal and the civil) have the effect in general of precluding public knowledge and discussion of the use and abuse of police and military powers.

OTHER CRIMES UNDER THE OFFICIAL SECRETS ACT

Various crimes which are part of the British law on official secrets, such as those relating to the receipt or retention of information,[41] have been taken over with insignificant variations in the South African Act. This applies also to the crime of harbouring offenders under the Act except that the provisions[42] dealing with harbouring in South Africa have been extended to incorporate a new crime of failing to report certain information. Any person who is aware that a foreign agent, or a person who has been in contact with a foreign agent is in the Republic, commits a criminal offence if he fails to report to the police the presence of such agent or person or to give to the police information that he has in relation to them.[43] This provision puts upon subjects who have information an affirmative duty to report to the police and no prior request is necessary. 'Foreign agent' is broadly defined to include a person reasonably suspected of being employed by a foreign state or of having committed acts prejudicial to the safety or interests of the state.[44]

The British crime of failing to give information about the crime of spying after demand, or of giving false information in response to such demand, has not been adopted as part of the South African Act. The Criminal Procedure Act[45] authorizes a magistrate upon the request of a public prosecutor to examine any person in connection with any suspected offence[46] and failure to co-operate is a crime.[47] There is clearly no need to make separate provision for obtaining information in the Official Secrets Act. The section[48] in United Kingdom law equating an act preparatory to an offence with the substantive crime has no counterpart in the South African Act; but the other provisions of that section governing attempts, incitements et cetera are part of South African criminal law in general.[49]

PROCEDURAL PROVISIONS OF THE OFFICIAL SECRETS ACT

The South African procedural provisions closely parallel those of United Kingdom law and provide for the Attorney-General's consent to prosecutions,[50] for trial either at the place of the commission of the offence or where the accused 'happens to be'[51] and for *in camera* hearings.[52] No special provision is made for arrest and search without warrant since this is in any event authorized by the Criminal Procedure Act.[53]

CLASSIFICATION AND D NOTICES

There is no law or public regulation relating to classification in South Africa. Classification is clearly practised but the rules governing it and the criteria employed are themselves secret. A letter written by the author to the Secretary of the Public Service Commission requesting information on the rules and procedures governing classification produced a three-line letter of reply stating that the enquiry would be dealt with by the Director of Archives. This brief and uninformative reply reached the author in an envelope marked 'confidential'. In his letter, the Director of Archives merely drew attention to the provision of the Archives Act[54] under which archives are presently available to the public up to and including 31 December 1930. In terms of the Act, the Minister of National Education may prohibit access to particular records in the archives on grounds of public policy even if they are otherwise available to the public.[55] He may also grant access to archives not available to the public.[56] In both cases his ruling is final. Declassification in South Africa is achieved by the application of the provisions of the Archives Act and takes place, unless the Minister decides otherwise, approximately fifty years subsequent to the date of the relevant papers and documents. Classification remains a matter of deep mystery. No formal system similar to the British 'D' Notice system is in operation.[57]

OTHER LEGISLATION LIMITING ACCESS TO INFORMATION

The near universal coverage of the Official Secrets Act has not deterred the legislature from enacting specific measures designed to limit and control the flow of information about public affairs. This body of specific measures may be subdivided into the following categories: (a) Defence and Atomic Energy, (b) Internal Security (including the Prisons Act and Publications Control) and (c) Miscellaneous.

DEFENCE AND ATOMIC ENERGY

The Defence Act[58] prohibits the *publication* of three classes of information without ministerial authority. The prohibited categories are

1. Information relating to the composition, movements or disposition of the South African Defence Force (including established auxiliary services) or of the forces of allied countries and of South African or allied ships and aircraft used for naval or military purposes or to services or property commandeered or requisitioned under the Act.[59]
2. Statements, comments or rumours relating to a member or activity of the South African or a foreign defence force 'calculated'[60] to prejudice or embarrass the government in its foreign relations or to alarm or depress members of the public.[61]
3. Secret or confidential information relating to the defence of the Republic, including information relating to actual or proposed works connected with fortification or defence.[62]

With regard to the third category of information, the statute provides that all information relating to the defence of the Republic is presumed secret or confidential unless the contrary is proved[63] and that any information relating to military equipment is *deemed* secret unless publication has been authorized.[64] Any person who has taken part in the publication of any of the prohibited categories of information is guilty of the offence;[65] but for prosecutions in respect of the first two categories the written authority of the Attorney-General, or a person he has designated in writing, is required.[66]

These criminal prohibitions of the Defence Act are both narrower and broader than those of the Official Secrets Act. They are narrower because the information protected is defence information whereas the Official Secrets Act covers all kinds of information. The provisions are broader mainly on account of the reference to the forces of allied or foreign powers. This has the effect of making defence information which is foreign a protected secret within South Africa. News of a build-up of military forces in a neighbouring hostile country could 'alarm or depress' members of the public and therefore fall under the second category of prohibited material. In *Minister van Verdediging* v *John Meinert (Edms) Bpk*[67] the court decided that a report about an alleged dangerous incursion into South West Africa (Namibia) of guerilla fighters was not prohibited by the Act only because it referred to the calling up of the police reserve and not the Defence Force reserve units. Otherwise the report was found to be one which could reasonably alarm or depress members of the public. Another sense in which the Defence Act prohibitions are narrower is that they punish 'publication' and not the broader act of 'communication' that constitutes a contravention of the Official Secrets Act. Publish must mean to make known to a substantial segment of the public, although there may be a difference here between the first two categories which may not be published 'in any newspaper, magazine, book or pamphlet or by radio or any other means' and the third category which may not be published 'in any manner whatsoever'. Whatever the difference is between these two restrictions on publication, neither can be equated with *communication* to a person or persons which does not have the connotation of being made known generally.

Whatever the extent of overlap between the Defence and Official Secrets Acts may be,[68] it is plain that the former has the effect of depriving the general public of the right to all information, whether directly or remotely connected with defence, unless publication is officially sanctioned. In order to fortify this blanket ban on knowledge about defence matters, the Act also makes it a crime for any government official or contractor with government (or any employee of such contractor) or any person to whom the information has been given in confidence, to communicate any secret or confidential defence information learnt by reason of office or employment to any other person unless disclosure was authorized by the Minister or a competent court or it was the duty of the communicator in the interests of the State to disclose the information.[69] Information is presumed to be secret or confidential unless the contrary is proved[70] and an accused who is or was an official, contractor or employee is presumed to have acquired the information by virtue of office or contract unless he establishes that he did not.[71] This crime closely parallels the offence of disclosing public information under the Official Secrets Act.[72] It makes the mere disclosure to a single unauthorized person of secret or confidential defence information a crime. Even information about general defence policy is covered unless the government chooses to make it known or the accused can show that it was his duty in the interests of the state to make it known. Whether a disclosure for the purpose of encouraging public debate on defence policy could be regarded as being in the interests of the state is doubtful.

The provisions of the Defence Act analysed above put newspapers seeking to publish anything relating to defence in an invidious position. Though there is no D-notice system to guide them, an 'agreement' between the Minister of Defence and the Newspaper Press Union is in operation.[73] This does not in any way lessen the impact of the Act on publication but essentially provides a procedure for the clearance of statements or reports which the press wish to publish. The agreement requires the press to refer such matters to a public relations officer or to the military chiefs or heads of sections but declares that statements on military policy must be referred to the Minister or Commandant-General. The press is enjoined not to publish even the fact that the Minister has been approached or has refused to comment, where he so requests. Gagging is itself a secret. Reporters are required by the agreement to understand that 'there should not be any arguments with the Minister' or his officials where news has leaked out and that a refusal to authorize publication of such leaks must be accepted. In one respect the agreement appears to assist the press: it authorizes the publication without clearance of a public statement of the Prime Minister, leader of the Opposition or other 'responsible official' of a foreign country on defence matters affecting South Africa provided that the person is named and the source of the news mentioned.

In view of the terms of the agreement, and the fact that it is adminis-tered solely by Defence officialdom, it is not surprising that virtually no advantages have accrued to the press. Under its operation, the press has frequently been prevented from making known locally news that has been widely publicized abroad, including such matters as the 1975 Angolan intervention and the recent visit of a military chief to the United States of America.[74] A great deal of information concerning operations in the so-called operational area on South Africa's borders is blacked out by the Act and the provisions of the agreement.

Until 1977 the Defence Act provided for the introduction of a general censorship only in times of war.[75] By amendments[76] introduced in that year, the State President is authorized to introduce a general censorship over postal, telegraphic, telephonic or radio services and over 'written or printed matter' by proclamation in the Gazette. He is authorized to do this either during 'operations in defence of the Republic' or for the prevention or suppression of terrorism or internal disorder. The amendment confers upon the government a limitless power to control communication and, of course, access to information about matters connected directly or indirectly with defence or internal security. While the measure does not appear to authorize direct censorship over newspapers such control could be achieved indirectly by chilling communication channels and sources on which the press relies.[77] This is a true garrison state enactment which will frustrate both knowledge and discussion of vital matters of general public interest when the law is implemented by the authorities.

The Defence Act contains a common statutory provision prohibiting the taking of photographs or the making of sketches, plans, models or notes of military places or installations without the authority of the Minister or a person designated by him.[78] The possession of cameras or other apparatus for the taking of photographs in such areas is also prohibited[79] and the authorities are empowered to seize and confiscate photographs, sketches, plans et cetera or cameras or other similar apparatus.[80] Finally, attention is directed to the power to prohibit entry to military premises[81] and to the provisions of the Military Code which prohibits service members from disclosing certain specified information such as watchwords or the numbers, movements, locations or preparations of the Defence Force.[82]

Various statutes relating to nuclear energy and installations incorporate provisions prohibiting the disclosure of information. The most important is a section of the Atomic Energy Act[83] which makes it a crime to disclose to any person or to publish without permission information relating to source materials[84] or ores containing source materials or relating to any research or any invention or discovery concerning source material, nuclear material or nuclear or atomic energy whether the information originates within or without the Republic.[85] It is also an offence to receive information knowing or having reasonable grounds to believe that it has been communicated in breach of the crime just described[86] or, having obtained possession of information which may not be communicated, to fail to take steps to safeguard it or to act so as to endanger its secrecy.[87] The offences do not reach disclosures to a patent agent, attorney or advocate in the course of a professional consultation[88] but otherwise their coverage is universal. Prosecutions require the written authority of the Attorney-General and may be held *in camera* if the Minister so directs.[89] The Atomic Energy Act also prohibits the disclosure of information gained by inspection or submission of returns under its provisions without the consent of the person from whom it was obtained.[90] A similar provision prohibiting disclosure of information obtained in the exercise of powers appears in the Nuclear Installations (Licensing and Security) Act.[91] Finally, regulations enacted under the Uranium Enrichment Act[92] create offences identical to those of the Atomic Energy Act already described except that in this case the material protected is information relating to anything done by the Uranium Enrichment Corporation of South Africa Ltd, whether within the exercise of its powers or otherwise.[93]

The provisions controlling information relating to nuclear energy and installations are in one sense broader than those prohibiting the disclosure of information under the Official Secrets Act. The latter Act in general prohibits disclosure of official information whereas the laws now under discussion generally protect all information in the defined class, whether official or unofficial. The reach of the law therefore extends outside the appropriate government departments or government created boards or corporations, to information in the hands of private bodies and citizens. It covers researchers in the field of nuclear science and even teachers who could breach the provision of the Act by discussion in the classroom or with colleagues. While there are no court pronouncements on the *mens rea* requirement of the crime of communicating protected nuclear or related information, it appears from the wording of the statute that the simple act of knowingly transmitting information that is objectively within the definition of protected material is a contravention of the law.

INTERNAL SECURITY LEGISLATION

Many and perhaps most of South Africa's wide-ranging security laws indirectly limit the availability of information about aspects of government administration. The 1976 riots and unrest have provided at least one striking example of this in the form of the detention of an entire team of reporters of the newspaper *The World*. The reporters were covering the riots and were arrested whilst on duty and detained in terms of the Internal Security Act.[94] Quite obviously their reporting, thus cut off by incarceration, would have included important information about government and police policy and activities in relation to the unrest. In a similar way the 'banning' under the Internal Security Act of either persons or publications may be an effective method of staunching the flow of information about aspects of public administration. The procedures for banning in themselves constitute a device for shielding government security operations since the Minister is required by the Act[95] to reveal only such facts and reasons underlying his decision to ban as in his opinion may be disclosed without detriment to public policy. While the self-prescribed limits of this work preclude discussion of the right of a party to a dispute to information from the other party, it is relevant to record that the denial of information to parties affected by banning necessarily involves a denial of information to the general public on an important aspect of administration. The leading case on the question, *Minister van Justisie* v *Alexander*,[96] clearly attributes the Minister's right to refuse reasons to a banned person, to a public policy principle derived from the Act that the information in question should not be spread abroad.[97]

Though it would be possible to give many other examples of indirect control of information through the internal security programme, the concern of this work is with laws directly affecting access to information and of these a few appear in security legislation. The Internal Security Act[98] authorizes the State President to ban a publication on the ground that he believes *inter alia* that it conveys *information* calculated 'to further the achievment of any of the objects of communism' or 'to endanger the security of the state or the maintenance of public order'. The review committee appointed under the same Act to make recommendations as to the detention[99] of persons operates in secret and it is specifically declared that its deliberations and recommendations shall not be disclosed except to persons who have a duty to deal with the 'subject matter of the disclosure'.[100] Only persons in the service of the state while performing their official functions have a right to inspect the committee's records.[101] The composition of the review committee has been a closely-guarded secret, thus depriving both the detainee and the public at large of knowing what persons, with what backgrounds and qualifications, are adjudicating upon the loss of liberty of subjects detained under the law. Since the detainees themselves have been denied information about the identity of members of the review committee they are thereby deprived of the power to raise against members of the committee such basic requirements of natural justice as the rule that no one shall judge a matter in which he has an interest. The Minister of Justice has stated that he would introduce legislation to prohibit even the publication of names of persons detained[102] when Parliament reassembled in 1978. At present such publication is not prohibited although the Minister has frequently declined to release the names or numbers of detainees. According to the Terrorism Act,[103] no person other than the Minister or an officer of the state about his official duties is entitled to any information relating to or obtained from a detainee under that Act. The Natal court in the case of *Nxasana* v *Minister of Justice*[104] held that the effect of this provision is not to make the information a state secret. The court said that it 'merely entitles the authorities to refuse, if they wish, to reveal the official information themselves' and that an outsider 'remains free to get it elsewhere when he can, and to pass it on when he likes'. Therefore the effect of the provision is to entitle the authorities to withhold the information if they so wish. In *Nxasana's* case the court held that it had the power to obtain evidence by interrogatory through the magistrate empowered to visit a detainee where a prima facie case of maltreatment is made out; but the court declared that on the facts no such case had been made out.

The Prisons Act[105] incorporates provisions which can be applied to restrict access to information. The first makes it a criminal offence to make a sketch or take a photograph of a prison or any portion of a prison or to publish any such sketch or photograph (or to cause it to be published) without the authority in writing of the Commissioner of Prisons.[106] A related prohibition forbids the making of a sketch or the taking of a photograph of any prisoner or group of prisoners without the written authority of the Commissioner unless it was made or taken at a court (or adjacent premises) at the time of the appearance of the prisoner or prisoners as accused and used 'in connection with' such court or adjacent premises.[107] The publication without authority of any sketch or photograph of any prisoner or group of prisoners is also forbidden unless it was made or taken in the manner just described and is published within 30 days of arrest or conviction.[108] Prisoner is widely defined in the Act to include any person detained in custody, whether convicted or not, or who is being transferred in custody, and for purposes of the prohibitions now under discussion includes even the corpse of an executed prisoner.[109] An amendment introduced in 1977[110] prohibits publication without the written authority of the commissioner of any 'writing, statement, life story or biographical sketch . . . of a prisoner concerning the offence as a result of which he became a prisoner' unless admitted in evidence at his trial.

Another relevant provision of the Act prohibits the publication of any false information concerning the experience in prison of any prisoner or ex-prisoner or relating to the administration of any prison.[111] The accused is guilty if he knew the information to be false or if he failed to take reasonable steps to verify its accuracy.[112] 'Publish' in this context was held in S v Kiley[113] to bear the same meaning as it does in defamation so that transmission to one other person could constitute an offence.[114] In S v South African Associated Newspapers,[115] where the prosecution was based on the revelations of a political prisoner about prison conditions, the court subjected publishers to unrealistically onerous duties under the requirement of the statute that the information must be verified prior to publication.[116] The onus of showing that reasonable steps to verify have been taken is on the accused and it was held not discharged in that case.

Those provisions of the Prisons Act which restrict the publication of photographs or sketches of prisons or prisoners or of statements or life stories connected with the prisoner's crime are arguably necessary to prevent the planning of escapes, the invasion of privacy or the glorification of crime. While they do prevent information from reaching the public, the general interest in such information is low and should perhaps yield to the interests sought to be advanced by the statute. The same cannot be said of the prohibition on the publication of information concerning experiences in prison or prison administration. It is true that what is prohibited here is the publication of *false* information; but the case of S v SA Associated Newspapers[118] has demonstrated the extreme difficulty of rebutting official information about what goes on within the walls of a prison. The provision comes very close to permitting criticism of government if the critic can prove his factual statements to be true.[119] In practice, the law now operates as an effective legal barrier to the publication of any adverse information about prison conditions, and the adjective 'false', which qualifies 'information' in the Act, can be taken as *pro non scripto*, at least for practical purposes. Significantly, no one has attempted a public exposé of prison conditions since the *SA Associated Newspapers* case. The result is that the important interest of full public knowledge about the treatment of society's criminals has been sacrificed in favour of a rather weak interest in personal privacy and to an even weaker interest of the government in being protected from harmful publicity. The balance of interests which this particular provision achieves is not one that a democracy can afford to tolerate.

The Publications Act 1974[120] is South Africa's chief instrument of censorship. Under its provisions, a powerful and elaborate state mechanism for controlling publications, films and entertainments has been set up. In general, the Act prohibits, on pain of criminal penalties, the distribution, publication or exhibition of publications, films or entertainments that have been found to be undesirable by the appropriate administrative bodies created under its terms.[121] It is also a crime to 'produce' an undesirable publication or object, and on such a charge the finding of undesirability may be made by a committee appointed under the Act at any time prior to the institution of the prosecution. The committee's finding binds the court in criminal proceedings under the Act. The right of appeal to the ordinary courts which was available under the previous Act[122] (except in relation to films) has been abolished and replaced by a right to review of the decisions of the appeal board set up under the current Act. In effect, therefore, government-appointed boards have the final say on censorship decisions unless a review lies on the basis of irregularity; and even then the court is required to refer the matter back to the appeal board for final resolution unless it finds that the Board acted mala fide.[123]

The criterion for a censorship decision under the Act is the undesirability of the material in question in the opinion of the appropriate committee or appeal board. The definition of 'undesirable' is broad enough to put the committee almost entirely at large in its findings.[124] For purposes of this study, which is concerned with access to information rather than the freedom to express opinions and beliefs, it is especially important that the definition could justify the suppression of information about public affairs. According to the statutory definition, material is undesirable if *inter alia* it 'is prejudicial to the safety of the State, the general welfare or the peace and good order'.[125] Publications intended to provide citizens with information about aspects of government administration can be censored under such broad descriptions of undesirability. An example of the use of the Act for such purposes was the banning in September 1976 of a Christian Institute publication entitled *South Africa—A 'Police State'?*[126] The publication listed people held in detention under various security laws, described details of the major political trials of the previous three years and indicated the type of torture that had allegedly been used by the police. While the Publications Act does not specifically restrict access to information, as this single example illustrates it is an effective law for preventing the distribution of information and thereby its availability to the general public. Many other similar prohibitions have been imposed since the banning of the Christian Institute publication.

MISCELLANEOUS LEGISLATION

A measure introduced in 1974[127] prohibits any person from furnishing information as to any business in response to any 'order, direction or letters of request issued or emanating from outside the Republic' without the permission of the Minister of Economic Affairs. The parliamentary debates on the introduction of this provision are not a model of clarity. The Minister of Justice said in moving the second reading that it was intended 'for the protection of South African and related undertakings against the furnishing of information which may be prejudicial to them'.[128] The true rationale of the law that emerged during the debates appears to be the protection of the employees of South African businesses against the assertion of jurisdiction by foreign courts or other authorities for the purpose of securing information outside the Republic.[129] The provision is likely to have as small effect on the subject's right to learn about public affairs within the Republic even though the word 'business' is wide enough to cover the work of semi-public corporations.[130] However, wage surveys such as those conducted in relation to British businesses operating in South Africa under direction of the House of Commons may well fall under the terms of this law. In that event, an indirect source of information about South Africa labour practices might be cut off in the future.

The Wage Act[131] prohibits on pain of criminal punishment the disclosure by wage board members and other designated officers of information 'in regard to the affairs of any person, firm or business' acquired in the exercise of powers or the performance of duties under the Act. Disclosure to the Minister, certain officers and statutory and other bodies is excepted and the Minister is empowered to release reports notwithstanding the prohibition so long as he does not disclose names and identities where information relating to finances or trade processes is revealed. The material protected by this prohibition is far too broad and it has been used to deny trade unions the official result of complaints taken up on behalf of their members.[132] Instead of protecting information relating to the affairs in general of 'any person, firm or business', the statute should be restricted to material the release of which would injure personal privacy or the competitive position of the individual or business involved. As presently worded the prohibition can be used to shield undesirable and even illegal labour practices. Equally broad restrictions on disclosure of a similar nature appear in the Industrial Conciliation Act,[133] the Bantu Labour Relations Act,[134] the Shops and Offices Act[135] and the Apprenticeship Act,[136] and all these measures could be used to limit general knowledge of important public issues. A more acceptable formulation appears in the Factories, Machinery and Building Work Act[137] where secrecy is required in respect of 'information relating to any trade process or trade secret or the financial affairs of any person'.

Another instance of an unnecessarily broad secrecy clause appears in the South African Reserve Bank Act[138] which prohibits officers and employees of the bank from disclosing, except to the Treasury or a court of law or in the performance of their duties, any information which they acquire in the course of their duties relating to 'the affairs of the bank, a stockholder or customer of the bank'. Not all the affairs of the bank require such protection and no attempt has been made by the legislature to designate the type of information which requires protection against disclosure.

There are several statutes which prohibit the disclosure of information in the interests of privacy. Examples are the Census Act[139] which requires the submission of certain information[140] but provides for the punishment of a census officer who divulges information obtained in the course of his duties;[141] the Statistics Act[142] which contains almost identical provisions[143] and the Income Tax Act[144] which provides for the preservation of secrecy in relation to information acquired in the course of its administration.[145] There is little point in providing an exhaustive catalogue of such measures.

BREACH OF CONFIDENCE

Any action comparable to breach of confidence in English law will have a restricted operation in the jurisdiction of South African courts on account of the absence of the 'broad principle of equity' on which the English remedy now rests. It is true that in *Goodman* v *Von Moltke*[146] a South African court somewhat uncritically took over the English doctrine and applied it to interdict publication of information derived from stolen letters ·or documents.[147] Subsequent judgments of the courts have been more cautious and have allowed an action only within the principles of the South African law of delict. In *Dun* v *SA Merchants Combined Credit Bureau*[148] and *Oude Meester Group* v *Stellenbosch Wine Trust*[149] the misuse of information complained of amounted to wrongful interference with trade activities and the court based liability firmly on Aquilian principles.

South African common law clearly offers more restricted possibilities of limiting access to public information. An action brought to achieve that end would have to be based either on contract or upon the general principles of liability in the law of delict. If based on contract, the action will be confined to the contractual parties and not, for example, to a journalist into whose hands the contractually secret information fortuitously comes. The journalist could not be restrained from publishing on the basis of 'implied contract' without introducing breach of confidence through the back door. The Aquilian action with its requirement of patrimonial loss has little relevance to public information and will be applicable mainly in interference with trade situations.

There remains the possibility of a delictual action based on injury to personal rights—the *actio injuriarum*.[150] Again the possibilities for restricting access to information about public affairs appear to be limited. Even where an invasion of personal privacy can be shown to result from the release of such information, the countervailing general interest in knowledge of matters of public concern will generally override the individual interest of personality. In *Goodman* v *Von Moltke*[151] the defendant advanced but was unable to demonstrate a broad public interest in learning about the contents of the stolen documents. The necessity for balancing the personal interest in privacy against the important public interest in knowledge of the affairs of society has occasionally been overlooked by writers who assert that the press will be interdicted from publishing information about secret organizations.[152] If the secret organization is one in which the public has an interest because, for example, it operates as a subterranean pressure group in the political decision-making processes, it is hard to accept that the law of delict can guarantee an absolute right of secrecy for that organization. The right of privacy is clearly qualified in our law by a doctrine of public interest similar to that which limits actions for defamation.[153]

COPYRIGHT LAW

The South African law of copyright is in all material respects similar to that of the United Kingdom in respect of the state ownership of copyright in 'literary' materials. The state is entitled by virtue of the Copyright Act[154] to the copyright in literary material 'made by or under the direction or control of the Government' and to material first published in the Republic if 'published by or under the direction or control of the state'.[155] The remarks made in relation to the law of the United Kingdom[156] are applicable to South African law except that by recent amendment to the South African law[157] the criminal penalties for infringements are now substantially higher[158] than those applicable in Britain. Other differences of note are that there is apparently no general defence that publication was in the public interest in South Africa;[159] and that there is apparently no self-imposed limitation on the enforcement of state copyright similar to the British restraints incorporated in a Treasury Circular of 1958.[160] Subject to these remarks, the South African law is at least as effective an instrument for controlling the flow of public information as the law applicable in Great Britain.

BRIEF EVALUATION OF THE SOUTH AFRICAN LAWS

Except for breach of confidence, the general body of laws designed to make government business secret is substantially similar to the *corpus* of laws that are operative in the United Kingdom. The Official Secrets Act is a little broader and cloudier than its British counterpart; and there are provisions relating mainly to internal security and publications which have no place at all in the British legal system. Nevertheless, the legal regulation of access to information in the two countries is surprisingly similar, and the differences between these two societies lie in the realm of the non-legal.[161] There is in the United Kingdom a current of legal reform, though it is at present running rather weakly. In South Africa, the direction of change has been the reverse, and contemporary signs indicate that the laws and practices will become harsher still. Though prosecutions in South Africa have taken place only occasionally, the political system is essentially a closed one on account of the socio-political situation rather than the laws. Paradoxically, the negligible degree of reliance upon law to enforce secrecy has not diminished the government's appetite for new restrictive laws. The outlook for reform of secrecy laws in South Africa is bleak.

NOTES

[1] For example, section 86(2) of the Local Authorities Ordinance 25 of 1974 (N) and section 23 of the Local Government Ordinance 17 of 1939 (T). Section 51(7) of the Municipal Ordinance 20 of 1974 (C) does purport to restrict the right of a council to resolve itself into a closed session to specific matters but one of the grounds specified is the belief of the council that an item of business to be transacted 'relates to any other matter prejudicial to the interests of the municipality'.

[2] These are generally open to inspection: See, for example, section 89(2) of the Local Authorities Ordinance 25 of 1974 (N), section 55(6) of the Municipal Ordinance 20 of 1974 (C) and section 33(1) of the Local Government Ordinance 17 of 1939 (T).

[3] Section 209 of the Municipal Ordinance 20 of 1974 (C) and section 84(1) of the Local Authorities Ordinance 25 of 1974 (N). The court held in *Gubb v Cape Town Municipality* 1977 (1) SA 249 (C) that section 52 of Ordinance 20 of 1974 (C) (prohibiting disclosure of certain confidential information) overrides even the discovery powers of the Supreme Court in litigation before it.

[4] 1953 (3) SA 525 (W) 528. See also *Bell v Van Rensburg* 1971 (3) SA 693 (C) at 722.

[5] The court was apparently untroubled by the dubious nature of this right when it is applied to public documents. It is not clear, for example, who 'owns' such documents.

[6] Act 16 of 1956.

[7] The Official Secrets Act 16 of 1956.

[8] Notice of its applicability to South Africa by virtue of sections 10, 11 and 12 was given in GN 472 of 2 April 1912 (GG 219 of 2 April 1912).

[9] Unchanged in the sense that it was unaffected by the changes brought about in Britain by the Official Secrets Act of 1920 and 1939.

[10] The Appellate Division held the Act applicable to South Africa in *R v Vorster* 1941 AD 472, confirming the Transvaal decision in *R v Wentzel* 1940 WLD 269. See also *R v Heard* 1937 CPD 401.

[11] *S v Marais* 1971 (1) SA 844 (AD). This case is discussed below.

[12] A S Mathews 'Disclose and be Damned—The Law Relating to Official Secrets' 1975 *THRHR* 348.

[13] Section 2 of the Official Secrets Act 1956, corresponding to section 1 of the Official Secrets Act 1911.

[14] The crime is bolstered by the same presumptions that operate in British law. However, section 7A, which was introduced in 1969, creates a presumption that material is useful to an enemy if the accused is an actual or suspected foreign agent or if he is employed or suspected of being employed by a foreign or international institution or if he entered or is within the Republic in contravention of any law.

[15] 1940 (2) PH H169 (W).

[16] Section 1 of the Official Secrets Act 1911.

[17] Section 2 of the Official Secrets Act 16 of 1956.

[18] Milton & Fuller in *South African Criminal Law and Procedure* (Juta, 1971) vol III 139 argue that the wording of the 1911 Act justified the restricted approach in *Wentzel's* case whereas the present wording dispenses with the requirement of intention to advantage an enemy. Yet it seems that a strict approach is compatible with both the earlier and the later provisions.

[19] 1941 AD 472.

[20] Of section 1(2) of the Official Secrets Act 1911.

[21] The other presumptions have been referred to briefly in the chapter on United Kingdom law. As Milton & Fuller op cit 140 point out, one of these (section 7(1)) has the effect of establishing both the *actus reus* and the *mens rea*.

[22] Section 3(1) of the Official Secrets Act 1956, corresponding to section 2 of the Act of 1911.

[23] There is a judgment on the corresponding section in the Rhodesian statute which holds that all information, regardless of its nature, is protected (in this case a government report on the suitability of an area as a park): See *R* v *Savory* 1973 (4) SA 417 (RAD).

[24] See chapter VI, p 110.

[25] See chapter VI, p 111.

[26] See chapter VI, p 107.

[27] Section 3(2) of the Official Secrets Act 16 of 1956.

[28] The reference in the British statute to communication to a foreign power has been dropped.

[29] The definitions appear in section 3(2)(*b*).

[30] Section 8(1).

[31] Ibid. For the requirements which must be satisfied before this presumption operates see *S* v *Niesewand* (2) 1973 (3) SA 584 (RAD) at 586–7.

[32] 1971 (1) SA 844 (AD).

[33] [1962] 3 All ER 142 (HL).

[34] *S* v *Marais (supra)* at 850–1.

[35] Report of the Commission of Enquiry into Matters Relating to Security of the State, RP 102/1971. (Referred to below as the 'Potgieter Report'.)

[36] Section 3(2)(*a*)(iii).

[37] In *S* v *Niesewand* (2) 1973 (3) SA 584 (RAD) the Rhodesian Appeal Court said in relation to the Rhodesian counterpart to section 3(2) that 'the purpose of the accused may in some cases be proved by the avowed purpose of the act itself, and in others on the basis that the accused must have known that the act which he committed would probably be prejudicial to the safety or interests of the state, irrespective of whether or not he wanted that object to be achieved' (at 586).

[38] A S Mathews loc cit 358.

[39] 1970 (2) SA 467 (C).

[40] The court was shown a copy of the material but did not reveal its content in its judgment.

[41] Also those relating to obstruction at prohibited places, wearing of uniforms without authority, making of false declarations, impersonation and forgery. The UK provisions regarding accommodation addresses and telegrams do not appear in the SA Act. Telegrams in South Africa fall under the extensive jurisdiction of the Postmaster-General: see section 78 of the Post Office Act 44 of 1958. Interception of telegrams is provided for in section 118A of the Act.

[42] Section 6.

[43] Section 6(*c*). The penalty provided is a fine of not exceeding R400 or imprisonment not exceeding twelve months, or both.

[44] Section 1(1).

[45] 51 of 1977.

[46] Section 205.

[47] Section 189. A punishment of imprisonment of up to two years may be imposed for each contravention. If the enquiry relates to certain offences under the Internal Security Act 44 of 1950, imprisonment of up to five years may be imposed.

[48] Section 7 of the Official Secrets Act 1920.

[49] Section 18 of the Riotous Assemblies Act 17 of 1956.

[50] Section 10. Offences for obstruction under section 5 do not require his consent.

[51] Section 9.

[52] Section 12.

[53] See generally chapters 2 & 5 of Act 51 of 1977.

[54] 6 of 1962.

[55] Section 9.

[56] Ibid.

[57] An 'agreement' between the Newspaper Press Union and the Minister of Defence will be discussed in the section below dealing with the Defence Act.

[58] 44 of 1957.

[59] Section 118(1)(a). A statement, comment or rumour having the effect of directly or indirectly conveying this information is also covered.

[60] 'Calculated' on a strict interpretation means intended. The courts are more likely to interpret it to mean 'having the effect of'. In Minister van Verdediging v John Meinert (Edms) Bpk 1976 (4) SA 113 (SWA) the court declared that 'calculated' means that there must be a reasonable probability that the statement will cause alarm.

[61] Section 118(1)(b).

[62] Section 118(2).

[63] Section 118(5).

[64] Section 118(6). 'Deemed' in this context appears to mean 'conclusively deemed'.

[65] Section 118(3). The penalties (prescribed by section 127) are a fine of not more than R1 000, imprisonment for not more than five years, or both.

[66] Section 118(IA).

[67] Supra.

[68] It is specifically provided that section 118 does not bar prosecutions under other laws: see section 118(7).

[69] Section 118(4).

[70] Section 118(5)(a).

[71] Section 118(5)(b).

[72] But it does not punish subsequent transmissions of the secret or confidential material. Such subsequent transmissions could be punished under the sections of the Act which prohibit publication or under the Official Secrets Act.

[73] The 'agreement' is summarized by K W Stuart in The Newspaperman's Guide to the Law 2 ed (Butterworths, Durban, 1977) 135. He speaks of the 'concessions' in the agreement but these are hard to discern. A more detailed account of the agreement is given by Strauss, Strydom & Van der Walt Die Suid-Afrikaanse Persreg 3 ed (J L van Schaik, Pretoria, 1976).

[74] A newspaper which did publish news of his visit was rebuked by the Defence Department.

[75] Section 101.

[76] Section 7 of the Defence Amendment Act 35 of 1977 introducing a new section 101(1).

[77] The provision refers to 'written or printed matter' which is 'addressed or intended to be delivered or conveyed to any person', an inappropriate wording if the intention was to cover the press directly.

[78] Section 119(1)(a). The prohibition extends to places used for military or defence purposes or under military control, and also to 'any object therein'.

[79] Section 119(1)(b). The penalty for this offence, and for the offence of taking photographs, making sketches etc is a fine not exceeding R200 or imprisonment not exceeding six months, or both.

[80] Section 119(2).

[81] Section 89.

[82] § 8 of Schedule I to the Defence Act 44 of 1957.

[83] 90 of 1967.

[84] As defined in section 1.

[85] Section 30(1)(a). The section has been summarized in the text. The maximum penalties are a fine of R10 000, imprisonment for twenty years, or both. The Atomic Energy Amendment Act 46 of 1978 extensively extended the range of protected material.

[86] Section 30(1)(b).

[87] Section 30(1)(c).

[88] Section 30(2).

[89] Section 30(3) and (4).

[90] Section 9(4).

[91] 43 of 1963 section 11.

[92] 33 of 1970 section 8(1)(*d*).

[93] § 6(2) of the regulations published as Proclamation R263 of 26 February 1971 (*Reg Gaz* 1404).

[94] Act 44 of 1950. The relevant section is 10(1)(*a*)*bis* introduced by section 4 of the Internal Security Amendment Act 79 of 1976. A report of the detentions appears in the *Daily News* of 27 October 1976. *The World* has since been banned and its editor detained.

[95] For example, section 9(2) of Act 44 of 1950.

[96] 1975 (4) SA 530 (AD).

[97] The court, by a majority, held that the Act displaced the moderately progressive rule of state privilege adopted in *Van der Linde* v *Calitz* 1967 (2) SA 239 (AD), which allows the court, at least in cases not involving national security, to determine the question whether disclosure should be prohibited on the ground of public policy. Section 29 of the General Law Amendment Act 101 of 1969 puts the issue of state privilege beyond the control of the courts where the Minister declares on affidavit that the material affects the security of the state and that disclosure would be prejudicial.

[98] No 44 of 1950 section 6(*d*) and (*d*A).

[99] Under section 10(1)(*a*)*bis*.

[100] Section 10*sex*(9).

[101] Section 10*sex*(10). No penalties for contravention of this subsection or of subsection (9) are provided.

[102] See *Daily News* 24 August 1976. In subsequent reports the Minister said the purpose was to protect the detainees and to avoid stimulation of unrest. He added that he might authorize publication with the consent of the detainee, an exception that appears to contradict his second reason: see *Daily News* 25 August 1976.

[103] 83 of 1967 section 6(6).

[104] 1976 (3) SA 745 (D). The court followed *S* v *Moumbaris* 1973 (3) SA 109 (T) and dissented from an unreported Transvaal case which held that even a court investigating maltreatment of a detainee could not obtain the official information by an interrogatory.

[105] 8 of 1959.

[106] Section 44(*e*)(i) and (ii). The section has been abbreviated in the text and reference to sketches or photographs of burials has been omitted. Photograph is widely defined in section 1.

[107] Section 44(*e*)(iii). Section 27A of the Police Act 7 of 1958 contains similar prohibitions on sketching or photographing persons in lawful custody (or fugitives from lawful custody) and on publishing such sketches or photographs prior to the commencement of the trial.

[108] Section 44(*e*)(iv). The prohibition also applies to photographs and sketches taken or made before imprisonment and these may not be published without permission after the expiration of the 30-day period even if they are used in a context unconnected with the crime. This aspect of the prohibition is far too broad.

[109] Section 1.

[110] Section 44(*g*) introduced by section 6 of the Prisons Amendment Act 88 of 1977.

[111] Section 44(*f*). The requirements for conviction were set out in *S* v *Theron* 1968 (4) SA 61 (T). An almost identically worded prohibition relating to the publication of false information relating to mental institutions appears in section 66A of the Mental Health Act 18 of 1973.

[112] Ibid.

[113] 1962 (3) SA 318 (T).

[114] This is a dubious interpretation: see A S Mathews *Law, Order and Liberty in South Africa* (Juta, 1971) 216.

[115] 1970 (1) SA 469 (W).

[116] A S Mathews op cit 214–17.

[117] If the provision is intended to further prison security, for example, by making it more difficult to plan escapes, the interest it seeks to further is more defensible but can only be ineffectually realized by such prohibitions.

[118] *Supra*. The court (at 473–4) rejected a narrow interpretation of the prohibition which would have confined it to publication of the personal experiences of an identified prisoner.

[119] Though the onus is on the state to prove that the information is false, grave diffi-

culties confront an accused who is charged under the section. Prison officials who are prepared to testify about malpractice in their prisons are rare birds, and the difficulty of persuading prisoners or ex-prisoners to give evidence in rebuttal of the 'five star' treatment usually alleged by authorities is very great indeed. A real fear of retribution exists among persons who have been victims of the system.

[120] 42 of 1974.

[121] Sections 8, 19 and 30. Very limited exemptions from control for technical, scientific, professional or religious publications were abolished by section 6(*a*) of the Publications Amendment Act 79 of 1977.

[122] The Publications and Entertainments Act 26 of 1963.

[123] Section 39.

[124] Section 47(2).   [125] Ibid.

[126] GN 1824 of 29 September 1976 (GG 5306 of 29 September 1976).

[127] Section 2 of the Second General Law Amendment Act 94 of 1974. The maximum penalties for breach of the provision are a fine of R2 000 or imprisonment for two years, or both.

[128] House of Assembly Debates 31 October 1974 col 7265.

[129] House of Assembly Debates 31 October 1974 col 7306.

[130] For example, the Iron and Steel Corporation.

[131] 5 of 1957 section 12.

[132] *Daily News* of 20 September 1977.

[133] 28 of 1956 section 67.   [134] 48 of 1953 section 21.

[135] 75 of 1964 section 25.   [136] 37 of 1944 section 15.

[137] 22 of 1941 section 8.   [138] 29 of 1944 section 20.

[139] 76 of 1957.   [140] Section 9.

[141] Section 12.   [142] 73 of 1957.

[143] Sections 5, 6 and 9.

[144] 58 of 1962.

[145] Section 4. The exessive protection of secrecy under this Act is illustrated by the fact that judgments of the special tax court are not publishable without the taxpayer's consent: *Estate Dempers* v *Secretary for Inland Revenue* 1977 (3) SA 410 (AD) at 420.

[146] 1938 CPD 153 at 157.

[147] The adoption by the court of the breach of confidence rule may have been unnecessary since copyright law would appear to afford adequate protection on the facts of the case.

[148] 1968 (1) SA 209 (C).

[149] 1972 (3) SA 152 (C).

[150] W A Joubert in *Grondslae van die Persoonlikheidsreg* (A A Balkema, Cape Town, 1953) 147n98 declares that *Goodman v Von Moltke* (*supra*) can only legitimately be based on invasion of the personal right of privacy.

[151] *Supra.*

[152] Strauss, Strydom & Van der Walt in *Die Perswese en die Reg* (J L van Schaik, Pretoria, 1964) 184 declared that breach of confidence is applicable to such situations. The most recent edition of this work (3 ed 1976 p 165) states that publication of affairs of a secret organization is not necessarily illegal.

[153] D J McQuoid-Mason 'Public Interest and Privacy' (1975) 92 *SALJ* 252; and by the same author 'Invasion of Potency' (1973) 90 *SALJ* 23 at 29–30.

[154] 63 of 1965.

[155] Section 33. Section 5 of the Copyright Bill 1978 would preserve the existing rights of the state.

[156] In chapter VI p 129.

[157] Section 3 of the Copyright Amendment Act 64 of 1975.

[158] The maximum penalties on first conviction are a fine of R500 or imprisonment for six months (or both) *for each article to which the offence relates*. On second conviction these penalties are increased to a fine of R1 000 or imprisonment for one year (or both) again for each article to which the offence relates: See section 22(6).

[159] The defence is not mentioned by A J C Copeling in *Copyright Law in South Africa* (Butterworths, Durban, 1969).

[160] Copinger & Skone James op cit § 886.

[161] Differences of a social or political nature (ie in the societal context of the laws) are analysed in Part III below.

PART THREE

The Background

CHAPTER VIII

Information Practices in the Three Societies

THE UNITED STATES

Judged by its laws America is probably the most open of all Western democracies. This is especially true of the laws which bear upon access to information about executive branch administration. The laws providing for criminal punishment for unauthorized release or transmission of information have a limited reach and apply in general only where an intention to harm the interests of the United States or to further those of a foreign nation is proved. Copyright is inapplicable to government papers and documents and the constitution ensures that the doctrines of breach of confidence and contempt of court cannot exercise the sway that they do in the mother country. But the United States, as we have seen, is characterized by more than the strictly circumscribed scope of the criminal-law regulation of access to information. Both at federal and state levels, there are laws, of varying range and effectiveness, providing the citizen with a positive right to information. Prior to statutory intervention, the unpropitious British common law was developed by courts in some states to achieve, though less effectively, what the statutes later gave the citizen. Though the laws in the United States are by no means perfect[1] and require improvement in many of the states, they do stand as a model worthy of emulation and adoption by other societies.[2]

The practice in the United States conforms broadly to the laws. A visitor to that country, or an observer of its public administration, cannot help being impressed, and sometimes alarmed, by the impunity with which official information can be disseminated to the public at large. The outstanding contemporary example is the publication of the Pentagon Papers, a classified history of America's tragic South-East Asia involvement commissioned by the Defence Department.[3] Daniel Ellsberg, it is true, was subjected to an abortive prosecution during which he was the victim of clumsy government harassment;[4] and an unsuccessful attempt was made to interdict publication of the papers. The fact remains that there are few countries, if any, in which an Ellsberg would be at large after the publication of similar papers or in which the courts would decline to enjoin dissemination. Another release (though less earth-shaking than the Pentagon Papers) which illustrates the contemporary practices in America was the publication by the *Village Voice* (a New York newspaper) of the uncensored version of the Pike report—a report of the House Select Committee on Intelligence. After copies of the report had been leaked to the New York Times and the CBS in January 1976, the Committee voted not to release it until after it had been censored by the executive branch. In defiance of this decision, the report[5] was published by the *Village Voice* and the nation learnt, for example, that the Committee considered that the 'intelligence agencies that are to be controlled by Congressional lawmaking are, today, beyond the lawmaker's scrutiny'; and that it believed that the intelligence budget, reported to Congress as about \$3 billion, was in fact nearer to \$10 billion.[6] As Edward Shils has observed, American society is characterized by a 'preponderance of publicity' over governmental secretiveness. While publicity may help to check government mismanagement and makes public opinion more informed, it has sometimes been pushed so far as to injure valid American interests. On 6 December 1975, for example, proposed options for the US SALT II negotiations with the Soviet Union were published within days of their drafting and shortly after they had been sent to President Ford for his approval.[7] An American publication *Counter-Spy* had identified Richard Welch as a CIA agent shortly before his assassination in Athens in 1975, and this disclosure has been condemned, with obvious justification, as a contributory factor in his killing. Whatever one may feel about the sins of the CIA, and there appear to be many, this form of disclosure offends against a rational secrecy/publicity policy. Though such excesses of publicity must be deprecated and controlled by tightly-drawn legislation, they should not blind the observer of the American scene to the manifold benefits public administration derives from the 'publish with impunity' policy.

The description of American practice as a preponderence of publicity over governmental secretiveness suggests quite correctly that publicity has not always held total sway. Prior to Watergate, J R Wiggins had written with remarkable prescience that '[t]here is abroad in this country . . . an impulse to secrecy';[8] and in the post-Watergate era, Arthur M Schlesinger has searchingly explored the 'secrecy system' that 'overpowered Congress and the nation' in the 1950s and 1960s.[9] The secrecy surrounding the operations of the intelligence agencies has permitted unauthorized and harmful covert actions abroad and illegal restrictions on American liberties at home. As a single example of apparent CIA folly abroad, the intervention in Angola may be mentioned since John Stockwell, the CIA's former Angola task force chief, has publicly exposed American activities there in an open letter published in the *Washington Post*.[10] The following extract from the letter expresses his estimate of the damage to United States interests that resulted from the Angolan episode:

'The CIA committed $31 million to opposing the MPLA victory, but six months later it had nevertheless decisively won, and 15,000 Cuban regular army troops were entrenched in Angola with the full sympathy of much of the Third World, and the support of several influential African chiefs of state who previously had been critical of any extra-continental intervention in African affairs. At the same time the United States was solidly discredited, having been exposed for covert military intervention in African affairs, having managed to ally itself with South Africa and having lost.'[11]

While this exposé demonstrates that there are areas of undesirable secrecy in intelligence agency operations which demand at the lowest prior executive branch and Congressional committee knowledge as a safeguard and corrective, the fact that it could be published without legal retribution underlines again the open nature of the American society.

Classification practices in the United States constitute another major exception to the general rule of publicity. A committee investigating classification of documents in the 1950s discovered that the Pentagon had classified reports on the use of bows and arrows ('silent flashless weapons') as secrets;[12] and other examples, both serious and comic, might be cited to illustrate the executive obsession with the secrecy of government papers and the only partially successful attempt to check the tendency towards massive overclassification. But again a reminder is in order that classification in America is not backed by an Official Secrets law of total coverage, and that transmission of classified information *simpliciter* is generally not a crime. What the exceptions to publicity reveal is a tendency of oscillation between publicity and secrecy,[13] the latter being emphasized in periods of crisis or upheaval. These oscillations seem to correspond to what Max Lerner has described as the 'violent alternations' in American politics;[14] but it needs stressing that American government at its most secretive is more open than most of the Western democracies.

BRITAIN

The whole weight of the laws in Britain is towards secrecy in government administration. The criminal law extends to the unauthorized release of any official information whatever and the citizen is as yet unarmed with a positive right enabling him to winkle information out of the executive crevices. The spirit of the law is reflected in the practices of government where the 'curse' of 'inner circle' secrecy still exerts a powerful influence.[15] Two American academics, in a study of the process of decision-making in the British Treasury, concluded that so far as information is concerned 'the Executive fortress . . . is proclaimed sacrosanct'.[16] What is particularly hidden from the public view in Britain is 'ongoing policy formation'[17] and the 'inner workings of state agencies and government'.[18] Secrecy is frequently justified on the ground of 'security' and the extent to which it has become ingrained as a habit of mind is revealed by the assertion of a British civil servant in the *Sunday Telegraph* case that embarrassment of the government and security are the same thing.[19] Though secrecy extends over the whole range of executive business its hold is nowhere firmer than in foreign policy where, as David Vital has said, 'the citizen is only implicated, as a rule, indirectly or by exclusion'.[20] This applies even to matters in the dead past with the result that the British involvement in the 1956 Suez crisis is still substantially in the dark in contrast, for example, to the open post-mortems which have been conducted in America on Vietnam and other major foreign involvements. British practices justify Edward Shils's conclusion that there is a preponderance of privacy and traditional government secretiveness over publicity.[21]

It would be wrong, however, to describe Britain as a 'closed' society and clearly much official information enters the public realm. The need to reconcile the laws with democracy has led to a policy of selective enforcement[22] of measures such as the Official Secrets Acts. The Acts have never been invoked against cabinet ministers who disclose inside knowledge in their memoirs or other writings and the Crossman Diaries, after the failure of the breach of confidence suit brought by the Attorney-General, have extended the boundaries of legitimate revelations about the inner workings of the British cabinet. Since the Acts are inapplicable where the transmission or publication of information is authorized and self-authorization is apparently permissible at the upper levels of the government hierarchy,[23] the press receives and publishes much information based on official leaks, though it must be remembered that information obtained in this way is frequently 'managed' to put the government or its officers in a good light. In recent times unofficial and unauthorized leaks have become more common and of these the most dramatic were those made in 1976 to the *New Society* concerning the government's reversal of its commitment to introduce a scheme of child benefits. Mr Frank Field, author of the *New Society* article which quoted classified cabinet documents on the scheme, has disclosed that he regularly received large amounts of classified information, including cabinet minutes, which had been delivered anonymously to the office of the Child Poverty Action Group 'in shopping baskets or carrier bags'.[24] In the generally tolerant climate of contemporary British democracy and liberalism, the public learn a substantial amount about public administration through official, quasi-official or unauthorized releases from government.

Yet, though Britain is not a closed society in respect of access to information, it would also be inaccurate to describe it as open. The evidence given to the Franks Committee by government departments and officials reveals a rigid and closed-minded attitude towards official information. The Attorney-General, Sir Peter Rawlinson, suggested that the range of persons to whom section 2 of the Official Secrets Act applies may not be sufficiently comprehensive and, while supporting a more precise definition of the information protected by the Act, was unable to offer a 'ready solution to this problem'.[25] The memorandum submitted by the Cabinet Office reveals that it continues to support 'a criminal sanction in respect of unauthorized disclosures over the *whole range of matter* transacted by the Cabinet'.[26] The Treasury wished to suppress, *inter alia*, 'assumptions about price and wage movements, the balance of payments, the level of employment, tax levels etc, unauthorized publication of which could prejudice the Government's ability to develop suitable policies to meet the emerging situation';[27] and the Home Office declined to suggest improvements to section 2 of the Official Secrets Act 1911, on the ground that 'all likely cures, if not worse than the disease, were not obviously better'.[28] The Prime Minister, the Rt Hon James Callaghan, justified criminal sanctions for the revelation of information by the following statement: 'If you can be prosecuted for riding a bicycle without a lamp, it does not seem to me by extension it is necessarily wrong that you should be prosecuted for disclosing information as a matter of principle.'[29] A society whose Prime Minister puts the public interest in the safety of cyclists on the same level as the general interest in an informed public and whose officials testify to a public commission as indicated above, is still a long way from being open to a meaningful degree.

Another reason why it is not yet possible to describe British information practices as being open without substantial qualification is that little information that reaches the public through the press is 'hard' information. Hard information is that which comes in a form which makes its official source and content difficult or impossible to deny. Most official information other than handouts which reaches the public through the press is a mixture of official gossip, rumour and journalistic speculation. It is the kind of information which a Minister or public official can usually deny or qualify without fear of contradiction. The difference between easily deniable information of this kind and hard information is well illustrated by the *Sunday Telegraph* case relating to its publication of the content of a confidential assessment written by the Defence Adviser at the British High Commission in Lagos about the then current Nigerian civil war. Prior to the publication of the report, the government had been able to get away with false denials of its heavy and controversial support, in the form of military supplies, to the Nigerian government. When the report was published, the falsity became transparent and the abortive criminal proceedings were commenced against the newspaper and other parties involved.[30] The important point which the case underlines is that the only stage at which the public could be said to have had real information about its government's involvement in the civil war was when hard information was published. Prior to that point the public could be kept in a state of confusion by newspaper allegations and official denials, neither of which was capable of effective verification. The publication of the 'hard' story ended the doubt but signalled the government's decision to prosecute—an unfortunately typical reaction when the official cover has been blown. It is a sobering thought that the prosecution would have succeeded had the journalist in question known (either actually or constructively) that the report was written by a Crown servant or had the newspaper editor not been advised that the report was not covered by a 'D-Notice'.[31] For this reason, Britain is likely to remain a society in which hard information is a scarce commodity.

SOUTH AFRICA

In South Africa the British Official Secrets Acts have been taken over, extended and rendered more vague and thus capable of arbitrary application. They are supplemented, moreover, by other sweeping laws, particularly in the security field, which make the control of information easy to maintain. Neither the common law nor statutes confers any positive right to acquire information upon the citizen. The situation in practice more than matches the expectations which the laws arouse, though paradoxically not necessarily as a result of the actual invocation of the provisions of secrecy laws. Without regular application of laws specifically designed to control information, the government possesses and exercises the ability to control what information the public receives and even to manufacture it in certain areas of public life. In short, information is not just rigidly controlled but also created.

The extent to which official secrecy is carried in South Africa may be illustrated by examples which relate to material ranging from trivial to profoundly important information. At the trivial end of the scale lies the experience of a university colleague who was commisioned by the SABC in 1977 to prepare a commentary for a series of programmes on South Africa filmed from the air. One of the buildings filmed was King's House in Durban, an official residence of the State President. Wishing to know whether the name of the residence was derived from the ownership of a person named 'King' or from the fact that a king of England had resided there during a visit to South Africa, the colleague telephoned the government official in charge of the residence. The official was adamant that he had no authority to assist but stated that if the request was put in writing, with supporting reasons, he would transmit it to Pretoria for authority to supply the momentous information.[32] A more serious case came to light when Professor Wolfgang Thomas, a member of the financial committee at the Turnhalle deliberations in Namibia (South West Africa) was deported by the government without reasons. In a subsequent press interview

Professor Thomas revealed that even as a member of this official committee he was denied information on matters such as the precise statistics of Namibia's gross internal revenue, its export potential and population figures. He stated that on one occasion statistics compiled by an official planner of the government had been briefly shown to the committee but that they were immediately withdrawn and could not be used as a working paper by members who had to rely on their memories.[33] If a person officially involved in constitution-making cannot obtain such information, the plight of the citizens is obviously lamentable.

It was South Africa's 1975 intervention in Angola which, more than anything else, starkly revealed official information practices and the impotence of the press to inform the public about a matter as momentous as the invasion of a neighbouring country by South African forces. By any standards the invasion of Angola represented a public policy decision of enormous significance to the South African people. It constituted a flagrant breach of South Africa's oft-reiterated policy of non-interference in the internal affairs of other countries with possibly portentous consequences for its future position in Africa. The invasion almost certainly led to a heightened Cuban and Russian involvement in Angola and elsewhere in Africa and, what is worse, lent a respectability to the communist presence in Africa which it had previously lacked in many Africa states. This was a question, as a *Cape Times* editorial put it at the height of the invasion, on which 'the South African public must be kept fully informed and not be dragged in total ignorance from the tested policy of non-involvement'.[34] One factor that a public or even parliamentary involvement in the decision would certainly have brought to the attention of an unseeing government was the American government's extreme wariness of involvement in land wars in either Asia or Africa and the consequent certainty (whatever the CIA may have said privately) that it would not want to be seen as a supporter of South Africa and its apartheid policies. Inadvertence to this factor was nothing short of a major blunder which men who make private secrets of public business are the more likely to commit.

The bulk of the South African population was kept in ignorance of their country's involvement in Angola until well after the withdrawal of troops. Some local newspapers, notably the *Cape Times*, strove valiantly to alert the public to the truth. But constrained by the laws and harassed by Defence Department censorship, it could only hint at the real position by informing its readers of the fact of censorship,[35] drawing attention to the folly of abandoning the tried policy of non-intervention and alluding to 'rumours' of the invasion that had appeared abroad.[36] The newspaper could not have published, without grave risk to itself and its staff, hard information which would be proof against official denials. Such denials were not lacking and served to confuse the general public even further. On 19 November 1975, it was reported that the Minister of Foreign Affairs had denied in London that the South African involvement went beyond protection of the Cunene water supply scheme at the border.[37] He repeated this denial in South Africa on 26 November. On 29 November, the Minister of Defence emphatically denied South African involvement in the civil war. In his New Year message, the Prime Minister refuted 'attempts to make us a scape-goat in this matter' and declared that 'we have committed no act of aggression'.[38] It has since appeared from the official account of the war released by the South African government that when these denials were made South African aggression had already begun; for example, a squadron of armoured cars and crews were sent to Silva Porto in mid-October 1975 and Novo Redondo was captured on 13 November 1975 where the first South African fatality was recorded. The official report also discloses that the major battle of the campaign fought by the Foxbat group raged from 9 to 12 December 1975, almost a month before the Prime Minister's denial. Confused by a welter of purely speculative reports and ministerial assurances the people in South Africa remained ignorant until the end of the war and even after. The people of all other countries in which effective and uncensored news services operate knew the true story almost from the beginning, as did the enemy against which South African troops were engaged. Thus it happened that the most ill-informed were those most entitled to know.

The three examples on an ascending scale of importance—King's House, Turnhalle and Angola—only partially illustrate the dimensions of the South African secrecy system. A few other representative examples will not be out of place. The cabinet in this country is truly a *sanctum sanctorum*, and no minister or ex-minister has ever published a detailed account of his cabinet experiences.[40] Foreign policy is completely shrouded, and, as John Barratt has said: 'The process is not exposed to public scrutiny, and therefore it is not possible to establish with any certainty who made specific decisions, or where the recommendations on which the decisions were based, originated.'[41] He also adds that Parliament has small influence in the making of foreign policy. Secrecy extends deep into the commercial sphere and keeps the public totally ignorant of such mundane issues of general concern as negotiations between the tyre manufacturers and the government for price increases, to cite a single example.[42] A research student attempting to obtain from the Legal Aid Board (a statutory body set up by the government) purely innocent information in the form of the qualifications of legal aid officers and the Board's policy relating to the means test, has been denied the material on the ground of inconvenience and embarrassment.[43]

These examples of concealment, though important, lack the sinister dimensions that the secrecy system has assumed in the security field.

It is currently impossible to obtain hard information about the treatment of detainees held under security laws, and even of the fact of detentions. The death in detention of Mr Steve Biko and the subsequent inquest gave an appalled outside world a brief glimpse of our hidden security operations, but since then the prison doors have clanged shut and once more deprived the public of any information about the treatment and fate of the approximately 700 detainees in custody for interrogation at the time of the inquest in November 1977. Even after the Biko revelations, Red Cross visitors have been denied access to detainees held for interrogation and permitted only to visit persons held under the Internal Security Act who in any event enjoy awaiting-trial status. On being asked for information in Parliament on the *number* of persons detained under the Terrorism Act since 1 January 1976, the Minister of Justice replied: 'Except to confirm that from time to time persons are being detained and released in terms of the Terrorism Act, I consider it not to be in the public interest to disclose particulars.'[44] The Terrorism Act provides that no person is entitled to official information about detainees and this provision, together with the isolation of detainees in solitary cells for purposes of interrogation, means that public knowledge of their treatment is either low or non-existent. In this vacuum the government is in a position to create information as it has attempted to do, for example, by explaining away the more than 30 deaths of detainees in suspicious or unsatisfactorily explained circumstances as instances of suicide devised as part of a communist master-plan for South Africa. This startling explanation has been offered without proof that the detainees are communist in any sense other than being opposed to the system of apartheid. The government's ability to bolster its own version of police operations in the riots is enhanced by the arrest and detention of journalists reporting on the black townships[45] and by the banning of publications which publish information contrary to the government position.[46] In the security field the control of information in the form of an official rewriting of contemporary history has markedly totalitarian features.

CONCLUSIONS

While the three societies that are the subject of this study all practise secrecy and exhibit examples of information blockages or distortions, they are significantly different in the nature and degree of information control. America and Britain are fairly close to each other in their secrecy practices, but in the former country secrecy has never become established as a rule or tradition and can be maintained successfully only for short periods. In Britain publicity rather than secrecy is the exception but the society can hardly be described as closed. South Africa, though originally characterized by laws and a constitution in the British tradition, now stands in sharp contrast to the other two countries. Despite the existence of a moderately free press, it is rapidly becoming a closed society. The information which the press can get is limited and that which it can publish even more circumscribed. Hard information about executive branch activities is a very scarce commodity and the publication of it when available attended by unacceptable risks. Government intervention is not limited to rigid controls but nowadays includes instances of 1984 style remaking of knowledge and information. The explanation of the similarities and differences between the three countries lies in the sphere of socio-political realities to which we now turn.

NOTES

[1] The Espionage Statutes, as we have seen, are hardly a model of clarity, and the exact meaning and scope of some of their provisions still has to be determined.

[2] Incorporation of these laws into other societies will certainly require carefully planned modifications and adaptations. This is attempted in Part IV below.

[3] Officially known as the 'History of US Decision-making Process on Vietnam Policy, 1945–1967'. The history was commissioned by former Defence Secretary, Robert S McNamara.

[4] The government withheld from the court before which Ellsberg was indicted a Defence Department analysis indicating that publication of the papers had caused negligible damage. The office of Ellsberg's psychiatrist was burgled and, in the midst of the trial, ex-President Nixon solicited the judge's possible interest in the directorship of the FBI: See Arthur M Schlesinger Jr op cit 348.

[5] The second section of the Report containing the Committee's findings on the intelligence agencies was fully published. The first part (a record of the Committee's frustrations in obtaining information) and the third part (recommendations, as yet not finalized) were omitted.

[6] I F Stone, in the New York Review of Books (1 April 1976), has argued that the report would have been published by the committee but for the leaks which enabled hostile House members to engineer the censorship resolution. However, he commends the *Village Voice* for rendering a public service in publishing in defiance of the resolution.

[7] The *Washington Post*, 17 February 1976 (A 8).

[8] J R Wiggins op cit X.

[9] Arthur M Schlesinger Jr op cit chap 10.

[10] And republished in the *Guardian Weekly*, 17 April 1977.

[11] Ibid.

[12] Arthur M Schlesinger op cit 342.

[13] Francis E Rourke op cit 227.

[14] Max Lerner *America as a Civilization* (Jonathan Cape, London, 1958) 358.

[15] Bernard Crick *The Reform of Parliament* 252.

[16] Hugh Heclo and Aaron Wildavsky, *The Private Government of Public Money* (Macmillan, London, 1974) 341.

[17] J A G Griffith 'Government Secrecy in the United Kingdom' in *None of Your Business: Government Secrecy in America* 330.

[18] Tony Bunyon *The History and Practice of the Political Police in Britain* (Julian Friedmann, London 1976) 7 and 9.

[19] Referred to by Anthony Sampson in 'Secrecy, News Management and the British Press' in *Secrecy and Foreign Policy* 222.

[20] David Vital op cit 47–8.

[21] Edward Shils op cit 57.

[22] Arthur M Schlesinger op cit 352.

[23] According to evidence given by the Rt Hon Roy Jenkins MP to the Departmental Committee on section 2 of the Official Secrets Act 1911, Cmnd 5104 (1972) vol 4, 375 (referred to below as the Franks Report).

[24] The *Guardian*, 25 June 1976.

[25] Franks Report vol 2, 5.

[26] Franks Report vol 2, 11 (italics supplied).

[27] Franks Report vol 2, 167.

[28] Franks Report vol 2, 108.

[29] Franks Report vol 4, 181.

[30] See Jonathan Aitken *Officially Secret.*

[31] Joseph Jacob, 'Some Reflections on Governmental Secrecy' 1974 *Public Law* 25 at 30–1.

[32] After making the position clear to my colleague, he added: 'By the way, who gave you permission to fly over King's House.'

[33] *Rapport*, 27 March 1977. It is interesting that Professor Thomas had personally calculated that Namibia had sufficient natural resources to be independent of South Africa and was opposed to a projected fiscal policy that would tie expenditure to the contributions made by each ethnic group.

[34] *Cape Times*, 18 November 1975.

[35] As it did on a front page article in the *Cape Times* of 17 November 1975.

[36] See *Cape Times* of 27 November 1975, in which reports were cited of 'South African accents' being heard as far north as Port Redondo.

[37] *Cape Times*, 19 November 1975.

[38] *Cape Times*, 1 January 1976.

[39] *Daily News*, 4 February 1977.

[40] *South Africa: Government and Politics* ed Denis Worrall (J L van Schaik, Pretoria, 1975) 39.

[41] Ibid 346.

[42] Eugene Roelofse, 'The Future of Private Enterprise' Lecture to the International Association of Commerce and Economic Students, delivered at the University of Natal, Durban, on 24 May 1977.

[43] Letter from Legal Aid Board dated 26 April 1977.

[44] *Sunday Express*, 27 March, 1977.

[45] *Daily News* of 30 September 1976 and *Natal Mercury* of 2 July 1977. The latter report refers to the detention of a *Rand Daily Mail* reporter who reported extensively on the 1976 unrest in the townships.

[46] Publications aiming to expose alleged police malpractices in the townships have been regularly banned: see, for example, GG 5539 (4 May 1977) banning the Rev D Russell's publication 'Riot Police and the Suppression of Truth', and making possession of the publication a criminal offence. The Rev D Russell has since been put on trial for producing and distributing this publication. In February 1977 a pamphlet entitled 'The Role of the Riot Police in the Burnings and Killings, Nyanga, Cape Town—Christmas 1976' was banned—GG 5411 (25 February 1977). Similar bannings continue.

CHAPTER IX

The Socio-Political Context

Analysis and comparison of the laws and their implementation in isolation from the social setting in which they have evolved and developed is frequently a sterile exercise. This observation carries a special validity in a study devoted to access to information about public administration where the relation between political traditions and social realities, on the one hand, and the laws and their administration, on the other, is immediate and direct. However difficult the task, the bare and white bones of the legal structure must be set into the flesh of living societies, especially if proposals for reform are to carry any conviction. The task is best undertaken by comparing in succession the dominant theories of political authority of the three societies, their constitutional make-up and political institutions, the underlying structural features of each and, finally, the political cultures that lie behind the legal institutions. The sketching-in of the background will necessarily be selective, the focus falling on those facets of the constitution and political and social tradition that seem particularly relevant to the subject of the study.

THE DOMINANT THEORIES OF POLITICAL AUTHORITY

Richard Rose has commented on the relevance of the expression 'We, the People . . .' in the American political tradition.[1] Political authority is regarded in the United States as having been derived from below—from the choice of the people.[2] If we follow Louis Hartz's theory[3] that the colonial fragments from European society all tended to incorporate a dominant teleology as opposed to the 'intertwined teleologies' of European societies, then the essence or spirit of the American fragment which it was destined to develop more 'purely and luxuriantly' is surely the belief in, and almost mystical importance of, the common man. This faith in the common man means that sovereignty in America is popular sovereignty and that democracy is of the Jacksonian, populist variety. From the beginning the American political tradition also emphasized as part of the Protestant individualistic culture a 'sense of responsibility wrought by the habit of political participation',[4] so that the citizen is seen not just as the source of authority in government but further as a regular and competent participant in it. The 'imbalance' in American democracy is 'on the participatory side'.[5] From these theoretical perspectives follow certain consequences for executive government which have been succinctly summed up by Alan Westin:

> 'The framers believed that executive affairs were not the private preserve of a President or his agents, in the classic mode of royal households, but an instrument of popular government, to be conducted mainly in public view or subject to public inspection.'[6]

Knowledge of public affairs in the American tradition is not something which political leaders may graciously concede but rather a right which the citizen may demand as effectuating the active, participatory role which that tradition envisages for him. Government is in principle continuously accountable and the citizens, in the words of a commentator, 'may not be regarded as closed-circuit recipients of only that which the state chooses to communicate'.[7]

The authority of government in Britain is derived not from the people but from the Crown.[8] The powers exercised by all three branches of government are still nominally those of the Crown from which they were derived. In a chapter devoted to the prerogative, two leading constitutional authors express the position in the following terms:

> 'Parliament is summoned and dissolved by the Queen; the powers of Ministers are exercised for and on behalf of Her Majesty; the courts are the Queen's courts.'[9]

However much tradition in the United Kingdom has been blended with modernity, British democracy has retained characteristics of its Tory origins; and while it may express the principle of government *of* the people and *for* the people, it has yet to yield fully to the idea of government *by* the people.[10] The system of representation, moreover, is best characterized by the term 'trusteeship'—a notion that implies the transfer of administration by the electorate to Parliament and by Parliament to the cabinet and denies the duty of continuous accountability or the right of regular and vigorous citizen participation. Trusteeship is strengthened and democracy qualified by the venerated maxim of English politics that politics is 'the rightful vocation of the privileged few, with the occasional participation of the many . . .'.[11] Government by the qualified few clearly depends upon trust on the part of the many, and trust of those in authority is a feature of British politics frequently commented upon and contrasted with the adversary style of government in America. All these features of British politics—derivation of authority from the Crown and government by the trusted few under a system of political trusteeship, bear directly upon the information practices of the society. Accountability operates upwards as much as in the downward direction; and in principle the subject's more passive participatory role does not carry an ancillary information right.

Because the British tradition of politics and the constitution became influential in South Africa at an early stage, the notion of the devolution of political authority from above and the requirement of trust in constituted political authorities are strong features of specifically South African theorizing about the source of political authority. But on account of the role of the Calvinist conception of the state and of the evolution of the Afrikaner civil religion, the 'altitude' from which political authority devolves is considerably higher than in the English tradition while the corollary of trust becomes transformed into the duty of obedience. This 'civil theology' is the subject of a detailed study by Dunbar Moodie who has said that it is 'rooted in the belief that God has chosen the Afrikaner people for a special destiny'.[12] The belief in the divine mission of the Afrikaner people has also incorporated the Calvinist notion of the providential election of the nation's leaders. In Calvin's thinking, the magistrates or civil authorities are divinely appointed and this had led to the rejection of the idea that the people can be the source of state authority as 'the myth of sovereignty as opposed to God'.[13] While it is true that Calvin qualified the duty of citizen obedience to the magistrates where a conflict arises between the command of the sovereign and the command of God,[14] he appears to be unclear on how and by whom the determination of conflict is to be made and what the subject's right of disobedience actually is. The result is that the notion of obedience to divinely appointed civil authorities comes through more strongly in his writing than any qualifications on the obedience owed to them; and Calvin himself pointedly declared that 'private men' have 'no authority to deliberate on the regulation of any public affairs'.[15] The Calvinist doctrine of the autonomy of the social spheres (soewereniteit in eie kring) also constitutes a highly qualified limitation on the authority of political leaders since the autonomy must give way to central authority if 'state policy as laid down is undermined',[16] a question which presumably will be settled by the political leaders themselves. Though André du Toit has convincingly demonstrated the dangers of attributing to Afrikanerdom any specific ideology of power,[17] the powerful role of political authority fortified by a religious sanction in South African history can hardly be seriously questioned. That political authority has been temporarily bolstered by such other props as 'the leadership principle and the idea of the authoritarian state' derived from 'fascist political ideas and sentiments'[18] is not something that weakens the argument but which proves rather a continuing need to validate a downwardly imposed authority for which the 'civil religion' has been the most consistent justification. Though the validation of authority in religious terms may nowadays be muted, its long and honourable role in Afrikaner history assures it a continuous contemporary relevance.

The principle of trust in the political leadership in Britain has always been contingent upon the condition that the rulers govern ably or justly; and it is therefore liable to be suspended when citizens no longer perceive these qualities in their government. The notion of trust has far stronger connotations in South Africa as Allen Drury discovered when questioning a young Afrikaner on the enactment of arbitrary laws: 'Mr Drury, I can just repeat to you—the Afrikaners are an honest people. We trust our government. . . . We trust our leaders and we know they will not misuse these powers.'[19] The principle expressed in this exchange with the author, as opposed to trust in the British context, is rather one of 'my leader, right or wrong'. The correct description of this attitude is 'obedience' rather than 'trust', and it is a natural corollary to the more heavily fortified concepts of political authority. It was perfectly caught up in a television interview with the Minister of Justice, Mr J T Kruger when, with total seriousness, he described a 'beautiful person' as one who 'clicks his heels when he speaks to you'.[20] The consequences of such notions for a citizen's right of access to information are depressing for, to the extent that authority has acquired a religious sanction, '[t]here is no arguing with the pretenders to a divine knowledge and to a divine mission'.[21] Even if today the political leaders have dropped their religious mantle, its influence in the past has helped to guarantee that the institutions of the society 'have been and still are set up in such a way as to imply that some body or some group of people is "the most objective authority in the world", and is therefore capable of finding ultimate solutions for all issues and conflicts'.[22] In such a situation the right to be *self*-informed is defined out of relevance.

CONSTITUTIONAL FACTORS

Constitutional arrangements are no doubt a reflection of political tradition; but since constitutions invariably come to acquire a life of their own it would be surprising if matters such as access to information were not materially affected by the fundamental law of the societies under consideration. In America, two features of constitutional law—the judicially enforced bill of rights and the separation of powers—have a significant influence on the law and practice affecting the citizen's right to information. It is not clear whether the bill of rights in the United States incorporates a guarantee of the right to gather information. Certainly there is no express protection of a right to information, but it has been persuasively argued that the first amendment protection of speech and press incorporates the right of the press to gather information subject to the usual restraints on the exercise of first amendment guarantees.[23] The statutory grant of access to information to the citizen both at federal and state level has made the constitutional issue less urgent, but even without a judicially declared right to information the generous interpretation given to the right to *publish* under the first amendment is of crucial significance. The possession of information without the right to publish is of small political value since it cannot then be used to create an informed public and to extend citizen participation. Because the first amendment right to speak and publish has received jealous, and sometimes zealous, protection from American courts, information about government that comes into private hands can be disseminated to the wider public with relative impunity. The fear of pre-publication censorship is only a minor and remote deterrent under the United States constitutional system—'[a]ny system of prior restraints of expression comes to this court bearing a heavy presumption against its constitutional validity'[24]—and post-publication criminal conviction for publication of information is in general unlikely outside the context of espionage. Although the acts of gathering and publishing information are notionally separate, the importance attached to freedom of expression in American constitutional practice has greatly enhanced access to information about public affairs. Moreover, the dependence of the one right upon the other underlines a principle of vital importance—the principle of the interdependence of civil and political rights. These rights appear to operate effectively only as clusters, with each right in the cluster adding strength and significance to the others. The right to information in America has been able to bloom more fully and maturely because of its place in a setting of constitutionally protected basic rights.

The second relevant feature of United States constitutional law is the separation of powers, perhaps more accurately described as a 'government (system) of separated institutions sharing powers'.[25] The distribution of political authority under the constitution has produced competing centres of power and, since information is a form of power competition for information—notably between the legislative and executive branches—takes place on a continuous basis. As two North American writers have observed, the 'separation and equality of the Executive and Legislative branches colors the whole process of information flow'.[26] The situation is basically one in which the powerful and semi-independent executive branch which possesses the information strives to keep it (or much of it) secret, while a powerful Congress (fortified by a constitutional investigative power) strives to extract the information held in the executive branch for the purpose of informing itself, the public or both. In the process a great deal more information gets out than would be the case if political authority were centralized and the holders of information operated from a virtually unchallenged power base. This situation which has been characterized as a 'kind of trial by battle and cleverness between the three estates and the fourth' has been criticized on the ground that it leads to 'rare, haphazard, fortuitous journalistic uncovering'.[27] The uncovering, moreover, may depend heavily on the extent to which the executive branch invokes executive privilege in the course of congressional enquiry. Nevertheless, an irregular flow of information is better than the non-flow which centralized systems of authority tend to create; and the criticisms appear to be directed at the lack of a sensible policy of accommodation between the branches rather than to deny the relation of separation of powers to the availability of information about government. In the result the position in the United States is that divided political authority puts more information into private hands and that the constitutional liberties, notably freedom of expression, facilitate the general circulation of such information.

Centralized power rather than divided authority characterizes the British constitutional system and non-separation of powers is unquestionably a powerful support for secrecy in that society. The constitutional position of Parliament, it has rightly been said, is that it does not govern but rather that 'the government governs through Parliament'.[28] Because in the British constitutional system the Executive and Parliament are intended to work 'along the same lines',[29] in contrast to the arm's length posture of the President and Congress, Parliament has not been able to establish itself as a centre of power for the purpose *inter alia* of communicating information about executive business to the public. As Andrew Shonfield has observed, the rules of the game 'allow the government to be endlessly teased but not to be seriously incommoded in the conduct of its ordinary work'.[30] The British system of representation and two-party politics has been subjected to searching analysis by J R Lucas, who describes it as a form of 'elective autocracy'.[31] His analysis demonstrates with a disturbing cogency how that system, by providing the electorate with packaged choices and limited alternatives, has reinforced the constitutional tendency to concentrate rather than distribute power. It is a system, as he says, which reduces participation in decision-making and operates on a principle of 'minimum communication'.[32]

Civil and political rights in the United Kingdom are at the mercy of parliamentary sovereignty and no constitutional guarantee restrains Parliament from enacting inroads into basic freedoms. British laws enacted to further secrecy have seriously inhibited not just the right to gather information but also freedom of expression. If the legislative intention to limit a right or freedom is clear from the statutory language, the courts are powerless to intervene. The present state of the law and the constitution in Britain makes a Pentagon Papers type of disclosure inconceivable and undoubtedly restrains the gathering and publication of less highly charged information about government. At the same time the social and political tradition has kept inroads into liberties down to a minimum and 'the freedom of political dissent and the legitimacy of criticism of political leaders are deeply etched in political practice'.[33] The significance of this fact is that were Parliament to pare down the secrecy laws and introduce a positive right to information the new information rights of the citizens thus enacted would be brought into congenial association with a cluster of meaningful basic freedoms from which they could draw nourishment even in the absence of constitutional protection.

The constitutional disadvantages in the British system are those that flow from the non-separation of powers rather than from the civil rights situation even though a judicially protected bill of rights would improve the citizen's chances of developing a more effective right to information. Unfortunately there are constitutional doctrines associated with the cabinet system of government which put Britain in a more deeply disadvantageous position. The doctrines or conventions of collective and ministerial responsibility have undoubtedly acted as powerful supports for the secrecy practices which the cabinet and civil service have so successfully maintained for generations. Collective responsibility originated in the transfer of executive authority from the monarch and his advisers to a cabinet responsible to Parliament and vested with 'the whole control over the direction of public affairs'.[34] The responsibility owed to Parliament and the exigencies of the two-party system[35] demanded that the cabinet stand or fall and speak together; and collective responsibility means in essence that, whatever differences may have been expressed in the making of executive policy, the finished decisional product should be seen to be unanimous and should be underpinned by a continuing duty of support and responsibility on the part of every member of the cabinet. It is not so much from the joint responsibility of members of the cabinet for government policy but rather from the need for an outward show of unanimity that the rule of secrecy for cabinet business springs. This outward manifestation of agreement is supposed to foster the mutual trust which the cabinet requires in order that its members may work effectively together[36] and revelations of disagreements or individual positions taken up by ministers during policy formulation are therefore proscribed, at least for a considerable period of time. Thus expressed, the doctrine imposes an obligation of secrecy in respect of any business whatever that comes before the cabinet. Individual ministerial responsibility extends the rule of secrecy to the internal affairs of the civil service on the basis that the Minister alone is responsible to Parliament for the decisions of his department and that parliamentary control depends on his personally taking the rap for departmental actions. It is not entirely clear why ministerial responsibility should entail a corollary of secrecy but various explanations have been offered, including the need to ensure civil service loyalty to successive governments and to develop a relationship of trust between ministers and their senior advisers. The important point is that collective and individual ministerial responsibility taken together provide a constitutional justification for blanketing the internal operations of the cabinet and the civil service.

During the past decade, the high sanctity that has traditionally surrounded the doctrines of collective and individual ministerial responsibility has begun to vanish. The Wilson government allowed members of the cabinet to dissociate themselves from the majority decision on the common market and to express their dissent publicly. The precedent has since been repeated under his successor. While it may in general be necessary in a functional sense for the cabinet to stand together and for members in fundamental disagreement with their colleagues to resign, this rule need not be associated with a policy of total secrecy for cabinet business. The joint responsibility aspect of the doctrine can be dissociated from the secrecy rule in an age which more readily accepts that disagreement is an anvil on which final policy decisions are hammered out. Moreover, the rationale of the doctrine is in part historical and the necessity, for example, of presenting a united front to the monarch hardly applies today. The endorsement of the secrecy aspect of convention by the court in the Crossman Diaries case is perhaps a belated judicial attempt to rescue a crumbling rule. Confidentiality in discussions leading to the formation of policy is certainly a desirable practice but it does not follow that it needs to be backed up by an enforceable legal rule or something as majestic as a constitutional convention. The American approach of qualifying the positive right to information by an exception protecting pre-decisional discussion seems more realistic since if the mutual trust and confidence which the secrecy rule is supposed to create actually breaks down, no convention or judicial decision will prevent knowledge of disagreement leaking out. Confidentiality is less a pre-condition of effective co-operation than a consequence of it. Individual ministerial responsibility has also lost both its historical justification and former attractiveness. It has recently been described as a 'survival from a concept of government where the governing class . . . did not feel it necessary honestly to account for their actions' and in which 'the authority necessary to government was maintained as a mystique . . .'.[37] It is questionable that secrecy is a necessary corollary to the rule that the Minister should take responsibility for departmental actions in Parliament and, in any event, secrecy frequently enables the Minister to evade responsibility in Parliament by confusing those who are ignorant of the real facts and background to government actions. The necessity of confidentiality for pre-decisional discussion between ministers and their advisers is conceded; but again it would be more realistic and less harmful to democratic accountability to make that confidentiality dependent upon the trust which actually exists and to qualify any positive right to information about government by an exemption protecting candid advice. In summary, the rationale for both conventions is today weak and unpersuasive but they have certainly not yet lost their grip upon official and judicial attitudes.

The South African constitutional structure is similar to the British, particularly in respect of the non-separation of powers between the executive and legislative branches. If there is a difference it lies in the more effective domination of Parliament by the executive. The conventions of collective and individual ministerial responsibility are applicable and the corollary of secrecy is clearer in the case of the former convention because minutes of cabinet meetings are not taken.[38] The conventions have not become matters of public controversy in South Africa partly because of the institutional support which secrecy enjoys in government. The two-party system is formally dominant in Parliament with the result that institutional challenge to the conventions in the form of an active and aggressive system of committees is inconceivable. Ministerial responsibility is more correctly ministerial unaccountability since no serious parliamentary probing into governmental activities is permitted. The South African experience has certainly stripped away the elements of myth and mystique that surround the conventions, making them, to the extent that reliance is needed, simple instruments of monolithic power.

The written constitution in South Africa incorporates no bill of rights and in this respect matches the situation in Britain; in their practices the two societies differ *toto caelo* mainly because of South Africa's politics of domination. Effective political rights exist for Whites only and civil rights for all have been eroded near to the point of extinction.[39] The most fundamental right—that of personal freedom—has been nullified by a series of detention-without-trial laws and broad statutory incursions into freedom of expression are the order of the day. There is limited support for such rights where they threaten to limit White hegemony and they therefore tend to lack socio-cultural roots. The outcome of this situation is that there is no context of rights and liberties into which an information right could be incorporated. Without a cluster of related rights to support it, freedom of information, even if formally established, would simply wither away.

POLITICAL INSTITUTIONS

Earlier discussion has shown that the division of power between separate institutions of government may have a powerful positive effect on access to information about public affairs. Experience has also demonstrated that the nature of political institutions and their manner of operation are equally crucial to freedom of information. The most important of these political institutions are legislative bodies and the public bureaucracies whose function, style and techniques of operation are frequently different in otherwise similar societies. As between the United States, on the one hand, and Britain and South Africa on the other, the differences are highly significant and result in widely divergent information practices.

The American Congress was conceived as a 'supreme watchdog' of the people's liberties from the earliest times. Francis Rourke's description of the functions of a legislative body is typical of American characterizations of the informing function of that organ of government:

> 'For a representative body is, intrinsically, an organ of publicity which ventilates grievances, exposes malfeasance on the part of executive officials, and constantly informs itself and the community of emergent issues in public policy.'[40]

The historical investigative and informing power is in part constitutional since the courts, as we have seen, have endorsed it as ancillary to the legislative function. Apart from legal/constitutional sanctions to give effect to the power Congress could (but rarely does) employ the weapons of impeachment, contempt or fund-blocking to secure information from the executive branch and to counter the use of executive privilege.[41] In fact, the use of the informing power is secured chiefly through the committee system which, for purposes of securing information, is a pre-eminent feature of congressional operations. The committees of the American legislature and their fact-finding function are deeply imbedded in the structure of government;[42] and while these committees have the dangers that McCarthyism underlined, they also carry with them the abiding virtue of being proven instruments for eliciting information. They were set up at an early stage of American history with sovereignty in their respective fields and with terms of reference 'deliberately drawn to correspond as closely as possible to the departmental structure of executive power'.[43] 'Continuous watchfulness' over administration was an explicit function and by being granted the means of achieving it the committees are nowadays 'industrious, self-contained, numerous, permanent and influential'.[44] The investigative function of Congress was given a powerful impetus by the Legislative Reorganization Act of 1946 which directed standing committees to exercise 'continuous watchfulness' over the administration of the laws by government agencies.[45] Of great practical importance is the fact that congressional committees have their own budget and staffs which enables them to develop into fully effective counter-centres of power and information. As a result Congress has developed into 'one of the best-informed parliaments in the world'.[46]

Parliament in the United Kingdom enjoys no constitutional separation from the executive and is dominated by the cabinet and the civil service even in respect of its legislative functions. Whereas the Senate and House of Representatives actually formulate legislation, the function of the House of Commons is different: 'It *examines* and *passes* legislation proposed by its government.'[47] While theoretically speaking the British member of Parliament exercises unlimited power through the House, the realities are different and have been well described by Anthony Sampson:

'But in practice, the member (like the shareholder) finds he cannot get hold of an issue until it becomes a *fait accompli*, and that the real battles for power are taking place away from his purview. The persons within his jurisdiction are too many and too secret to be known, let alone controlled'.[48]

The ancient and unlimited power of enquiry[49] has been subdued by cabinet government, the two-party system and the growth of bureaucracy; and an exhaustive study of the Treasury has revealed that 'parliament plays little direct part in expenditure decision-making'.[50] The committee system, in contrast to the position in the United States, is poorly developed and, as a result, 'parliament is powerless to interrogate Ministers fully, question the permanent secretariate, or call for departmental papers down to the lowest, but often most revealing, levels of administration'.[51] Though there are both standing and select committees, these tend to lack teeth since they are without adequate research and secretarial staff and are dependent on the House to enforce their right to send for persons and papers. British parliamentary committees, it has been rightly said, 'are not sources of power but vehicles for detailed work'.[52] The power to send for papers, in any event, is a limited one since only documents of a public or official character are covered.[53] It is not surprising that a survey in Britain has disclosed that most members of the House of Commons feel that they are ill-informed about the administrative acts of government and the civil service.[54] With Parliament lacking adequate information the general public will obviously be substantially in the dark.

Parliament in South Africa is also not constitutionally separated from the executive but its subordination to the cabinet is far more extreme than in the United Kingdom. It hardly exercises an enquiring and informing function under the exigencies of the power politics that nowadays characterize government in South Africa. Whereas the committee system in Britain is underdeveloped, in South Africa there has been no significant progress whatever. British select committees have made some progress in achieving their intended purpose of informed criticism and scrutiny of the aims and actions of the executive;[55] and some committees 'specializing over a period in areas of government activity rather than specific actions or events'[56] have been set up.[57] The result, though unimpressive by American standards, is that already in the 1960s a new balance between Parliament and the executive had been struck.[58] Similar developments have occurred in Canada where under the Trudeau government in 1968 a structure of eighteen standing committees governing a broad range of governmental administration and with power to send for persons and papers was set up.[59] Corresponding developments in South Africa are entirely lacking and no attention has been given to the idea of maintaining a balance between Parliament and the executive. Dissatisfaction in South Africa with the 'Westminster system' appears to spring from the opposite desire for stronger and more unfettered executive government; and it is usually forgotten that the Westminster system has not remained static in Britain and elsewhere as it has in South Africa. In the circumstances, critical reference to that system is to a petrified institution deprived of the opportunity to develop and of its normal context of political freedom,

It has been said that the supreme authority of the cabinet and a weak committee system make secrets easier to keep.[60] In South Africa the appointment of committees *over a period of time* to supervise branches of government business is unknown. There are sessional committees such as the Public Accounts and Railways and Harbours committees but their functions are substantially related to expenditure control and no tradition of independent scrutiny and criticism of the aims and general actions of the administration has been developed.[61] The British convention that the Public Accounts committee is chaired by a member of the Opposition has found no local favour, nor has the recently authorized practice of certain select committees in the United Kingdom to travel abroad. Under such conditions the keeping of secrets is virtually guaranteed and Parliament is incapable of monitoring the administration or acting as a communications system between the government and the public.

Even such institutions as question time in Parliament have ceased to have any real informing function in South Africa. They have a limited value in societies that take them more seriously,[62] mainly because members of Parliament lack the information enabling them to ask the right questions.[63] Parliamentary question time in South Africa has become an institution for the denial of information rather than its provision. Refusals to answer tabled questions relate to such non-sensitive information as negotiations for foreign loans, the *names* of members of a review committee appointed to hear appeals from persons detained under the Internal Security Act, details of submissions from the public relating to the banning of a film entitled 'The Rocky Horror Picture Show' and the qualifications of persons appointed to censorship committees under the Publications Act.[64] The government's conception of what is sensitive is now so broad that even narrowly defined factual material is proving hard to get during question time.

Public bureaucracies, especially at the senior adviser or upper civil servant level, have become semi-independent centres of political power in modern states. The very fact that the bureaucracies are our chief storers of information means that they possess great power.[65] For a variety of reasons related to the nature and functions of bureaucracies, there is an inevitable drive or momentum towards secrecy in such organizations. The reasons include the fear of harming the state upon which members of the bureaucracy are dependent for security, the belief that efficiency (the dominant principle of bureaucratic organization) is furthered by secrecy, and the need to protect bureaucratic interests against other centres of political power. Quite apart

from tendencies inherent in bureaucratic organization, other factors
connected with the tradition, nature and style of operation of particular
bureaucracies may either further or retard the drive towards secrecy.
It is these other factors that concern us here.

The civil service in Britain has 'steadfastly adhered to secrecy as one
of the first principles of sound government'.[66] Richard Crossman spoke
of its 'delight in secrecy' and 'passion for keeping the public in the
dark'.[67] The origin of this closed tradition, it has been said, is that
government in the late nineteenth century was in the nature of a club;[68]
and the atmosphere in Whitehall today remains one of hushed discretion and dignity. The tradition also stems from the privileged class
composition[69] of the civil service which has only recently begun to
change. As a variety of writers have said, this has meant the relations
between the civil service and the public have traditionally been characterized by aloofness, suspicion and even hostility.[70] Even where such
pejorative terms are not justified, the tradition has at the lowest resulted
in a deficiency in human touch[71] which has served to maintain a
barrier between bureaucracy and public. In the result it seems that the
lack of channels of communication between the civil service and its
environment, a serious problem with most bureaucracies,[72] has been
acute in Great Britain.

The tendency to cover up has been exacerbated by a frequently
venerated feature of the British civil service—the 'cult of high-minded
amateurism'.[73] In an age which increasingly requires specialists in the
managerial and administrative aspects of government, there will be
an almost natural tendency, on the part of a civil service which has
notoriously lacked such skills, to cover up mistakes and incompetence
in order to protect the Whitehall image.[74] However, reasons of this
kind merely fortify the old tight-lipped and sealed-lipped tradition
maintained by strong internal discipline, which included punishment
for disclosures. Finally, secrecy has been used by the civil service, as in
the case of many other power groupings, to enlarge its political power
even to the extent of concealing the secrets of past governments by
removing documents from old files and creating new ones.[75] The
keepers of secrets of outgoing governments thereby fortify their
positions vis-à-vis the incoming politicians.[76] Even though the contemporary recruitment of previously non-privileged groups into the
civil service has begun to erode old traditions,[77] the public bureaucracy
in Britain remains a substantially closed and inaccessible community.

Though there is virtually no searching and critical writing on the
civil service in South Africa,[78] it is undoubtedly an impregnable fortress
for state papers and documents. In his inaugural lecture, an alien
appointed to a chair of public administration in South Africa, said that
'[o]ne of the things that strikes one, as a foreigner in South Africa, is
the amount of secrecy and confidentiality to be found everywhere'.[79]
He also observed, with undeniable accuracy, that it was 'almost

impossible' to obtain any real information on prison administration in the country.[80] An American journalist, assigned to write a report on South Africa for the journal *Town and Country*, described his task his toughest yet because of the uncommunicativeness of officials in government. He described their lack of co-operation as 'incredible' and 'terrible'.[81] One of the major reasons for the absolutely closed nature of the public bureaucracy in South Africa is its largely White composition. The following quotation indicates the racial composition of the public service in 1972:

> 'The government employs, in one way or another, 26 per cent of the white population, 12 per cent of the Coloured, 8 per cent of the Indian population, and 7,8 per cent of the Bantu population.'[82]

If one takes into account the fact that all senior and certainly key appointments are in White hands and, increasingly, in the hands of government supporters, the 'loyalty' of the civil service as keepers of official information is not at all surprising. It is significant that one of the few instances when that loyalty broke down in recent years was at the time of the right-wing break-away of the HNP from the ruling party in 1969. For a short period, official documents (including one on telephone tapping) were mailed anonymously to the right-wing politicians who split off from the ruling party;[83] but the ranks closed again soon after. The disclosure of information which might embarrass the government in the Black versus White political contest, as opposed to the internal conflicts of White politics, is today completely unthinkable in the light of the predominantly White composition and total White control of public administration. A final underlying reason for the reliability of the civil service in controlling information, is the job security which the public service has traditionally provided for a large percentage of the White population, and especially the Afrikaner White population. This dependence virtually guarantees that employees will not embarrass the government which employs them by disclosing its secrets.

The qualities of loyalty and efficiency, so heavily emphasized in British and South African public administration, are counterbalanced in America by the requirement of responsiveness and accountability. This is in substantial measure due to the fact that 'a democratic political system was already well established . . . when a bureaucracy of substantial size first began to emerge in the latter part of the nineteenth century'.[84] In the European societies, and equally in South Africa, democracy (to the extent applicable) has had to accommodate itself to the bureaucracy,[85] whereas in the United States it was the other way round. From early times the American public has suspected officialdom—'[t]he popular feeling about government bureaucrats combines mistrust, dislike, and contempt with a degree of fear'.[86] As a result, bureaucracy has been seen as the servant rather than the master of the public; and its members recognize a loyalty to the public together with their responsibility to the employing government. Loyalty to the public finds expression in practices such as that of 'blowing the whistle' which government officers frequently indulge in to alert the public to malpractices and corruption.[87]

The more open tradition of American bureaucracy is strongly reinforced by its openness to outside penetration.[88] This is due partly to the fact that a 'much larger segment at the top . . . is filled by political appointments'[89] (the so-called spoils system) and to the mobility between government and the private sphere. Another specifically American feature of bureaucracy is the extensive use made of outside advisers who in the course of their work come into contact with much official information. The changing composition of American bureaucracy, especially at the upper levels, is responsible for much of the flow of information about government to the press and public. The result is that the tradition, style and composition of the public administration in the United States all tend to further public knowledge about official administration.

STRUCTURAL FEATURES

The social structure of a society may have a direct or indirect influence upon patterns of information flow within that society. 'Structure' in this context refers not just to the class structure of the society in question (though that is obviously included) but more broadly to social arrangements and processes which have solidified sufficiently to be termed characteristic of it.[90] These arrangements and processes are of various kinds and will include references to such matters as economic inequality, political pluralism, the machinery of coercion, and so on. The structural aspects discussed in this section will be those that seem to bear upon the citizen's right and power to secure information about government administration.

Both the United States and Britain are fully enfranchised political communities in which all citizens are vested with political and civil rights to a satisfactory degree. The correspondence of the political arrangements of these societies to 'procedural democracy', as opposed to 'substantive democracy',[91] is very close. In different language, all subjects are formally equal in respect of the right to vote, to hold political office and to exercise the basic freedoms of speech, assembly, press and the like. The formal equality is not matched, however, by a substantive equality due mainly to inequality of income and wealth and differential patterns of political influence and access to political office. While it seems clear and agreed that the disadvantaged classes in both America and Britain have a considerably higher income in absolute terms than four or five decades ago, in relative terms there has been an insignificant change in their share of income or wealth.

Gabriel Kolko, in commenting on the situation in the United States, has said that 'the basic distribution of income and wealth in the United States is essentially the same now as it was in 1939, or even 1910'; and he adds that 'most low-income groups live substantially better today, but even though their real wages have mounted, their percentage of the national income has not changed'.[92] A table of income for American families in 1962 shows that while the lowest fifth earned 6% of the total income, the highest fifth took 43%. In 1941 the figures were 5% and 48% respectively.[93] Figures for Great Britain point towards a similar situation, and it has been estimated that at the end of the sixties 'a minority of one in twenty between them took a larger share (of income) than went to the third of the population with the lowest incomes'.[94] In 1967, the poorest 30% of the population earned only $11\frac{1}{2}$% of the total value of allocated income.[95] Though the statistics are a little dated, it does appear from comparative analyses that the distribution of income of Britain and America follow almost identical curves[96] and that in each society the *relative* share of the poor has not improved significantly in relation to the wealthy or wealthier segments of the population. In both countries there is also a gross inequality of wealth, the position in Britain being somewhat worse than that in the United States.[97] Notwithstanding the great complexities surrounding the calculation of income and wealth distribution and continuing disputes about matters such as the evaluation of the contribution of government services (health, housing, etc) toward redress of the imbalances, it seems indisputable that a large degree of economic inequality is still a feature of these two Western democracies.

What are the consequences of a structural inequality in which a minority have a monopoly of 'material resources, status and political power'[98] of which a large section of the majority is deprived to a corresponding degree? The most important result for our purposes is that there will inevitably be a sharp divergence between the formal and the substantive rights of citizens, including the right to information and the cluster of associated rights upon which its effectiveness depends. In the United States where an affirmative right to information does exist, and where associated constitutional rights are available to all, the poorest and weakest section of the population is obviously less able to enjoy and enforce these rights where they conflict with the interests of the wealthy and the powerful. If, as is frequently alleged,[99] there are close links between big business and government, the exercise of rights by the disadvantaged sections of the community can be frustrated all the more easily. Moreover, as Claus Mueller has shown, structural inequalities tend to produce an 'arrested'[100] political communication due to 'class specific language codes'.[101] The powerful minorities will couch policies, explanations and data 'in a language which itself contains pre-definitions and interpretations that serve the purpose of maintaining an undisturbed exercise of political power'.[102] Information which is 'doctored' in this way, while legally available to any person or group, does not reach those whose closed language codes prevent a deciphering or reinterpretation. Paradoxically therefore information may be withheld as it is given.

Notwithstanding these negative tendencies, certain structural and other social features in the United States have tended to modify T B Bottomore's maxim that 'the economic dominance of a particular class has very often been the basis for its political rule'.[103] In other words, the political consequences of economic inequality have been checked by the countervailing force of other social realities. The most significant reality of a structural kind is undoubtedly the political pluralism that is characteristic of the United States. Pluralism in this sense means a specialized and relatively autonomous political infrastructure of 'subsystems such as political parties, pressure groups and the media of mass communication . . .'.[104] While the levelling effect of pluralism has frequently been exaggerated, it has acted, in the words of William Kornhauser, as a 'guarantee against the aggrandizement of power by elites'[105] to a not insignificant degree. Even if that statement claims too much for pluralism, there can be little argument about its decisive role in making the right to information meaningful. After observing that pluralism implies that 'the same stocks of data are differently used and interpreted by influential voices in the decision process', Harold Lasswell states the need for 'pluralist elements' in modern nations to 'seize promptly on modern methods of documentation' in order to inject new initiatives into the political process and thereby to create a 'public order in which power is genuinely shared'.[106] This has been happening to an increasing degree in the United States, especially since statute law has conferred a positive right of access to information upon the citizen. Private groups such as the American Civil Liberties Union and the Freedom of Information Clearing House[107] have assisted individuals and organizations to obtain information from government offices and agencies, and this information is frequently the basis of political initiatives that were not possible without it. The Freedom of Information Clearing House, acting for Carl Stern, a newscaster for NBC, won access to FBI documents relating to the establishment and disestablishment of certain counter-intelligence programmes. Following this the Attorney-General had the FBI counter-intelligence activities investigated and concluded that they had no place in a free society.[108] Pluralism in America has also made possible what Kent Cooper has described as 'unrestricted publication by private enterprise'[109] of which the aggressive, independent newspaper is the best example. Though all newspapers are undoubtedly limited by the policies and controls of proprietors, many newspapers in the United States have demonstrated impressive editorial independence and have contributed to open government by publication of official documents like the Pentagon Papers. Where a healthy political pluralism prevails, it is also possible for the new élite of information keepers within government to be balanced by private experts and specialists outside government. Outside pressure groups, led by their own experts, are taking advantage of the positive right to information which American law confers. Such activity is undoubtedly an important preliminary to social reform.

Both state-sponsored[110] and private systems of civil legal aid are available to poor citizens or groups that wish to enforce information access laws. As already observed, the Freedom of Information Act gives courts the discretion to award costs against the government where the plaintiff has substantially prevailed.[111] The effects of inequality on the information right are materially mitigated by rules of this kind and by private institutions (and, sometimes, even public institutions such as the Office of Economic Opportunity) which flourish under American political pluralism. Inequality undoubtedly hampers the use which the poor and dispossessed can make of information which comes into their hands; but it appears to have only a limited effect upon the enforcement of the information right itself.

As previously indicated income inequality and especially the inequality of wealth is serious in Britain as well as the United States. The British problem is compounded by the tenacity and prevalence of class distinctions which have restricted the social mobility that changes in economic conditions and educational policies ought to have brought about. Bottomore has said that there is today 'no general sense of greater "classlessness" nor of great opportunities for the individual to choose and create his way of life regardless of inherited wealth or social position'.[112] At the same time the countervailing forces of political pluralism are weaker in Britain than in the United States. This is partly because membership in 'secondary groups' is not as high (60 per cent of Americans as opposed to 50 per cent of Britons belong to secondary groups)[113] so that pressure groups tend to be less active than in America. The press in Britain is notably weaker than its American counterpart and probably could not undertake contests with the government of the magnitude of the Pentagon Papers dispute. The inevitable result of these factors is that the substantive inequality of rights formally held by British subjects is a greater problem that across the Atlantic.[114] Since, however, there is no positive right to information which any class or group can enforce in the United Kingdom, this inequality is not directly relevant to access to information about government. Of course, much information gets out through informal channels and institutions such as the 'old boy' network ensure differential access to such information. The principle of limiting the need to know to the 'right' persons is still very strong in Britain.

Disparities of wealth and income are severe in South Africa. In a recent study it has been estimated that the top 10% of the population take 57% of the personal income while the bottom 80% receive only

26%.[115] Reliable studies of the relative shares of wealth are not available but the disproportions can be assumed to be gross in view of the income situation. Of course the social structure in South Africa is not simply economic and to a considerable degree the classes are constituted, to borrow Bottomore's terminology, by specific legal rules.[116] The caste-like social structure of the society has frequently been commented upon and the following passage from Kinloch is representative of sociological descriptions of the specifically South African class structure:

> 'Role assignment in South African society is thus based mainly on ascriptive characteristics (i.e. race) and generally represents a highly closed system in which caste elements determine the shape of the opportunity structure. . . . Social mobility is only possible within each racial caste and is highly limited among the non-whites.'[117]

A major consequence of the legal entrenchment of social classes is that economic inequality runs largely along racial lines. We have seen that 57% of personal income is taken by the top 10% of the population. This top group is 97% White annd only 3% Black.[118] The relative shares of income earned by the different population groups has hardly changed in three decades. In 1946–7 the percentages were

   White 71,3   Coloured 4,5   Asian 2,0   African 22,2.

In 1970 these figures read

   White 71,9   Coloured 6,4   Asian 2,3   African 19,3.[119]

While it has been demonstrated that the Black share of personal income improved measurably in the period 1970–5, thereby producing over this period an estimated 6% increase in the share taken by Blacks,[120] the economic recession since 1975 and the consequent heavy increase in Black unemployment have diminished if not eliminated these gains. Even allowing for recent changes, the figures confirm that there is 'an extreme degree of racial income inequality'.[121] In evaluating the figures account should be taken of the fact that the Whites are only about one-sixth of the total population.

   South Africa is distinguishable from Britain and America by much more than the fact that wealth and poverty run closely along racial lines. There is a fundamental inequality in South Africa in respect of political rights since Whites have a virtual monopoly of political power. The impact of the 'homelands' policy and of the special political institutions created for Coloureds and Asians has had only a marginal influence on the distribution of political power and there are no indications of any substantial change in this situation. The Coloured and Asian people, and the very large number of Africans who are permanently settled outside the Transkei and Bophuthatswana,[122] remain effectively disfranchised. The loss of basic civil rights as a result of the enactment of preventive detention laws and laws providing for banning and house arrest (to mention only some examples) affects both the Black and White populations in the country, but Blacks carry other legal disabilities which are inapplicable to Whites. Africans are subject to the influx control and pass laws and to residential, business and employment restrictions. All Blacks are educated under different and inferior educational programmes. In sum, inequality in South Africa is severe and operates both at the formal and the substantive levels.

The institutionalization of inequality along racial lines has necessarily produced discontent and reaction which in turn have been responsible for certain other structural characteristics of the social system. The most obvious is the powerful machinery of coercion which White rulers have created to control challenges to the system. However the coercive machinery is characterized—Heribert Adams's 'dictatorial terror' as opposed to irrational terror of the Fascist or totalitarian kind seems the most acceptable description[123]—there is no denying that it is a material element of the social system. Extensive reliance on coercion means that institutions for the regulation of conflict are noticeable more by their absence. South Africa is not a society 'whose institutions are characterized throughout by the recognition and rational canalization of conflict'.[124] Conflict tends to be kept outside the political system and to be dealt with by coercion wherever it becomes serious. This is strikingly evident when a strike of Black workers occurs as the first on the scene are usually the police, and refusal to return to work is frequently met by arrests and criminal charges. The heavy reliance on coercion as a response to conflict has meant the destruction or rigid control of intermediate institutions and secondary centres of autonomy. Political bodies have regularly been banned outright (for example the ANC and PAC), others forced out of existence by statutory restrictions (for example the Liberal Party)[125] and a whole range of organizations intimidated, harassed and neutralized. The press, which even the authorities still like to proclaim as the freest in Africa, has lost a little of that freedom each year and the basis for the boast may soon disappear altogether. The restraints under which the South African press is forced to operate are numerous. A new newspaper may be denied registration unless a deposit of up to R20 000 to ensure 'good behaviour' is lodged with the Minister of Justice; and a newspaper whose conduct is disapproved of by the Minister will forfeit the deposit if it is thereafter banned.[126] Newspapers may be banned by the State President[127] and this has happened on several occasions. In October 1977, the newspaper *The World* was banned and its editor placed in detention. Journalists are sometimes banned, detained or harassed where their activities displease the authorities. Broad political crimes restrict what newspapers may print and prosecutions for publication of 'offensive' material are not uncommon. Examples of such prosecutions are for publication of material relating to prison conditions or matter which expresses anti-White hostility (the SASO and BPC trials under the

Terrorism Act). In 1977 the government introduced a bill to control the press but later withdrew the measure after the press had agreed to a stricter voluntary code administered by the Press Council set up by the Newspaper Press Union in 1962. Political criticism has moderated since these developments but this has not prevented government ministers from threatening to close down newspapers or to reintroduce the withdrawn measure if the press does not 'put its own house in order'. Nor has it prevented the banning of *The World*, the detention of its editor, or the banning and detention of other editors (such as Donald Woods) and many journalists. Finally, it is noteworthy that under the Publications Control Act newspapers not falling under the Newspaper Press Union are regularly banned on political grounds. In the first seven months of 1977 approximately 40 student publications were banned under the Act. Control over the press and numerous other organizations and institutions in South Africa has curtailed political pluralism to the extent that it hardly qualifies as a counter-vailing or restraining force.

In the language of Dahl, the South African political system may be characterized as one of limited polyarchy for Whites and hegemony over Blacks.[128] Competition between White groups is currently of minimal significance and the politics of the country revolves around the conflict between the politically entrenched White group and the excluded Black groups. The political rulers respond to this conflict largely by strengthening the sinews of political power and there is at best a limited attempt at accommodation. Halting and ineffectual steps have been taken to institutionalize conflict between the White group and the Coloured and Asian groups. Conflict canalization in response to Black demands is almost non-existent and these are dealt with more by exclusion than incorporation, by coercive power rather than accommodation. The inevitable result is that politics in South Africa is largely a matter of power and domination with the inevitable result that basic rights, including the right to information, stand no chance of realization. Secrecy, we have seen, is practised as an adjunct to power. Where politics is reduced to a naked power struggle, information becomes one of the major weapons of the contest, and the information right, and other basic political and civil rights, the inevitable victims. Secrecy increases (and information diminishes) proportionately to the degree to which power is used as a response to social conflict. It is therefore deeply imbedded in the South African social structure.

POLITICAL CULTURE

Current information policies and practices are attributable in part to the political cultures of the three societies with which we are concerned. The term 'political culture' refers to the 'attitudes, beliefs and sentiments that give order and meaning to the political process'.[129] In attempting a brief description of political culture in each society, the focus will again fall on those aspects that seem specially significant for access to information about public administration. In the United States and Great Britain there appear to be relatively uniform political cultures of which the main features are fairly easily identified and agreed upon by social scientists. The fragmented nature of South African society makes it impossible to speak of a single political culture and in this instance we shall concentrate on the political culture of the dominant White group whose attitudes have a determinative influence on information laws and practices. Within the White group, the political culture of the ruling Afrikaner majority is clearly crucial.

The earlier description of the theory of political authority in America as one which emphasizes the derivation of authority from the people is a good starting point for a brush-stroke account of American political beliefs and attitudes. An egalitarian tradition, though modified by 'capitalist élitism',[130] has characterized American politics from the earliest stages and is responsible for certain attitudes that have a profound influence on citizen access to information. That tradition has freed American politics from the tyranny of 'authority and revelation'[131] and explains the 'passionate bent against hierarchy'[132] in the society. Egalitarianism is one of the major roots of the political demand that the executive be accessible to the people[133] and the rejection of hierarchy is present in most societies in which information is freely available. Egalitarianism can be traced back to the sturdy and self-reliant citizens that were the product of an early 'protestant individualist culture'[134] and which bred a powerful sense of civic responsibility. The belief in civic competence has generally been associated with (possibly in a causal sense) a lack of deference towards, and trust of, political leaders.[135] There is almost a natural tendency to suspect and even distrust political leaders in America and a pervasive belief, in the words of Henry Steele Commager, that 'democracy cannot function unless the people are permitted to know what their government is up to'.[136] The confidence of the American citizen in his civic competence is associated with a mentality of bargaining and compromise in politics[137] and with widespread support for fundamental political and civil rights. It follows that the typical American citizen believes that he has a right to participate in politics and to all the rights that are required to make that participation meaningful. Over and above that he does more than subscribe to the belief that citizens have a right to know about government business—he also actually wants to know what his political representatives have been doing. Of course political realities do not always rise to the level of articulated beliefs, and there have been periods in which, for example, an 'unquestioning popular fear of communism'[138] has led to an attitude of 'our leader knows best'. These periods are undoubtedly aberrations in the American cultural tradition which is in general favourable to an effective right of access to government information.

While Britain shares with the United States a general belief in basic political and civil rights, the sense of citizen initiative has always been combined with an attitude of deference towards authority.[139] Hierarchy and acceptance of the notion that 'the greater in degree govern the lesser'[140] are historically strong features in British culture. They account for the popular presumption of trust which has so long characterized politics—a trust which Richard Rose found still to be present in his recent work on English politics:

> 'They (Englishmen) continue to trust the goodwill and bona fides of their governors and the civil servants who do most of the day-to-day work of the government.'[141]

Even if trust and deference are beginning to break down in the United Kingdom they have been relevant until recent times and account substantially for the state of the law and current information practices. Moreover, the United Kingdom has yet to develop, as a replacement for trust and deference, a tradition of informed participation in the affairs of government. It is significant that the principle 'if only you knew what we (the leaders) know' has had a respected place in British politics and is even now not completely discredited.

The earlier description of social structure in South Africa revealed the existence of a racial oligarchy in which White rulers respond to challenges to their privilege and exclusive power through legalized instruments of coercion. Historically this dominance has been strongly fortified by an appropriate political culture. The racial elements had their origin in early frontier society for, as MacCrone has observed, 'the intense and exclusive group consciousness of the frontier found expression in a consciousness of race and social supremacy which coincided almost uniformly with the distinctions based upon creed and colour.'[142] Though official justifications for present policy rest upon differentiation rather than inferiority, the racial basis is still the foundation since every citizen's political and legal status is conclusively determined by racial categorization under the Population Registration Act.[143] Also observable from the earliest times was a 'civil theology' according to which the Afrikaner people had been chosen for a special destiny, an election which rendered 'demonic' all threats to Afrikaner separateness.[144] From this theology flows a fanatical insistence on 'volkseenheid' and unity and the notion of the small, beleaguered nation pitted against a veritable ocean of hostile forces. T Dunbar Moodie has graphically illustrated the durability of the theme of conflict with (as opposed to incorporation of) South African Blacks in the following quotation from Dr D F Malan:

> 'In that new Blood river, black and white meet together in much closer contact and *a much more binding struggle* than when one hundred years ago the circle of white tented wagons protected the laager, and a muzzleloader clashed with an assegaai.'[145]

In such a conflict disunity or 'skeuring' is seen as a social crime of a specially heinous nature.

The doctrine of divine election is one which appears to vest a special authority in leaders and to lead more generally to a high social value being placed upon authority and revelation. Authority was bolstered from the outset by a patriarchial family structure and by an imperious frontiersman tradition which MacCrone characterizes as the 'aristocracy of a rude society'.[146] Dahrendorf's observation that in Imperial Germany the words 'nation, state, tight control, the interest of the whole, adaptation and subordination'[147] came up again and again in policy discussions is applicable also to contemporary South Africa where a slightly different usage puts the stress upon discipline, authority, obedience and order. It goes without saying that the elevation of authority and order imply a lower respect for rights and participation, and belief in basic political and civil rights has always enjoyed a precarious hold in South African political culture.

Though it has been argued that some of these features of political culture have been substantially modified and that nationalism particularly is less exclusive and less reliant on a well-defined authority structure,[148] it seems nearer the truth to regard their hold as being substantially undiminished. Nationalism may have broadened sufficiently to incorporate the English but this is clearly subject to the rider that the disposition of the affairs of state remains in Afrikaner Nationalist hands. Very recently, Otto Krause, an enlightened or 'verligte' nationalist by reputation, said that 'speaking as an Afrikaner and a Nationalist, I think one can say that Afrikaners one way or another do not intend, nor would they want to share power with anybody'.[149] The divine origin of authority and leadership is much less a part of English political culture and is hardly part of explicit Afrikaner rationalization of power today; but this is of limited significance since, as Dunbar Moodie has argued, ethnic exclusivism is likely to give way to a 'common White "anti-communist" authoritarianism'.[150] English political culture contains powerful strains of authoritarianism[151] and the principle that the leader knows best enjoys widespread English support, as in the following statement of F N Broome, an ex-Judge President of the Natal Supreme Court: 'But I am bound to credit the government with more knowledge of the facts than I, or the press, possess.'[152]

It seems reasonable to conclude that belief in White political control, in the coercive (security?) machinery, in ruling party unity and a veneration of authority continue to characterize the political culture of South Africa. Each one of these factors is hostile to access to information and the information right. White control through coercive measures indicates a preference for power over accommodation—and power politics and secrecy have always gone hand in hand. Afrikaner or White unity associated with the sin of 'skeuring' imply that official secrets should never be shared with the excluded groups. Veneration for authority concedes to the leaders the right to decide what to keep secret and simultaneously implies a low or non-existent desire on the part of the subject to discover what government is about. An independent survey conducted in 1977 among White voters has provided clear empirical confirmation that the enfranchised public simply do not regard the government as obligated to respond to citizen requests for information on important questions if the information would embarrass it.[153] A substantial proportion of the respondents supported the general proposition that political representatives have an obligation to account to the public for their actions during their term of office. The detailed breakdown of the responses to this question is as follows:

	Total %	Afrikaans %	English %
Agree completely	76,7	74,7	79,3
Agree partly	16,7	18,8	13,8
Disagree entirely	1,9	1,9	1,9
Uncertain	4,0	3,8	4,4
No response	0,7	0,8	0,6

In an attempt to make the issue more concrete and specific, respondents were asked to indicate their attitude to the proposition that citizens have still not been adequately informed about the South African government's Angolan intervention, the reason for it and the consequences of it. The returns to this question read as follows:

	Total %	Afrikaans %	English %
Agree completely	44,1	34,7	56,6
Agree partly	25,8	26,7	24,7
Disagree entirely	22,1	30,1	11,5
Uncertain	7,2	7,5	6,7
No response	0,8	1,0	0,5

The most revealing response was to the proposition that the press and public have a right of access to the reasons for government decisions and to government documents (other than obviously secret documents) even if the government would be embarrassed thereby. In this instance the responses were:

	Total %	Afrikaans %	English %
Agree completely	35,0	21,6	52,7
Agree partly	26,1	25,6	26,9
Disagree entirely	29,6	42,9	12,1
Uncertain	8,2	8,5	7,8
No response	1,1	1,4	0,5

These results indicate that while citizens tend to support broad propositions of a democratic kind, their actual understanding of democratic processes is shallow and their adherence to them very weak. The likelihood of embarrassment to the government is sufficient to nullify their claims to explanations of government actions[154] and their participatory role, as conceived by themselves, is seriously qualified.

CONCLUSIONS

The social climate in America is benignly in favour of an information right and its enforcement. The established theory of political authority, the constitution, the nature and style of political institutions and the political culture permit and even encourage the recognition of a citizen right to know. While the value of the right may be diminished by a structural inequality of income and wealth, there are even here countervailing forces which give substance to what would otherwise remain purely formal. In Britain the atmosphere is simultaneously clement and inclement. Theories of political authority, certain constitutional rules and practices, the style of administration and the political culture do not strongly favour more open practices of government but neither are they irrevocably opposed to them. If an information right were to be introduced structural inequality would present a more serious problem than in America but there are methods of overcoming this. The social factors in South Africa make up a climate that is almost entirely inhospitable if not menacing to the information right. The structure of inequality is harsh and rigid and the grossly inflated power aspect of politics promises increasing secrecy and inaccessibility. Movement towards an open society will require profound policy changes at the national level of government.

NOTES

[1] Richard Rose *Politics in England Today* 67.

[2] Almond & Verba *Civic Culture* 178–9.

[3] Louis Hartz *The Founding of New Societies* (Harcourt, Brace & World, Inc. New York, 1964).

[4] Ibid 76.

[5] Almond & Verba op cit 315.

[6] Alan Westin 'The Technology of Secrecy' in *None of Your Business: Government Secrecy in America* 290.

[7] Leonard B Boudin 'The Ellsberg Case: Citizen Disclosure' in *Secrecy and Foreign Policy* 306.

[8] Richard Rose op cit 67.

[9] E C S Wade & Godfrey Philips *Constitutional Law* 8 ed (Longman, London, 1970) 184.

[10] Samuel H Beer *Modern British Politics* 95.

[11] Walter A Rosenbaum *Political Culture* (Nelson, London, 1975) 71.

[12] T Dunbar Moodie, *The Rise of Afrikanerdom* (Univ of California Press, London, 1975) 12.

[13] Leo Marquard *The Peoples and Policies of South Africa* (Oxford Univ Press, 1969) 228.

[14] John Calvin *On God and Political Duty* (Bobbs–Merrill Co Inc, 1956) 81.

[15] Ibid 52.

[16] T Dunbar Moodie op cit 219.

[17] André du Toit 'Ideological Change, Afrikaner Nationalism and Pragmatic Racial Domination in South Africa' in *Change in Contemporary South Africa* eds L Thompson & T Butler (Univ of California Press, Berkeley, 1975) 19.

[18] Ibid 35.

[19] Allen Drury *A Very Strange Society* (Michael Joseph, London, 1967) 99.

[20] The Minister was commenting on the transformation of a typical young recruit to the Police Force and said: 'Hulle maak 'n pragtige mens van hom. Hy klap sy hakke as hy met jou praat.'

[21] Walter Lippmann *The Public Philosophy* 80.

[22] Ralf Dahrendorf *Society and Democracy in Germany* 137.

[23] Note: 'The Right of the Press to Gather Information' 71 *Colum L Rev* 838 (1971). The Supreme Court has yet to determine the constitutional status of the right to gather information but there are conflicting determinations in the lower courts: see 848 et seq. Recent cases on the right of press access to individual prisoners indicate that gathering information is an embryonic and still heavily qualified right: See Robert A Taft 'Prisons and the Right of the Press to Gather Information' (1974) 43 *Univ Cinc L Rev* 913. The Supreme Court has thus far declined to grant the press any greater gathering rights than are held by the public generally: see Randall P Bezanson 'The New Free Press Guarantee' (1977) 63 *Virginia L Rev* 731, 754.

[24] *New York Times* v *United States* 403 US 713 (1971) at 714 (the Pentagon Papers judgment).

[25] Senator Charles McC Mathias Jr quoting Richard Neustadt in 'Executive Privilege and Congressional Responsibility in Foreign Affairs' in *Secrecy and Foreign Policy* 70.

[26] Thomas M Franck & Edward Weisband 'Dissemblement, Secrecy and Executive Privilege in the Foreign Relations of Three Democracies: a Comparative Analysis' in *Secrecy and Foreign Policy* 425.

[27] Louis Henkin 'The Right to Know and the Duty to Withhold: The Case of the Pentagon Papers' (1971) 120 *Univ of Pa L Rev* 271.

[28] Kenneth Bradshaw & David Pring *Parliament and Congress* (Constable, London, 1972) 9.

[29] Ibid 355.

[30] Andrew Shonfield *Modern Capitalism* 392.

[31] J R Lucas *Democracy and Participation* chap 10.

[32] Ibid 197.

[33] Walter A Rosenbaum *Political Culture* 71.

[34] Wade & Phillips *Constitutional Law* 87.

[35] David Williams *Not in the Public Interest* 41.

[36] See the evidence of Sir John Hunt quoted by Hugo Young in *The Crossman Affair* 96.

[37] Quoted in Hugo Young *The Crossman Affair* 129.

[38] J P verLoren van Themaat *Staatsreg* 159.

[39] The extent of the erosion may be gauged from studies like A S Mathews's *Law Order and Liberty in South Africa* (Juta, Cape Town 1971) and J D van der Vyver's *Die Beskerming van Mensregte in Suid-Afrika* (Juta, Cape Town, 1975).

[40] Francis E Rourke *Secrecy and Publicity: The Dilemmas of Democracy* 62.

[41] These 'weapons' have been described as too crude and heavy to justify a ready resort to them: See Charles McC Mathias Jr 'Executive Privilege and Congressional Responsibility in Foreign Affairs' in *Secrecy and Foreign Policy* 81–3.

[42] Max Lerner *America as a Civilization* 421.

[43] K Bradshaw & D Pring *Parliament and Congress* 210–18.

[44] Ibid 218.

[45] Malcolm E Jewell & Samuel C Patterson *The Legislative Process in the United States* 2 ed (Random House, New York, 1973) 515.

[46] William C Olson 'The Role of Congress in Making the Foreign Policy of the United States' (1975) 56 *The Parliamentarian* 151 at 157.

[47] Stanley B Wheater 1974–5 *Parliamentary Affairs* 8 at 10.

[48] Anthony Sampson *The New Anatomy of Britain* 20–1.

[49] Raoul Berger *Executive Privilege: A Constitutional Myth* 31.

[50] Heclo & Wildavsky *The Private Government of Public Money* 243.

[51] Richard Middleton 'The Problems and Consequences of Parliamentary Government: A Historical View' 1969–1970 *Parliamentary Affairs* 55 at 58.

[52] Malcolm E Jewell & Samuel C Patterson op cit 219.

[53] J A G Griffith 'Government Secrecy in the United Kingdom' in *None of Your Business: Government Secrecy in America* 337–8; Erskine May *The Law, Privileges, Proceedings and Usages of Parliament* 647.

[54] Anthony Barker & Michael Rush *The Member of Parliament and His Information* (Allen & Unwin Ltd, London, 1970) 149.

[55] Erskine May op cit 670.

[56] Ibid 671.

[57] Examples are the select committees on Public Accounts, on Science and Technology, on Race Relations and Immigration and on the Parliamentary Commissioner for Administration.

[58] K Bradshaw & D Pring op cit 4.

[59] Michael Rush 'The Development of the Committee System in the Canadian House of Commons' (1974) 55 *The Parliamentarian* 86 at 154–6.

[60] Patrick Gordon Walker 'Secrecy and Openness in Foreign Policy Decision-making: A British Cabinet Perspective' in *Secrecy and Foreign Policy* 42–3.

[61] For a brief account of these committees and their functions, see R Kilpin *Parliamentary Procedure in South Africa* 3 ed (Juta, Cape Town, 1955) 122 et seq.

[62] R A R Maclennan, 'Secrecy and the Right of Parliament to know and Participate in Foreign Affairs' in *Secrecy and Foreign Policy* 138.

[63] David Williams op cit 59. See also K Bradshaw & D Pring op cit 366–70 who say that questions are only of real value in eliciting 'specifically defined factual information'.

[64] Many of these examples are cited in a special investigation published in the *Sunday Express* of 27 March 1977.

[65] Almond & Powell *Comparative Politics: A Developmental Approach* 155.

[66] David Williams op cit 55.

[67] Quoted by Stanley de Smith 'Official Secrecy and External Relations in Great Britain: The Law and its Context' in *Secrecy and Foreign Policy* 312.

[68] Jonathan Aitken *Officially Secret* 210.

[69] Max Nicholson *The System: The Misgovernment of Modern Britain* 463.

[70] Ibid. See also H Heclo & A Wildavsky op cit *passim*; Anthony Sampson *The New Anatomy of Britain* 376.

[71] Andrew Shonfield *Modern Capitalism* 425.

[72] Michael Crozier *The Bureaucratic Phenomenon* (Tavistock Publications, London, 1964) 194.

[73] Max Nicholson op cit 463.

[74] Jonathan Aitken op cit 39.

[75] Anthony Sampson *The New Anatomy of Britain* 233.

[76] Ibid 234.

[77] As shown, for example, by the previously discussed leak of cabinet papers to the New Society.

[78] J S N Cloete *Inleiding tot die Publieke Administrasie* 3 ed (Van Schaik, Pretoria, 1976) deals with public administration in general. Where his treatment is specific, it tends to be uncritical as in his categorical statement that the Republic of South Africa is a democratic state (p 24). He states that public business should not take place behind a curtain of secrecy (p 25) but fails to discuss the extent to which this occurs in the South African public service.

[79] J F Beekman 'The Power of Administration', Inaugural Lecture delivered at the University of Cape Town on 14 March 1973, 11.

[80] Ibid 12.

[81] *Daily News*, 3 June 1977.

[82] J F Beekman loc cit 14.

[83] One of the receivers of this information was unsuccessfully prosecuted in *S v Marais* 1971 (1) SA 844 (AD); but in *Minister of Police v Marais* 1970 (2) SA 467 (C) a civil interdict to prevent publication of the 'leaked' documents was granted.

[84] Francis E Rourke *Bureaucracy, Politics and Public Policy* (Little, Brown & Co, Boston, 1969) 56.

[85] Ibid.

[86] Max Lerner *America as a Civilization* 411.

[87] The whistle-blower has been described as the 'muckraker from within, who exposes what he considers the unconcionable practices of his own organization'. See *Blowing the Whistle: Dissent in the Public Interest* eds Charles Peters & Taylor Branch. (Praeger, NY, 1972) 4.

[88] Francis E Rourke op cit 102.

[89] Andrew Shonfield 'Britain in the Postwar World' in *Style in Administration: Readings in British Public Administration* eds Richard A Chapman & A Dunsire (Allen & Unwin, London, 1971) 413.

[90] This discussion of social structure seeks to avoid the debate about the meaning of the concept and the jargon in which some of that debate is conducted. The characterization of structure in this discussion is loose but this has been deliberately done in the interests of a clear and simple exposition of factors which do not fall under other headings such as political theory and culture, constitutional features and public administration.

[91] The expressions 'procedural democracy' and 'substantive democracy' are used by I Katznelson and M Kesselman in *The Politics of Power* (Harcourt Brace Jovanovich, Inc, NY 1975) chap 2.

[92] Gabriel Kolko *Wealth and Power in America* (Praeger, NY 1970) 3. Kolko has been criticized, for example, by H P Miller, 'Income Distribution in the United States' in *Wealth, Income and Inequality* ed A B Atkinson (Penguin, 1973) 114n1; but Miller's own figures do not derogate much from Kolko's conclusions.

[93] H P Miller loc cit 113.

[94] Westergaard & Resler *Class in a Capitalist Society* 41.

[95] Ibid 40.

[96] See A B Atkinson, *Unequal Shares: Wealth in Britain* (Penguin, 1974) 20.

[97] Ibid.

[98] Katznelson & Kesselman op cit 463.

[99] See, for example, Katznelson & Kesselman op cit 136 et seq and Edward S Greenberg *The American Political System: A Radical Approach* (Winthrop Publishers, Inc Cambridge, Mass 1977) 199.

[100] Arrested communication is distinguished by the author from 'directed' communication (achieved mainly by censorship and similar controls) and constrained communication (the successful structuring of communication by powerful groups to foster their interests): see Claus Mueller *The Politics of Communication* 19.

[101] Ibid 84.

[102] Ibid 87.

[103] T B Bottomore *Classes in Modern Society* (Allen & Unwin, Ltd, London, 1970) 14.

[104] Almond & Powell *Comparative Politics: A Developmental Approach* 46–7.

[105] William Kornhauser *The Politics of Mass Society* (The Free Press of Glencoe, Illinois, 1959) 236.

[106] Harold D Lasswell, 'Policy Problems of a Data-Rich Civilization' in *Information Technology in a Democracy* 196–7.

[107] The Freedom of Information Clearing House was established in 1972 with two principal objectives. The first is to gather information on government access laws and to disseminate it to individuals and groups with a view to assisting in the effective use of these laws. The second objective is to litigate cases under access laws which the Clearing House has done extensively since its establishment.

[108] Information obtained from Freedom of Information Clearing House circular dated 10 December, 1975. The judgment referred to is reported as *Stern v Richardson* 367 F Supp 1316.

[109] Kent Cooper *The Right to Know* 14–15.

[110] The most extensive state scheme is the Legal Services Program of the Office of Economic Opportunity. A South African commentator has described this service as 'a development of enormous magnitude': P H Gross, *Legal Aid and its Management* (Juta, Cape Town, 1976) 90.

[111] 5 US CA 552 (3) (E).

[112] T B Bottomore op cit 41. See also J Westergaard & H Resler op cit 314 who argue that there has been no significant acceleration in social circulation in Britain over the past half century.

[113] Walter A Rosenbaum op cit 70.

[114] Ibid.

[115] M D McGrath 'Trends in Income and Material Inequality in South Africa' (as yet unpublished paper, August 1974) 16. The figures quoted in the text were for the year 1970.

[116] T B Bottomore op cit, 17.

[117] G C Kinloch *The Sociological Study of South Africa: An Introduction* (Macmillan, Johannesburg, 1972) 149.

[118] M D McGrath loc cit 16.

[119] M D McGrath, *Racial Income Distribution in South Africa* (Dept of Economics, Univ of Natal, Durban, 1977) 23.

[120] Jill Nattrass 'Narrowing Wage Differentials: Some Dynamic Implications for Income Distribution in South Africa' (1977) 45 *SA Journal of Economics* 408.

[121] Ibid 24.

[122] The only two 'homelands' that are independent at present.

[123] Heribert Adam 'Internal Constellations and Potentials for Change' in *Change in Contemporary South Africa* 305.

[124] Ralf Dahrendorf *Society and Democracy in Germany* 144.

[125] This party disbanded in 1968 when the Political Interference Act 51 of 1968 required political parties to limit membership to a single race group.

[126] Section 6*bis* of the Internal Security Act 44 of 1950. At least ten newspapers have been unable to register on account of this provision.

[127] Section 6 of the Internal Security Act 44 of 1950.

[128] Robert A Dahl *Polyarchy: Participation and Opposition* 29.

[129] Walter A Rosenbaum *Political Culture* 6.

[130] Max Lerner *America as a Civilization* 366–8.

[131] Ibid 718.

[132] Ibid 413.

[133] Richard R Fagen *Politics and Communication* 62–3.

[134] Louis Hartz *The Founding of New Societies* 75.

[135] Walter A Rosenbaum op cit 82.

[136] Quoted by Raoul Berger *Executive Privilege: A Constitutional Myth* 207.

[137] Walter A Rosenbaum op cit 76.

[138] Arthur M Schlesinger Jr *The Imperial Presidency* 341.

[139] Almond & Verba *Civic Culture* 35.

[140] Samuel H Beer *Modern British Politics* 4.

[141] Richard Rose *Politics in England Today* 394.

[142] I D MacCrone *Race Attitudes in South Africa* (Oxford, 1937) 130. See also Newell M Stultz *The Nationalists in Opposition: 1934–1948* (Human & Rousseau, Cape Town, 1974) 155–6 where he speaks of a policy of 'racial exclusivism in all matters'.

[143] 30 of 1950.

[144] T Dunbar Moodie *The Rise of Afrikanerdom* 12 and 15.

[145] Ibid 199 (emphasis supplied).

[146] I D MacCrone op cit 107–8.

[147] Ralf Dahrendorf *Society and Democracy in Germany* 42.

[148] Denis Worrall *South Africa: Government and Politics* 213.

[149] SASH, 1 May 1977 (vol 19) 12.

[150] T Dunbar Moodie op cit xi.

[151] See, for example, David Welsh *The Roots of Segregation: Native Policy in Colonial Natal, 1845–1910* (Oxford, 1971) especially chapter 8 entitled 'The Langalabalele Affair and its Consequences'.

[152] This statement appears in a chapter entitled 'The Individual and the Community' in *White South Africans are Also People* ed Sarah Gertrude Millin (Howard Timmins, Cape Town, 1966) 164.

[153] Survey by Market and Opinion Services Pty Ltd in September 1977.

[154] English-speaking respondents, however, supported the proposition to the extent of 52,7%.

PART FOUR

The Solution

Introduction

A belief in open government and a commitment to its advancement are central to this book. Open government implies both the absence of broad restraints on access to information and the presence of a positive, legal right enabling the citizen to inform himself about the government of his society. One of the hard kernels of democracy, it has been rightly said, is the proposition that it rests not upon trust in the government or in officials, but upon a faith that is guaranteed and implemented by legal rules and techniques.[1] This is quite obviously a condition or state of affairs that characterizes very few contemporary societies. The elusive nature of open government should serve as a warning that its virtues are not self-evident and that the clime and soil favourable to its nourishment are fairly rare.[2] It can flourish only in democracies that are of the non-totalitarian type and also of the non-consociational kind, though effective information-sharing might characterize the latter. In some of the non-totalitarian democracies the tradition of citizen participation is passive and therefore discouraging to a positive information right which appears to be an outgrowth of an activist style of citizen involvement. Even where that is present developments within modern industrial societies (such as the growth of bureaucracies and the creation of a vast security and intelligence apparatus) have tended to put formidable obstacles in the way of a right to self-information about public affairs. Moreover, since the exercise of power is an element in all governments (though it is obviously a smaller element in the constitutional democracies), and since power is more effectively wielded when its nature and purposes are disguised, open government is necessarily locked in a perpetual struggle with the coercive elements of political rule.[3] All these difficulties are compounded by the realities of international relations between those countries in which power and secrecy are carried to extremes and the constitutional democracies whose increasingly open practices could make them relatively vulnerable and weak.

The focus of this study on the political and social environment of 'open' and 'closed' societies, and on the problems and obstacles that confront the believer in a positive information right, is intended to invest a desirable political movement with a sense of reasoned realism. The pursuit of open government as a slogan has often distracted attention from the heavy ground-work necessary for its achievement. Sloganeering has also tended to present openness in government as an unqualified political virtue whereas it is at best a partial one, like all the principles and institutions of politics. The public interest may sometimes demand confidentiality rather than publicity; though, as J R Lucas has said, 'blanket invocations' of the general interest in secrecy are objectionable and there is a need to establish by careful investigation those instances, *limited in number*, in which the public interest in secrecy is more compelling than competing private and public interests which favour openness.[4] The balance of interests which is struck may be different as circumstances change and will be heavily contingent upon the social and political configurations of the society in which the investigation is being conducted. It is with these general considerations in mind that proposals for change are put forward in this final part under the somewhat arrogant rubric of 'The Solution'.

The 'solutions' proffered in the ensuing pages are little more than broad directions of change. Before a course of reform is charted intensive thought and analysis are required in relation to such matters as the responsiveness of the constitutional and political system to change, the institutional obstacles that have to be overcome and traditional patterns of acting which need to be modified. Some of that thinking and analysis was attempted, hopefully with a measure of success, in Parts I and III above. While hard thought is a necessary preliminary to the adoption of a policy of change, it remains essential throughout the entire process of working that policy out. Frequently the creative work, in the form of relevant categories and distinctions, mechanisms and techniques, has been done in other societies, and only a little intelligent plagiarism will be needed in the reforming society. Some examples of the products of creative thinking in progressive countries might be helpful. It is widely agreed that policy-making in the formative stages needs to be shielded from public scrutiny. The protection of the deliberative process, however, does not necessarily require concealment of factual material considered during policy formulation or of the decision or action that is the outcome of it.[5] Communications to the decision-makers from private pressure groups likewise carry no persuasive claim to protection and should not be regarded as exempt from disclosure. The blanket application of a secrecy rule in science and research is both harmful and unnecessary. A helpful distinction here is between 'facts in nature' which can be discovered by others and other facts such as the stockpile and location of atomic weapons.[6] Secrecy may be harmful to its keepers in respect of facts in nature but is clearly necessary in relation to a nation's atomic stockpile. Another relevant distinction is between the general ideas of science in which there should be a free exchange and specific applications of those ideas which could require protection.[7] Policy questions can frequently be debated in public though they relate to sensitive subjects such as atomic energy. The Flowers Committee appointed to investigate the environmental aspects of Britain's nuclear energy policy declared that it was important 'openly and deliberately to weigh the risks and costs of embarking on a major nuclear programme' with a view to enabling 'major questions of nuclear development to take place by explicit political process'.[8] Blanket secrecy in matters of foreign policy is also undesirable and distinctions in this area could be made between the economic aspects of foreign policy (where secrecy is frequently unnecessary) and other more sensitive matters such as the security aspects of international relations. One might also allow foreign relations to be subject to fairly open post-mortems while preserving secrecy on current diplomatic exchanges.

What these examples primarily illustrate is that once a government or a people abandon a mindless adherence to total secrecy (or publicity, for that matter) there is the clear prospect of the successful construction of a rational and reasonable information policy in which the requirements of confidentiality and openness can be successfully compromised and accommodated. Comparative study will yield some of the criteria on which accommodation may be based; but others will have to be newly evolved. The important thing is for the nation to embark on a programme of thoughtful reform.

NOTES

[1] *Hoe Openbaar Wordt Ons Bestuur* eds B de Goede & H Th J F van Maarseveen (Vuga-Boekerij, The Hague, 1969) p 6.

[2] Provision of information will not necessarily increase participation especially where the population is not educated or sophisticated. In such a situation, the general public may feel overpowered by the mass and technical nature of the material that is provided and become apathetic or mistrustful: See *Hoe Openbaar Wordt Ons Bestuur* 24.

[3] Power, in this sense, means the ability to affect adversely the interests of an unwilling subject. If power is defined more widely as the ability to persuade others to accept restrictions upon their interests, then it is not directly in conflict with open government.

[4] J R Lucas *Democracy and Participation* 104.

[5] Norman Dorsen & John H F Shattuck, 'Executive Privilege: The President Won't Tell' in *None of Your Business: Government Secrecy in America* 33.

[6] Walter Gellhorn *Security, Loyalty and Science* 9–10.

[7] Suggested to the writer by Sir Brian Pippard, Clare Hall, Cambridge.

[8] Royal Commission on Environmental Pollution—Sixth Report: Nuclear Power and the Environment (Cmnd 6618, Sept 1976) ¶¶ 522 and 524.

CHAPTER X

The United States

From the perspective of South Africa, where non-official sources of information have virtually dried up and where independent fact-gathering about public affairs is scarcely possible, there is a temptation to portray the United States, and its laws and institutions, as the Promised Land of the believer in the right to know. Such euphoria would be mistaken notwithstanding the real progress that has been achieved in America in the past ten years. For one thing, the struggle for information (like freedom) is never conclusively won or settled. The supply of background information, for most officials, politicians or bureaucrats, runs against the psychological grain unless, of course, the information will reflect favourably on the disclosing agency or its officials. On 17 September 1977 the *International Herald Tribune* reported that a new Executive Order on classification of papers and documents was being prepared on behalf of the President. An enquiry by the writer to the Office of Press Relations at the White House produced an evasive and totally uninformative response which dealt with the five-year-old Executive Order of President Nixon. This non-reply came from an administration which launched itself with a pledge of open government.[1] A more serious example of the stubborn survival of secrecy is the clandestine American involvement in Angola which took place in the immediate post-Watergate era.

A 'state of the nation' report on secrecy and openness in the United States would distort reality if it did not record blemishes as well as achievements, and some of the weaknesses which counterbalance the strength of the open government movement. The most fundamental of the weaknesses is one of process which in America is best characterized by the phrase 'information by combat'. The observer of the process and techniques of open government *à la Americaine* cannot help gaining the impression that the purpose of extracting information is frequently the desire to do a political opponent a shot in the eye rather than to enhance the quality of decision-making. Information sometimes seems to be merely a by-product of a bitter combat between political rivals. No doubt this process is structurally related to the political system which is characterized by division of power, an adversary style in politics and an aggressive litigiousness in the legal system. While these are the very factors that have made American governmental processes more visible than many others, the information flow in such a society tends to be unreliable, halting and irregular. By contrast the Swedish system appears to produce a regular, routinized flow of information; and less of it is lost in the din of political conflict. Information in Sweden also seems to be got more cheaply and with less expenditure of forensic or political effort. There would be little point in making proposals that run counter to the basic structural features of United States politics, but an attempt to moderate some of their worst consequences might prove rewarding. Such moderation could be achieved by the constitution of a system of administrative boards with two basic functions:

1. The provision of regular advice to agencies on administrative techniques (such as early categorization of documents as exempt or non-exempt, indexing and methods of facilitating public access) aimed at routinizing the provision of information;[2]
2. The interposition of an independent administrative hearing between the agency decision to release (or otherwise) and the intervention of the ordinary courts. The administrative hearing should be informal and subject to appeal in limited circumstances only, for example where the board itself believes that the appeal would settle an important issue or where a divisional court grants leave to appeal (*certiorari*) for the same reason.

At state level we have already noticed the Oregon system of an initial appeal to the Attorney-General, an elected official, against an agency refusal to disclose documents. In practice, where the Attorney-General orders disclosure by the agency, it will initiate proceedings before the Supreme Court if it believes the order to be unwarranted. Sweden is a relatively small country and Oregon one of the smaller states in America and their rules and practices may not transplant easily into more populous and complex jurisdictions. Yet with adaptations their systems could make disclosure at the federal level of government an altogether smoother affair attended by less cost and work burdens. A recent report on the Freedom of Information Act in the popular press concluded that unless that statute is amended 'the government may drown in its own regurgitated material' and, as evidence, cited the example of the FBI which has a full-time staff of 379 people handling 16 000 requests per year at a cost of $9 million.[3] Even allowing for the backlog of FOIA requests, this is a formidable burden on the government generated by one federal agency alone.

The advocates in America of more and of less information about government affairs tend to push each other to extreme positions, leaving few in occupation of the middle ground. One of the results of this polarization is that agreement to amend the Espionage Statutes is presently unattainable. The former Senate bill known as S I which incorporated extensive amendments to the Espionage Statutes has been reintroduced with the provisions of the Espionage Statutes left intact.[4] All proposed changes are probably doomed to stalemate because influential legislators and public figures occupy two conflicting basic positions:

(1) that in the interests of free speech and full public canvassing of important issues, the release or transmission of sensitive information *simpliciter* should never be a criminal offence;[5]

(2) present laws in America facilitate the pouring of the nation's secrets into the public domain where they become available to enemies of the country. In order to check this flow, an official secrets law covering defined classes of sensitive information must be introduced.

Behind each of these approaches there lie two complexes of values and assumptions which are obviously irreconcilable. At the risk of over-simplification the underlying beliefs may be represented in the form of a contest between, on the one hand, those who think that the open society strengthens itself most effectively, against both internal and external foes, by virtual unqualified adherence to the principles and institutions of freedom to which it is dedicated, and, on the other hand, those others who believe that democracy's implacable enemies can be neutralized only by enacting inroads into those same principles and institutions. Clearly such a contest cannot be resolved in the abstract, but in relation to laws which criminalize disclosure there may be some hope of compromise in the specification of categories of infomation, rigorously limited in number and scope, whose protection by the law would do limited harm to the American concept of freedom but simultaneously go some way towards satisfying the critics of its unqualified pursuit and application.

In a nutshell the current state of United States federal legislation with a negative impact on disclosure of information may be expressed in three summarizing propositions:

1. Classic espionage in the form of the wilful communication of defence information to a foreign power is a clear and enforceable crime which has frequently been invoked with success against spies.

2. The provisions of the Espionage Statutes which penalize the simple disclosure or release of defence information are probably unen-forceable in the light of constitutional difficulties and the legislative intent to preserve freedom of debate.

3. Two narrowly drawn provisions which penalize (1) the disclosure *simpliciter* of classified information concerning codes, crypto-graphic systems and intelligence communications and (2) the trans-

mission of any information classified as affecting the security of the United States to the agent of a foreign government or a member of a communist organization, are on the statute book and are fully enforceable without proof of any intent to injure the United States or advantage a foreign power.[6]

A workable compromise between proposals for broadening the enforceable provisions of the law by official secrets legislation and the maintenance of the *status quo* according to which only two categories of information are clearly protected, might take the following form:

(a) The retention (obviously) of the classic espionage crime in terms of which the communication of defence-related information to a foreign power with the intention of advantaging that power or injuring the United States is a federal offence. This crime should apply even to defence-related information which is lawfully in the public domain contrary to the finding in *United States* v *Heine*[7] that 'whatever it was lawful to broadcast throughout the country it was lawful to send abroad'. A statutory amendment to nullify the ruling in that case should not attract constitutional difficulties in a crime which is restricted to defence information and which requires a guilty intention.[8]

(b) The retention (with amendment) of the crime of transmitting classified information to an agent of a foreign power or a member or official of a communist organization. The reference to a communist organization in the law reads oddly today although it no doubt had an historical justification. The suggested amendment would substitute transmission to a member or official of an organization which has as one of its objectives (whether expressed or tacit) the use of force or violence against the government of the United States or any subdivision thereof or of assassination against any of its officers. This crime (as amended) will enable the state to punish those who transmit classified information to foreign governments or hostile organizations without intent to harm the United States but who act for other reasons or purposes such as financial inducements, blackmail or misplaced political motives.[9]

(c) The introduction of a new crime for the punishment of any person who without authority discloses to any other person information in certain specified categories which at the relevant time is classified 'Top Secret' with knowledge or reason to believe that the information was so classified. The recommended specified categories are—

   (i) information concerning codes, cryptographic systems and communications intelligence;[10]
   (ii) information which identifies agents engaged in intelligence operations;

(iii) plans, designs and technical specifications of military weapons or research directly related thereto;[11]

(iv) tactical military operations and strategies for the defence of the nation (excluding the policies on which these are based);[12]

(v) in time of war (whether declared or undeclared) the movement or disposition of troops or servicemen and the location of strategic military equipment.

Disclosure of information falling into these categories should be a crime only while such information remains classified 'Top Secret' and would cease to be a crime when it is automatically downgraded under current declassification procedures. It follows that mere disclosure of information classified as 'Top Secret' but falling outside the specified categories or of information classified in a lower category (such as 'Secret' or 'Confidential') will not be a crime but the state will not be required to reveal such information under laws (like the FOIA) conferring a positive right to information. Misclassification should be allowed as a defence but the courts should in general limit their enquiries to the correctness of classification procedures and only evaluate the content of classified material by *in camera* inspection where a blatant misclassification seems probable.[13] While this crime stops far short of being an official secrets law it does guard against the irresponsible or misguided revelation of vital information. The classification system with which it is linked should be an enlightened one providing in general for rapid downgrading of material so as to prevent a Pentagon-type disclosure coming under the law.

The changes thus far proposed in this chapter affect both the positive right to information (the Freedom of Information Act) and the laws restricting disclosure of information. In sum, the recommendations are for a smoother system of disclosure controlled by administrative boards at the federal level and for replacement of confused and unworkable provisions of the Espionage Statutes. These proposals are obviously general in nature and modest in scope. They do not touch specific problems which positive federal legislation on records and meetings has brought into prominence, let alone the numerous state open records and meeting statutes. Open-meeting legislation at the federal level is in any event comparatively recent and it is too early for an alien outsider to venture criticism and reform. To an outside observer the Oregon open-meetings model seems to be one of the most practical and balanced in contrast with others which either go too far[14] or not far enough; but detailed proposals are beyond the scope of this work, which like a road sign aims to point out the route without travelling the whole journey.

The lack of detail in these reform proposals will probably be found less reprehensible than the modesty of the changes actually proposed. Measured against the radical changes suggested by two American authors in a recent book[15] they do indeed seem timorous. The essence of the reform put forward by these authors is a legislated system of classification tied to an amended Freedom of Information Act which will in effect extend the positive right to government information to everything but a few highly sensitive categories such as weapons systems, intelligence methods, military plans and on-going diplomatic negotiations.[16] All other categories will be either disclosed automatically (if falling into certain specified categories) or released in the discretion of the classifying authority subject to review of the decision by a review board and ultimately the courts. The modesty of the proposals put forward in this chapter is quite deliberate. Radical extension of the positive information right is attended by problems which the authors hardly trouble to address. The manpower and fiscal burden of the present system on the federal government is already heavy and would be increased to an intolerable degree by a revolutionary extension of the right of access. The courts will be drawn into a form of decision-making for which they manifestly have neither the desire nor the capacity. Whereas under present law the courts are guided by moderately clear definitions or categories of exemption, a broadened information right will compel them to take substantive decisions in which the task of weighing considerations favouring disclosure and confidentiality will be imposed upon them. Because the envisaged scheme will therefore commit to the ultimate jurisdiction of the courts a new area of responsibility which is essentially political, it has distinctly undemocratic potentialities and appears to rest upon the (unwarranted?) assumption that judges can be relied upon, now and in the future, to adopt a liberal disclosure policy. Finally, the disclosures envisaged by the authors sometimes have a surprising air of political unreality about them as in the unqualified adoption of a scheme that would 'require the United States to reveal that it was engaging, or about to engage, in military operations against another country'.[17] All in all it appears more sensible to work for immediate improvement of the processes by which information is presently provided than to attack the bureaucratic fortress in such a head-on fashion. Apart from the processes of information flow, specific proposals to narrow the presently exempt categories (especially the defence and foreign policy exemption) and to improve Congressional access to sensitive information[18] appear to be more realistic goals than the radical overhaul of the current system.

Arguably, the most serious blot on the American open government record is the clandestine activitiy of its intelligence[19] and national security services. The findings of the Church Committee on the United States intelligence operations have already been mentioned[20] and confirm that any society that values both openness and freedom must subject the intelligence and security agencies to both oversight and control. Secrecy is without question an essential element in any effective intelligence and security programme but total secrecy is undesirable and dangerous even in relation to intelligence and national security. Francis O Wilcox has shown how intelligence misinformation, which is frequently a product of over-restrictive policy of access to intelligence estimates, affected political judgements in the Dominican intervention and the Gulf of Tonkin incident.[21] In relation to the latter incident he has said: 'Meticulous reconstruction of the Tonkin incident, based on these messages and the ships' logs, revealed a substantially different set of circumstances and sequence of events than had been presented to Congress and the public at the time.'[22] Unless access to intelligence materials and estimates is broadened to incorporate effectively elements of the legislative branch (without actually subverting the intelligence and security operations) major errors in political decision-making are likely to occur from time to time. Another danger of too much secrecy and too little control over intelligence operations is that the rights of citizens are put in jeopardy. A carefully written analysis of political intelligence in the United States has underlined the threats to political freedom that are possible consequences of such activities even in a society of guaranteed freedoms:

'The apparatus maintains a readiness to round up dissidents. It spreads fear through leaks and hearings, with the conscious, although seldom acknowledged goal of discouraging what it sees as a dangerous activity. It attempts to direct dissent toward violent action'.[23]

The dangers of excessive intelligence and security secrecy are easy to point out but exceedingly difficult to remedy. Reforms will of necessity be of an institutional kind, the principal elements being an oversight apparatus involving the legislature and an independent board or body. In the post-Watergate period, President Ford made a good start by setting up an Intelligence Oversight Board with a specific mandate (*inter alia*) to investigate and report on 'activities that raise questions of legality or propriety'.[24] This was followed up early in 1978 by a new reorganization plan introduced by President Carter. Under the plan rigorous controls over the domestic activities of the intelligence agencies are introduced with the specific objective of protecting the rights of American citizens. A major feature of the new system is the power of review accorded to the Attorney-General over a broad range of intelligence operations.[25] The Executive Order embodying the plan was the product of executive collaboration with Congress and the President envisaged the subsequent enactment by Congress of a statutory charter on the intelligence community. The important goal of executive and legislative co-operation on intelligence operations is now within reach. Since these institutional changes do not directly bear upon the citizen right of access to information any further investigation is beyond the scope of this work.[26] It needs stressing, however, that no fair assessment of the state of openness of government in the United States can ignore or play down the problems created by intelligence operations.

NOTES

¹ This pledge, admittedly, was not made to foreign researchers like the writer. Even to him, however, the administration might have explained either that the *Herald Tribune* leak was false or, if true, that the details of the new Executive Order were still in the confidential stage of formulation.

² Compared with Sweden, the task in America is fraught with problems of magnitude and scale; but this provides all the more reason to work out routines and techniques to facilitate access. American writers have suggested the introduction of 'a new administrative element', in this instance an ombudsman, to improve public access: see Andrew C Gordon, John P Heinz, Margaret T Gordon & Stanley W Divorski, 'Public Information and Public Access: A Sociological Interpretation' (1973) 68 *NW Un L Rev* 280 at 305.

³ *Time Magazine* of 19 December 1977.

⁴ Letter dated 9 November 1977 from Congressman John E Moss to the writer.

⁵ At present only information relating to codes and intelligence communications is clearly so protected. Supporters of this first basic proposition would resist any further extension of the criminal sanction, for example, to troop dispositions, weapons designs etc.   ⁶ These laws are analysed in detail in chap IV above.

⁷ 151 F 2nd 813, 816 (2nd Cir, 1945).

⁸ The rationale of the *Heine* decision is hard to perceive. Spying may reasonably include the transmission of any defence-related information to a foreign power with the requisite intention.

⁹ The retention of the crime of disclosing the content of code or diplomatic transmissions applicable only to federal employees is also desirable. The crime is briefly described in chapter IV above.

¹⁰ This would replace the existing provision referred to earlier.

¹¹ The category is adapted from William Birtles 'Big Brother Knows Best: The Franks Report on Section Two of the Official Secrets Act' 1973 *Public Law* 100, 111.

¹² This category has also been adopted from the article by William Birtles.

¹³ See chap IV above on classification.

¹⁴ For example, the Florida Sunshine Law, under which officers have been prosecuted for discussing official business at a luncheon meeting: see Joseph W Little & Thomas Tompkins 'Open Government Laws: An Insider's View' (1975) 53 *North Carolina L Rev* 451. A useful review of state open-meeting statutes has been conducted by William R Wright 'Open Meetings Laws—An Analysis and a Proposal' (1974) 45 *Miss LJ* 1151.

¹⁵ Morton H Halperin & Daniel N Hoffman *Top Secret*.

¹⁶ Ibid chap V.   ¹⁷ Ibid 66.

¹⁸ As Halperin and Hoffman themselves point out (43 et seq) Congress has already acted in two troublesome areas of secrecy, war and executive agreements, by requiring the executive to provide it with certain information. Increasing Congressional knowledge of defence and foreign policy matters seems to the writer to be a more attainable political goal than providing the general public with a direct right of access.

¹⁹ The principal divisions of the intelligence community are the CIA, the Defence Intelligence Agency, the National Security Agency, the intelligence division of the Department of State and the FBI.   ²⁰ Chapter II above.

²¹ Francis O Wilcox *Congress, the Executive and Foreign Policy* (Harper & Row, London, 1971) 48–9.

²² Ibid 49. Halperin & Hoffman op cit 9 declare more forcibly that 'both the unprovoked nature of the North Vietnamese action and the spontaneity of the administration's response were fabrication.'

²³ Nick Egleson 'The Surveillance Apparatus' in *State Secrets* eds Paul Cowan, Nick Egleson and Nat Hentoff (Holt, Rinehart and Winston, NY 1974) 3, 59. For evidence of interference with citizen rights the reader may consult Note 'The Central Intelligence Agency: Present Authority and Proposed Legislative Change' (1976) 16 *Virginia L Rev* 332.

²⁴ Executive Order No 11905 of 18 February 1976, section 6.

²⁵ Executive Order No 12036 of 24 January 1978.

²⁶ It should be observed, though, that citizens are currently obtaining some information about intelligence operations under the FOIA. A survey of proposed legislative controls appears in Note: 'The Central Intelligence Agency: Present Authority and Proposed Legislative Change', *supra*.

CHAPTER XI

The United Kingdom

If the access to information situation in America is not quite as good as it seems, in Britain it is probably not as black as it is frequently painted. The author of a recent study of open government in Britain has identified a number of liberalizing trends such as the issue by the government of Green Papers,[1] the modification of the doctrine of crown privilege by the courts and a recent government declaration that more information would be made available on the administration of public affairs.[2] He concludes that while 'there is no acceptance of the general principle that the public have the right of access to official information' it is also true that 'by a series of pragmatic arrangements such information is in fact quite widely available for particular purposes'.[3] These improvements are arguably more than crumbs and to be welcomed; but they are counterbalanced by the maintenance of quite needless secrecy in many areas of government. The author, for example, sought information in October 1977 on whether legislation was being (or had been) drafted in the Home Office to amend the Official Secrets Acts and to introduce a positive right to information. The response to this enquiry was that information on that question was not available and could not be obtained.[4] The example may be trivial but it is revealing as to the official attitudes which appear to be little affected by the 'liberalizing trends'.

Whatever improvements have been introduced in British society all remain subject to one major flaw: the government alone decides what should be released, to whom material should be released and at what stage the disclosure should take place. As William Pitt said in 1741 a system of that kind 'will produce no great information if those whose conduct is examined are allowed to select the evidence'.[5] The vesting of a sole discretion to authorize disclosure in the executive branch is an aspect of the principle of trust in the political leadership which has been so deeply imbedded in political culture as to become as English as steak and kidney, if that is the equivalent of the cherry-pie across the Atlantic. Though the present situation in the United Kingdom might be improved by more government handouts, it is time that

Western democracy's mother country conferred upon its citizens a legal right of access to papers and documents concerning the administration of public affairs.

The introduction of a fully-fledged and judicially enforced positive right to information is not conceivable in Britain, at least not by a one-jump process. For one thing, because under the Westminster parliamentary system power is effectively concentrated rather than divided as in America, the right cannot be wrung from a recalcitrant executive by some other branch of government. Parliament, for reasons that have frequently been analysed and exposed, is the captive of the cabinet and is unlikely to act unless bidden. The present government, moreover, holds a precarious position in Parliament and has had to form an alliance with the Liberal Party to survive. Vis-à-vis the Opposition it stands in a position of weakness and is unlikely to increase the difficulty of governing by conferring a right to information which could be exploited by political opponents to enhance their own power position. Our analysis of the political culture and institutions of the society has underlined the ingrained habit of secrecy that affects officialdom from the highest down to the lowest echelons of government. In short, neither the cabinet nor Whitehall is likely to bid Parliament to act—at least not in a dramatic or revolutionary way.

Pressure for reform from interest groups and the public (which have recently generated some momentum) will have to take account of these political and social realities in advocating a positive right to information. A carefully staged programme along the following lines will have the advantage at least of political realism:

1. The enactment of a statutory obligation on departments of government and other specified agencies (including the nationalized industries) to publish and make available for inspection in a visitors room:

(a) a description of the organizational structure, the functions and the location of branches and divisions of all departments or agencies together with information about the name and designation of an officer responsible for providing the public with further available information about such department or agency;

(b) rules, final opinions and orders, statements of policy and interpretation, staff manuals and instructions which have been adopted by the agency and which affect members of the public, but excluding purely domestic rules and practices and manuals or instructions revealing investigatory or law enforcement techniques.

These two classes of information correspond to what was earlier designated as 'the publication and secret law' requirements of the Freedom of Information Act.[6] They aim to ensure that the public can find out about government departments and agencies that implement law and about the rules and criteria employed in that implementation.

Departments and agencies should be required to comply with these publication requirements by a designated date, being not later than one year after the enactment of the statute.

2. The enactment of a statutory obligation on the departments and agencies referred to in para 1 above to make their records available to inspection by members of the public subject to the exclusion of materials falling into categories of exemption similar to those appearing in the Freedom of Information Act.[7] The following rules and principles should be made applicable to the right of inspection:

(a) Only *new* documents and papers generated after a specified date (not later than two years after the enactment of the legislation) will fall under the law. This will avoid the enormous cost and work burdens resultant upon backlog requests and will enable departments and agencies to determine in advance which documents or materials are exempt or non-exempt and to file and index them accordingly, thereby reducing the cost of searching for and extracting materials.

(b) Any member of the public has the right to inspect without the need to demonstrate a special interest;

(c) Time limits for compliance are essential to give the law the necessary efficacy and failing compliance after expiry of the limits there ought to be an automatic appeal to the departmental or agency head (eg the First Secretary of the Department). A fixed period for disposing of the appeal is desirable.

(d) Where internal remedies have been exhausted without success, the law should provide for a further appeal to a Parliamentary Commissioner on Public Information, an officer appointed by statute with a status similar to that of the present Parliamentary Commissioner for Administration. In general this decision will be final unless on application he decides to allow an appeal to the ordinary courts on the ground that the case presents difficult and important issues of interpretation. It seems desirable that the matter should be argued *de novo* before the ordinary courts which should have the power of *in camera* inspection.

(e) The excellent suggestion of a Parliamentary Select Committee on Official Information made by the Outer Circle Policy Unit should be adopted.[8] The main function of the Committee would be oversight of the law and its application, the consideration of an annual report from the Parliamentary Commissioner and the recommendation of new legislation where considered desirable.

The general idea behind these proposals for a right to inspect records is to construct a system like that of Sweden 'where the registration of documents and the provision of an index is a normal part of the established systems of departmental record-keeping . . .'.[9] Such a system will be less formal and costly than the American and should

avoid excessive litigation, thereby putting its benefits within the reach
of all. Simultaneous reform of other branches of the law such as copyright, breach of confidence, classification and Official Secrets will
obviously be necessary to prevent the new right coming into conflict
with them.

Of all the other laws that will need amendment prior to, or simultaneously with, the introduction of a positive right to information,
the Official Secrets Acts loom the largest across the reformer's path.
Though the Franks Report was published in September 1972 and
successive governments have undertaken to implement it, legislation
revising the Official Secrets Acts is not yet in sight. The investigations
of the Franks Committee were extremely thorough and its report is a
scholarly document; but when its actual recommendations are considered it does not seem exaggerated to say that the Committee laboured
manfully to produce only an unimpressive squeak. Most reformers have
greeted it with what Damon Runyon liked to call a 'weak hello'. This
unenthusiastic response is due primarily to two factors. The report, in
the first place, does not propose radical change but retains the criminal
sanction in all but those areas where its application under present law
is an absurdity. Secondly, it does not deal with a citizen right of
information and this, at the present time, gives its proposals a distinct
air of anachronism. Unless changes to the Official Secrets Acts are
accompanied by the introduction of a positive right of access they are
better left in their present justly derided form.

As they now stand, the Official Secrets Acts extend the criminal
sanction to the unauthorized release of official information of any
description whatever. The Franks proposals would alter this so as to
make that sanction applicable to the following categories of material:

(a) Defence, internal security, foreign relations and matters relating
    to currency and the reserves, provided that in each case the material
    was properly classified at the time of disclosure. (The Committee
    did not envisage any independent scrutiny of classification decisions
    and the Minister's certificate would be binding on a court of law.)
(b) Matters relating to the maintenance of law and order the disclosure
    of which would facilitate either the commission, prevention or
    detection of offences or escape from custody, or harm prison
    security.
(c) Cabinet documents, whatever their nature.
(d) Information supplied to the government by private individuals
    whether or not submitted under compulsory powers and whether
    or not provided in confidence.

In all these cases the unauthorized disclosure of the information by
a Crown servant or the knowing transmission of it by an ordinary
citizen is to be a criminal offence subject in general to a defence that
the accused did not believe, or have reason to believe, that disclosure

was unauthorized or contrary to his duty. The Committee also recommended that it should be an offence for persons possessing or entrusted with official information to communicate it for purposes of private gain and that mere receipt of official information by a citizen should no longer be an offence.

If carried into effect these proposals would narrow the present law but the narrowing is one that preserves the basic coverage of the Official Secrets Acts. The *Sunday Telegraph* disclosures, the revelations by the Oxford undergraduates in the publication *Isis* and even the release of information about military uniforms (which falls under the Franks category of 'military . . . stores and equipment of all kinds') could result in a successful prosecution if the information is classified;[10] and classification under the Franks proposals is put beyond the reach of independent adjudication. Even with the improvements to Franks announced by the Home Secretary in November 1976[11]—the removal of cabinet documents and material relating to currency and the reserves from the scope of the criminal law—the protected categories are too broad and could effectively inhibit public knowledge and discussion of important policy issues. The democratic process is surely harmed by making it a criminal offence to leak *any* classified material relating to foreign or defence policy even if the disclosure is meant to facilitate public debate and will not harm the interests of the nation.

The continued belief in a law of almost universal coverage rests upon some unquestioned (or too little questioned) assumptions of British political and legal life. One of these is the tendency to equate legal protection with the criminal sanction. There seems to be in British official circles a feeling of reverence for the criminal law and a widespread belief in its desirability and efficacy. Contrary to this assumption, it does *not* follow that because it is good policy to keep some matters confidential the use of criminal punishment is the most desirable method of achieving confidentiality. There is nothing necessarily inconsistent in the belief that certain secrets ought to be kept (by means, for example, of internal controls and safeguards) and the simultaneous rejection of the criminal sanction as something altogether too majestic and forbidding to invoke in the protection of those same secrets. The reflex tendency to rely on the criminal law should give way to a rational calculation not just of its efficacy but especially of the balance of public and private interests that are advanced and injured by its invocation. It will sometimes be better to protect material by exempting it from a statutory duty to disclose rather than by subjecting disclosure to criminal sanctions. A second assumption of British public life is that the courts are by nature disqualified from anything but a marginal and innocuous role in this branch of public law. The assumption is expresssed in the almost derisory functions that the Franks Report envisages for the courts in classification matters and seems to spring partly from the fear that an enlarged judicial authority will tempt judges to displace rather than control executive decision-making. In America, for example, where the tradition is more activist and the courts are specifically authorized by the Freedom of Information Act to make *in camera* inspections, the judges have demonstrated sensitivity to executive claims for the need for secrecy and tend to resort to inspection only after affidavit evidence has established its necessity.[12] A dangerous usurpation of executive authority seems even less likely in Britain whose courts, it has been suggested in a recent book, are essentially upholders of the system.[13] There seems to be no reason to doubt that if judges were to be given a larger authority in classification and related matters they would approach their new function with a strong sense of the desirable limits of judicial intervention in delicate matters of state policy. In this sphere the judicial role will be the prescription of the outer boundaries of executive conduct rather than the displacement of executive decisions.

A third assumption in British political and legal thinking relates to the role of the law rather than that of the courts. Official secrets, it is widely assumed, raise matters of broad political policy which cannot be expressed in, or regulated by, definite concepts or exact legal rules. This point of view was perfectly expressed by the Attorney-General's written evidence to the Franks Committee in which he said that great difficulty arose 'in establishing categories and giving definitions which can be translated into terms amenable to the application of the criminal law' and concluded that 'it is not practicable to categorise information which should be protected, either by the method of listing subject matter or by the method of security grading of all documents'.[14] Here we encounter a typical example of English pragmatism in the form of a disbelief in the value of theorizing, of drawing distinctions and setting limits and of exercises in conceptualization. The sphere of politics with which we are concerned is admittedly a difficult one but hardly so thorny as to justify either the Attorney-General's pessimism or his implied belief that in these matters the final decision must be left to the judgment of executive officials. The earlier analysis of the Freedom of Information Act[15] was very largely a survey of the distinctions and concepts evolved by Congress and refined by court adjudication and subsequent amendment. If the task is feasible in relation to a positive right of information, there is no reason to assume that it would be a futile exercise in the realm of criminal law.

In a modern democracy, the range of material protected by the criminal law should be far narrower even than the 'liberalized' version of the Franks proposals announced by the Home Secretary in November 1976. (It is worth stressing again that lack of protection by the criminal law does not imply the absence of other forms of protection such as internal discipline and control and the exemption of material from a positive obligation to allow inspection.) There seems to be no real need for the criminal law to extend beyond the specific categories suggested in the previous chapter on American law,[16] that is, codes and intelligence, military weapons, tactical defence operations and strategies, identification of intelligence agents and, in time of war, the disposition of troops or military equipment. If this is thought to be unbearably radical for modern Britain, the categories could be broadened a little to include:

1. The disclosure by officials of certain kinds of information submitted to the government by private individuals. In general, this can be achieved by penalty provisions in the laws requiring the submission of information, as is already the case.
2. The communication by any person of information that would be directly helpful in the commission of a crime or escape from prison or that would prevent the detection of crime.

The extension, however, of the criminal sanction to the revelation of any classified defence information or foreign affairs material is far too broad when one considers the incredible range of public business encompassed by these two categories. Could British legislators not borrow a leaf from the American statute book and make it a crime to transmit any classified information to a foreign agent or hostile organization?

Public opinion in the United Kingdom is now reaching a point at which the mere narrowing of the criminal law will be seen as manifestly inadequate. The time is ripe for the government to evolve and introduce an overall information policy, including a positive right to inspect government material. A review of the current law will have to take in other areas such as copyright and breach of confidence. State copyright, if not abolished as in America, should at least be inapplicable to materials required to be revealed under a disclosure statute. There is no need for breach of confidence to extend beyond private law interests. Classification of documents needs to be brought under statute with a view to the establishment of an oversight committee, the introduction of automatic declassification[17] and a limited judicial involvement. The intelligence services, *horribile dictu*, might be brought under some kind of parliamentary oversight though this would necessarily be limited to matters of broad policy so as not to impair their effectiveness.[18] The time is hopefully past when the advocate of a coherent policy of reform embracing all these aspects could be accused of pointless dreaming.

NOTES

[1] A 'Green Paper' unlike a White Paper does not represent settled government policy but sets out lines of thinking on a particular problem with a view to receiving a public response.

[2] Ronald Wraith *Open Government: The British Interpretation* (Royal Institute of Public Administration, London, 1977) 18 et seq.

[3] Ibid 22.

⁴ Letter dated 7 November 1977 to British Vice-Consul in Durban who transmitted the author's request to the Central Office of Information.

⁵ Quoted by Raoul Berger op cit 7.

⁶ See chap V above.

⁷ We need not examine in detail here the precise scope and wording of these exemptions. They would cover the areas of defence, internal security, foreign relations, internal advice, law enforcement, privacy, litigatory privilege and business and financial information. Obviously, the categories would have to be tightly defined to prevent evasion of the law.

⁸ See *An Official Information Act* 31.

⁹ *An Official Information Act* 15.

¹⁰ These examples are taken from prosecutions under the Acts and are discussed in chap VI above.

¹¹ The announcement is summarized by Ronald Wraith *Open Government* 63.

¹² The discussion on *in camera* inspection under the FOIA in chap V is relevant here.

¹³ John Griffith *The Politics of the Judiciary* (Fontana, 1977).

¹⁴ Franks' Report vol 2, 5–6 (evidence of Sir Peter Rawlinson QC).

¹⁵ See chap V above.

¹⁶ Chapter X.

¹⁷ With a corresponding amendment to the Public Records Act 1958. The thirty-year rule for disclosure could be abolished and the release of materials governed by declassification procedures.

¹⁸ Halperin & Hoffman op cit 63 suggest that the legislature should concern itself with questions such as whether the intelligence organization should exist, what its functions should be, and how much money should be voted.

CHAPTER XII

South Africa

If we turn our attention from Britain to South Africa, we confront conditions that make the forecaster of progressive reform seem like a demented dreamer. The earlier analysis and discussion of the social structure and the political culture and institutions of the society revealed no circumstances or tendencies that would favour enlightened reform. The most recent political events of significance, far from altering that judgment, have merely seemed to confirm the system's intractability and rigidity. In November 1977 the White electorate went to the polls on the issue of a new constitutional dispensation for Indian and Coloured people in South Africa. No official document in the nature of a White Paper was issued to explain the constitutional proposals and voters had to rely on press 'guesstimates' and party political explanations of the government's intentions. In effect the voters went to the polls blindfolded on an issue actually submitted by the government for electoral decision. Many months after the election major features of the envisaged constitutional changes remained obscure and unclarified. The information system of a country that makes a state secret of important elements of a plan submitted to electoral test must clearly be an extraordinary one.

Another retrogressive tendency is evident in recent actions taken under the Publications Act.[1] On 21 October 1977 a committee appointed under the Act banned a publication issued by the South African Institute of Race Relations entitled 'Detention Without Trial in South Africa 1976-7'.[2] This publication was mainly a compilation of information about detentions that had been published in the regular press previously and the material it contained was almost exclusively of a factual kind. The reasons given the Institute for the proscription of the document are full of ominous auguries for the South African information policy of the future. The Director of Publications declared in a letter to the Institute that its publication created a false picture in 'order to embarrass the authorities' and for the purpose of 'giving grist to the Communist, ANC, PAC and AAM mill'.[3] This incident shows how government-appointed committees in South Africa decide on the

reliability and accuracy of information about public affairs and proscribe allegedly distorted information in order to protect the authorities from embarrassment or to deny advantages to its political enemies.
The effect is to exclude or limit alternative interpretations of public
business and create an official truth on crucial aspects of the administration of government policy. Though the assiduous researcher may still
be able to discover facts that contradict official truth, the effect of
regular bannings under the Publications Act is to deprive the general
South African public of such information.

The Publications Act is now emerging as a censorship instrument of
frightening dimensions. Acting under its provisions the police regularly
engage in 'search and seizure' operations against various organizations
involved in publication, especially student organizations. Material may
be seized prior to publication and submitted to a committee operating
in terms of the Act for a finding on its 'desirability'. If, as frequently
happens, the material is found to be undesirable, a prosecution for
production of the offensive material is launched in which the committee's finding is binding on the criminal courts.[4] This form of police
and prosecutional operation therefore acts as a prior restraint on publication and, because the standard of undesirability is completely vague,
as a form of *ex post facto* law imposing guilt retrospectively. In many
cases it is opinion or political interpretation which is so proscribed but
the potentialities of the statute for stemming the flow of information
about public administration to the public are obvious and are as yet
in the early stages of exploitation by the authorities. Since the finding
of undesirability may be coupled with a prohibition on possession (as
happened in the case of the publication 'Detention Without Trial in
South Africa 1976-7') both the flow of facts and access to their sources
can be disrupted. The law is now unique in the Western world since
it regulates and controls access to information about government
emanating from *private* sources and institutions.

In October 1977 the government banned eighteen organizations
and a number of persons and newspapers, and detained numerous
people under the Internal Security Act.[5] Though this 'night of the
long knives' operation was ostensibly taken to curb unrest there are
aspects of it which are relevant to access to information. Some of the
banned organizations and persons were undoubtedly engaged in providing the public with sets of facts and interpretations of them which
were strongly disapproved of by the government.[6] The bannings reveal
a fierce determination by the government to bring under its own control, as far as it possibly can, the information in circulation about the
current situation of internal unrest. On such fundamental issues the
government desires to present the public with an official truth and to
eliminate ambiguity. The same purpose has long been evident in the
application of laws like the Defence Act; but the Publications Act is
proving to be a far more effective instrument for depriving citizens of

alternative facts, sources and interpretations. The ability to put forward, and have access to, such alternatives is what democracy is really all about.

The developments just described are a reflection of an underlying tendency towards the comprehensive authoritarian control of politics in South Africa. Power is being established in a position of primacy and will soon occupy the whole political stage. The recent acceleration of the drive towards power has fateful consequences for citizen access to information in the society. We have seen that information policies and programmes are partly contingent on power configurations within America and Britain. In America divided power ensures that the process of political combat will yield up some information for the general public. Power in Britain is more centralized and the information situation is exacerbated by this fact as well as by the current weakness of the Labour government which is unlikely to jeopardize its power position by arming its opponents with an independent information right. If anything, the relation between power and information is more decisive in South Africa. The burgeoning will to power virtually guarantees that whatever sources of independent information remain are destined to systematic obliteration. Absolute power limits secrecy to those in authority and would be contradicted by the relaxation of secrecy laws or concession of an information right.[7]

The shift from ideology to an emphasis on strategy and procedures which an acute commentator on South African politics has discerned[8] is not necessarily inconsistent with the thesis that current South African politics is predominated by the extension and consolidation of state power. The ideology (or ideologies) that are associated with the rise of Afrikaner nationalism was essentially 'a moral justification for what is basically the will to power'.[9] The fact that the justification is nowadays more muted and that there is much talk about the process of change does not signify that the power-drive which that justification concealed has been abandoned together with its moral trappings. On the contrary power is now being asserted and expanded in a more naked fashion. Moreover, two of the models of change described by the same commentator—the models of coercion and of consultation—are reconcilable with the maintenance of overriding power even whilst they signify a muting of ideology. The negotiation model which implies power-sharing between political equals is no part of government policy.

The crisis of the Afrikaner rulers in South Africa today has been said to be the crisis of their political power: 'Today the Afrikaner is in danger of suffering the consequences of the political confrontation which has been created by his own power politics and power thinking.'[10] While power and confrontation remain in the forefront of attempts to deal with the country's daunting political problems (and there are few omens to indicate that they will not so remain) information relating to all the fundamental actions and decisions of government will be increasingly restricted to a coterie of reliable supporters. Public knowledge of the reasons for and background to the most important decisions and actions of government will be meagre or non-existent. The influences upon executive decision-making and the processes by which it takes place will continue to be blanketed in secrecy. There are indications, given credence by recent newspaper reports,[11] that secret power is exerted directly upon the executive by the Broederbond, a clandestine organization of influential Afrikaners that was in considerable measure responsible for the political break-through of Afrikaner nationalism. Power and secrecy were fused in the crucible of Afrikaner politics and will continue to reinforce each other in the foreseeable future.

The preceding analysis leads irresistibly to the conclusion that laws like the Official Secrets Act and the secrecy provision of the Defence Act will remain and that no moves of any kind will be made to confer a right of access to information. Because laws restricting access to information are part of the underpinnings of White power in South Africa, they seem to favour the interests of the electorate and the government which rules in its name. Nevertheless, the advantages so conferred by the laws are likely to be of short duration. They enable the government to restrict policy options to those that it favours and even to eliminate choice in politics. It does this by the selective use of information, presenting only that which supports approved policy decisions and screening out unwelcome facts and interpretations. By this process government decisions acquire a flavour of inevitability while the opposition (both parliamentary and extra-parliamentary) cannot develop alternatives that will appear viable to the public. There is no doubt that by manipulating information relating to the adminis-tration of security laws the government has been able to present many political opponents, prepared to work for change within a framework that is both democratic and peaceful, as subversive enemies of the public. When security information is both concealed and distorted, there does not seem to be a viable alternative of negotiation with men of goodwill among the politically powerless. The concealment of the alternative creates political frustration which contributes in time to its elimination, so that the government in effect structures choices out of the political agenda. Today's myth that the conflicts of the society are not nego-tiable may become tomorrow's reality; and extensive secrecy in the society may disable it from responding without disaster to pressures for social justice. There are many other examples outside the security field of a similar manipulation of information in order to narrow political alternatives.[12] Taken together they constitute overwhelming evidence that a political system characterized by a tragic non-respon-siveness to future needs is in the final stages of construction.

Does it follow from this gloomy analysis that all reform proposals to improve South Africa's information laws and practices are condemned to failure? Where reform will touch the central issues of public policy and affect the power-balance adversely to the present rulers, the answer to that question is a strong affirmative. Enlightened change at the national level of politics is probably precluded even in respect of the peripheral issues of politics. The protection of the consumer, for example, seems at first blush to be an innocuous area in which information might be given more freely than in something as sensitive as defence or foreign policy. But a powerful government that has occupied office for 30 years will have established close and possibly lucrative ties with the private economic sector which it will be reluctant to jeopardize. Members of the government may be as heavily involved in price-fixing as private business, and the consumer who seeks to expose such connections through the reform of information laws and practices will get short shrift from government. The provincial and local levels of government might be more promising areas for the inauguration of change. Questions of national security and foreign policy hardly impinge on the lower levels of government and disclosure will not be attended by the same perceived risks as in national politics. Of course provincial and local governments are affected by the same dead-weight of tradition that clogs up the institutions of central government; and their officials are drawn from the same secrecy-bound communities. The suggestion by the writer to a local government official in Durban that files should be accessible to the public (with exceptions for exempted material) was received with sufficient incredulity and discomfort to demonstrate how great a revolution of mind and attitude will be needed to achieve the smallest of improvements in South Africa. Provincial government records fall under the Official Secrets Act but the provincial council has power to legislate for open government at the municipal level.[13] The government in office in the province of Natal is still an opposition government (i e a non-Nationalist party) and could set reform in motion by requiring local authorities in Natal to open committee meetings (subject to suitable exceptions when sensitive matters such as staff appointments and dismissals and property acquisitions are discussed) and to make local government records available to inspection with exceptions similar to those that have been applied in other societies.[14] This suggestion is made not simply because it is always easier to get some other person or body to revolutionize its practices. The Natal provincial government appears to be the only one in South Africa sufficiently freed from the constraints of national politics to give an enlightened lead; and it would be doing so in the least sensitive area of government where public interest is low and the effects of change are likely to be entirely manageable. If the Natal government is unwilling to act in this way it will deservedly retain a reputation for holding as benighted an attitude on many issues as that of the central government.

The emerging Black governments are also conceivably agents of desirable reform in South Africa. The Inkatha organization[15] launched by Chief Buthelezi, the Chief Minister of KwaZulu, has adopted a Statement of Belief which incorporates the principle of 'the elimination of secrecy in public administration'.[16] The government in KwaZulu is currently not in favour of assuming independence and the continued application of the laws of the Republic (including the Official Secrets Act) together with limited KwaZulu legislative power are impediments to the full realization of that principle.[17] The government in Bophuthatswana might also be amenable to proposals for an open style of government but Transkei, which repealed and then reintroduced in a compendium measure most of South Africa's most sweeping security laws, appears committed to an authoritarian rule that is quite incompatible with access to information. In the 'homeland' areas much will depend on the willingness and ability to reject Pretoria's example in politics and administration.

Reform in quasi-public institutions such as public corporations like the Iron and Steel Corporation or the South African Broadcasting Corporation is precluded by reason of the control which the government exercises through key appointments and the subservience of these institutions to the broad requirements of official policy. This leaves private organizations and institutions which, though not the subject of this study, might conceivably generate from the base of the pyramid of power a ripple of change that will ultimately affect the controlling groups and institutions. The style and practices of the formalized institutions of state are in large measure a reflection of behaviour in primary groupings like the family, the church, and the work situation. It is inadequate and perhaps pointless to demand reform from government whilst maintaining the closed tradition at the basic levels of organizational life. In South Africa the lead will have to come from bodies like the churches, businesses and the universities in which a process of open management could be introduced without the backing of legislative and policy reorganization that is needed in the public sector. Reform from the base of the pyramid is a long and daunting task and its further progress will be contingent on the resolution by the power groups in the society of at least the most threatening political conflicts. It was probably this last factor which prompted an eminent political scientist in America, with whom the socio-political context of open government was discussed, to remark that in relation to South Africa his contribution was limited to an offer of sympathy.[18] That is regrettably the most realistic note on which to end this chapter and book.

NOTES

[1] 42 of 1974. For a brief discussion of the Act in relation to information control, see chap VII above.
[2] Government Notice 2222 (GG 5785 of 21 October 1977).

[3] Letter to legal representative of the SA Institute of Race Relations dated 10 November 1977.

[4] The legality of this form of proceeding is presently before the Appellate Division. Unfortunately, there appears to be little doubt that the statute requires a finding of guilt where the accused is proved to have produced material which a committee declares to be undesirable at any time prior to the institution of the prosecution: See section 8 of Act 42 of 1974.

[5] Proclamations R282–R302 of 1977 inclusive (GG 2551 of 19 October 1977) bring about the banning of the organizations and of the publications *Pro Veritate* and *The World*.

[6] This comment applies with special force to the banning of a body like the Christian Institute and the proscription of the newspaper *The World*.

[7] The relation between power and secrecy is examined in chap III above. It is argued there that power and secrecy are inevitably linked. The South African case demonstrates that extreme forms of power imply high degrees of secrecy, and vice versa. Reform of secrecy laws and practices in South Africa are conceivable only if the ruling party decides to share power on an orderly basis. In the initial stages of this process information could also then be shared with the leaders of groups that are incorporated into the power system, as in consociational democracies. At the same time, open forms of government could be inaugurated within groups (and even between them) at regional and local levels of government. Such a co-ordinated plan of reform cannot be commenced while monolothic power dominates politics and threatens to build up against itself competing forms of monolithic power.

[8] André du Toit in a lecture delivered at Natal University in November 1977.

[9] W A de Klerk *The Puritans in Africa* (Pelican, 1975) XIII.

[10] André du Toit 'Confrontation, Accommodation and the Future of Afrikanerdom' (address delivered at the University of Cape Town Summer School, January 1977).

[11] See, for example, the *Sunday Times* of 15 January 1978 on Broederbond access to, and influence upon, cabinet policy-making in South Africa.

[12] An example outside the security field relates to the Republic's relations with the United States. The government, relying primarily on a single remark by the American Vice-President, has persuaded the White public that conflict with America is inevitable in view of an insistence on a 'one man one vote' policy for South Africa. This is manifestly not official American policy and a different picture is likely to come out if (when?) authentic diplomatic communications on the question are released. In the meantime the alternative of productive co-operation with the USA towards a moderate solution in southern Africa cannot be developed.

[13] The legislation that already exists is exclusively restrictive in nature and was briefly described in chap VII above.

[14] See, for example, the Oregon Statute discussed in chap V above.

[15] Inkatha Yenkululeko Yesizwe (National Cultural Liberation Movement).

[16] Paper delivered by Gibson Thula entitled 'The Process of Power Sharing', January 1978 Conference of the SA Institute of Race Relations held in Cape Town. Mr Thula is the chairman of the Publicity and Strategy Committee of the Inkatha movement.

[17] There may be some flexibility prior to independence. Section 3 read with Schedule I of the Bantu Homelands Constitution Act 21 of 1971 vests legislative authority in Homelands governments over municipal institutions. Open government could therefore be introduced for municipalities without any difficulty. Homeland governments have power under section 5 of the same Act to control their own departments but the Official Secrets Act continues to apply and any repeal of such legislation would require the assent of the State President. However, the appropriate officials in the departments are presumably authorized to permit disclosure of departmental information and could thereby take much of the sting out of the Official Secrets Act as it affects departmental business.

[18] Discussion with Professor Gabriel A Almond of Stanford University in February 1976.

Postscript

On 16 March 1978 the Minister of Finance introduced the second reading of the Secret Services Account Bill. After being passed by Parliament the measure was published in the *Government Gazette* of 17 May as the Secret Services Account Act,[1] but it had already come into force on 1 April 1978.[2] In a nutshell the Act provides for the creation of a Secret Services Account, for the appropriation by Parliament of moneys to the account and for transfer, by agreement between the Minister of Finance and any minister of state, of moneys from the account to a department of state to be utilized for services of a secret nature.[3] Though the account established by the Act is subject to audit by the Auditor-General, the accounts maintained by a department to which the money has been transferred, and the utilization of that money in the department, are subject to audit by the Auditor-General only to the extent determined by the Minister of Finance after consultation with the Minister whose department is involved and the Auditor-General himself.[4] This means that secrecy can (and probably will) be maintained both as to the *amount* allocated to a department[5] from the account and as to the utilization of the money allocated in that department. That Parliament was willing to authorize a secret fund in any department of state is certainly surprising, not the least because it appears thereby to have diminished its own powers to scrutinize the executive branch for maladministration and to restrain such activities. Prior to the enactment of the measure there was statutory authorization for secret funds in three instances only—Defence, Foreign Affairs and the Bureau for State Security.[6] Reduced public scrutiny ought to be reluctantly conceded even in these areas where the case for secrecy does carry some conviction. Wholesale extension of secrecy to every branch of executive government, whether or not justified by reference to the Manichean struggle in which the government believes itself to be involved,[7] is reckless and unwise.

Just how unwise the government was to force enactment of this law has been made patent by the recent disclosures concerning the secret operations of the Department of Information. From press revelations it seems beyond dispute that the department conducted operations which were financed by unidentified sources of money lodged in secret accounts, both official and unofficial. At the time the

233

department was not one of those authorized to maintain secret accounts and serious questions have arisen as to the propriety of these operations, and their legality in terms of the Exchequer and Audit Act.[8] The report of the Auditor-General on the department disclosed, and investigations by the Select Committee on Public Accounts has confirmed, a number of irregularities in departmental spending. But these disclosures of irregular actions by departmental officials have only scratched the surface of the problem and both the Auditor-General and the Select Committee have declared that they are unable to report fully on the source and use of secret funds.[9] Except for a few items that were initially reported to Parliament arising out of the Auditor-General's report, there has been no effective scrutiny by Parliament (or its committees) of the 'dark' side of the department's affairs.[10] Disturbing but inconclusive press reports on secret fund activities have touched upon such matters as breaches of currency control, the possible use of public funds for private advantage, clandestine backing through 'laundered' accounts of a certain newspaper and even a possible link between the murder of Dr Robert Smit and the secret operations of the Department of Information.[11] There has been more than enough information to trigger the alarm bells of the society and to prompt an open post-mortem. The response on the government side has been quite the reverse; and far from being lifted, the veil of secrecy has been more tightly drawn over clandestine activities despite alarming intimations of possible improprieties and perhaps even crimes.[12]

There is a powerful tendency in South African government administration to regard publicity, rather than the misdeeds that it might reveal, as an evil. There is an investigation being conducted into the Information Department's clandestine activities, but it is a secret one being conducted by a person appointed by the Prime Minister. Further investigations into secret operations of the department will be undertaken by the retiring Secretary for Security Information[13] (General H J van den Bergh, head of BOSS), an appointment that is revealing as to the government's belief that high secrecy should continue to surround the entire affair notwithstanding a clear public interest in the exposure of apparent maladministration. The government already knew that there were irregularities in the department when it published the Secret Services Accounts Bill, and although the Information Department scandal had not broken when the Bill was being debated, the measure can reasonably be regarded as part of the government's response to it. Removal of some of the officials of the department and even the dissolution of the department itself, while probably inevitable in the light of the revelations, does not even begin to solve the problem. The disease which led to the Information débâcle was secrecy; and the cure that we are being offered is essentially more secrecy.[14] It may seriously be asked whether further disclosures of the kind that occurred in relation to Information can realistically be expected when secret funds are now officially sanctioned in every department of government.

NOTES

[1] Act 56 of 1978.

[2] Section 4.

[3] Sections 1 and 2.

[4] Section 3.

[5] See House of Assembly Debates of 16 March 1978 cols 3160, 3167, 3172, 3267 and of 17 March 1978 cols 3229–30 and 3231. An amendment by the New Republic Party, which would have required revelation only of the *amount* allocated to each department, was not accepted by the government: See House of Assembly Debates of 17 March 1978 col 3227.

[6] Defence Special Account Act, 6 of 1974; Foreign Affairs Special Account Act, 38 of 1967; Security Services Special Account Act, 81 of 1969.

[7] The parliamentary debates on the Bill are full of references to the 'abnormal times' in which we live, to the determination of 'South Africa's enemies', and to the irrelevance of 'Queensbury rules'.

[8] 66 of 1975. It has been suggested that a department authorized to operate a secret account may appoint officials in other departments its agents and thereby legally authorize them to make use of funds without violating Parliament's appropriations. This violates the spirit and possibly also the letter of the Act.

[9] See Natal Mercury Report on 13 June 1978.

[10] See the article by Ken Owen and Martin Welz in the *Sunday Times* of 18 June 1978.

[11] Speculation on this link appears in the newspaper *Rapport* on 28 May 1978.

[12] There has even been a threat to extend the scope of the already overbroad Official Secrets Act: See report in the *Daily News* of 11 May 1978.

[13] This appointment was announced by the Prime Minister on 15 June 1978.

[14] The response of the legal and political processes in America to Watergate throws into relief the failure of these same processes in South Africa. Watergate underlined some of the strengths of American democracy. The Information affair has confirmed that the democratic processes that remain operate feebly in South Africa.

Index